FOUNDATIONS OF DEMOCRACY

RELIGION AND CIVILIZATION SERIES

RELIGION AND THE WORLD ORDER

WORLD ORDER: ITS INTELLECTUAL AND CULTURAL FOUNDATIONS

FOUNDATIONS OF DEMOCRACY
F. Ernest Johnson, *Editor*

GROUP RELATIONS AND GROUP ANTAGONISMS

CIVILIZATION AND GROUP RELATIONSHIPS

UNITY AND DIFFERENCE IN AMERICAN LIFE
R. M. MacIver, *Editor*

FORTHCOMING VOLUMES

WELLSPRINGS OF THE AMERICAN SPIRIT
F. Ernest Johnson, *Editor*

LABOR'S RELATION TO CHURCH AND COMMUNITY
Liston Pope, *Editor*

GENERAL EDITORIAL BOARD

Louis Finkelstein

F. Ernest Johnson   R. M. MacIver

George N. Shuster

RELIGION AND CIVILIZATION SERIES

FOUNDATIONS OF DEMOCRACY

A series of addresses

EDITED BY
F. Ernest Johnson

*Professor of Education, Teachers College
Columbia University*

Published by
INSTITUTE FOR RELIGIOUS & SOCIAL STUDIES

Distributed by
HARPER & BROTHERS
NEW YORK AND LONDON

COPYRIGHT, 1947
BY INSTITUTE FOR RELIGIOUS AND SOCIAL STUDIES
3080 BROADWAY, NEW YORK CITY

*All rights reserved including the right
of reproduction in whole or in part
in any form.*

PRINTED IN THE UNITED STATES OF AMERICA
BY THE VAIL-BALLOU PRESS, INC., BINGHAMTON, N. Y.

THIS VOLUME IS
DEDICATED IN GRATEFUL MEMORY TO

HARLAN FISKE STONE

*who as jurist, educator and citizen
stood firmly upon the foundations of
democracy.*

The authors contributing to this volume were invited to address the Institute for Religious and Social Studies because of the special competence each could bring to the discussion. Each chapter represents solely the individual opinion of the author. Neither the Institute nor the editor assumes responsibility for the views expressed.

FOREWORD

The Institute for Religious and Social Studies was established at the Jewish Theological Seminary of America by means of a gift from Lucius N. Littauer, Esq. Its purpose is to enable ministers of all faiths to study under the guidance of scholars in various fields, representing different religious groups.

The series of lectures contained in the present volume was given during the academic year 1944–1945. The design of the series grew out of some academic experimentation on the editor's part aimed at bringing into one perspective the sources and various expressions of the democratic idea embodied in Western culture. So many strands enter into the development of democracy, and its expression has so many facets that their adequate presentation requires the collaboration of minds familiar with a variety of disciplines. It is true that the resulting symposium contains elements not fully reconcilable. Yet it is believed that each lecture presents an aspect of the theme which cannot be ignored if one would gain an understanding of democracy as a force in the world today.

The preceding volumes in the series focused attention upon the problem of establishing a world order consistent with religious and moral principles which have common acceptance in our culture. The present volume has a less pragmatic purpose, directing attention rather to the exploration of our tradition in terms of its assumptions concerning the bases of human association. All three volumes deal with problems of democracy, but the one now appearing undertakes a more systematic exploration of democratic concepts.

The variety in form which will at once strike the reader's eye is due not only to differing styles of address but to the fact that in some cases the lectures were submitted in manuscript while in others stenotype reports of addresses informally given were used as the basis of the text.

The next volume in the series will bear the title, "Wellsprings of the American Spirit."

THE EDITOR

February, 1946

CONTENTS

			PAGE
	Foreword		7
I.	The Crisis in Modern Democracy	F. Ernest Johnson	3
II.	Classical Origins	Irwin Edman	18
III.	Hebrew Sources: Scriptures and Talmud	Louis Finkelstein	27
IV.	Mediaeval Sources	George N. Shuster	35
V.	Reformation Sources	John T. McNeill	44
VI.	Humanistic Sources	Horace M. Kallen	62
VII.	Literary Sources	Amos N. Wilder	87
VIII.	The Founding Fathers	Moorhouse F. X. Millar, S.J.	109
IX.	Democracy and Economic Liberalism	George H. Houston	125
X.	The Role of Economic Groups	A. J. Muste	151
XI.	Democracy in a Collectivist Age	Goodwin B. Watson	166
XII.	Education for Freedom	Scott Buchanan	177
XIII.	Democracy in Educational Practice	Harrison S. Elliott	192
XIV.	Democratic Conceptions of Authority, Revelation, and Prophecy	F. Ernest Johnson	202
XV.	Democracy and Ethical Realism	Justin Wroe Nixon	214
XVI.	Organized Religion and the Practice of Democracy	H. Paul Douglass	227
XVII.	Democracy and Zionism	Mordecai M. Kaplan	239
	Index		267

FOUNDATIONS OF DEMOCRACY

I

INTRODUCTION DEPICTING THE CRISIS IN MODERN DEMOCRACY

BY

F. ERNEST JOHNSON, D.D.

Professor of Education, Teachers College, Columbia University; Executive Secretary, Department of Research and Education, Federal Council of the Churches of Christ in America

The purpose of this introductory lecture is to depict the situation with reference to democracy as a crisis in our history. I do not mean a crisis that has developed in a year or in five years or ten, but one that has been gradually shaping up over a much longer time. And I am thinking of crisis not merely in the sense of grievous involvement, but in the sense of a historical situation that carries impulsion to a decision of major importance. Inherent in the word "crisis" is the necessity of decision. A crisis has in it the possibilities of creative thought and action; it is not necessarily nor altogether a misfortune.

To say that democracy is in crisis is to accent elements in the human situation of which we are now more acutely conscious than formerly. I was talking with an academic colleague a few weeks ago about the world situation. He is an ardent believer in democracy, but he had a rather sad face that day as he said, "I am pretty much discouraged and disillusioned." I said, "About what?" He replied, "About man. When the Lord made man He put in a little too much hog and a little too much tiger and I am afraid there isn't very much we can do about it." That will do very well, I think, for a terse characterization of the predicament of man today in the Western world as he seeks to govern himself and to manage his affairs: too much egocentrism, too much self-seeking, too much pugnacity.

In an often-quoted remark, Edmund Burke once said he did not know how to draw an indictment against a whole people. More difficult, still, is it to draw an indictment against the human race. That is one of the things, I take it, that we have to accept as given, and, if democracy is going to succeed, it must succeed in spite of such limitations as are inherent in the human situation. But the democratic faith requires the assumption that there are resources of the human spirit by means of which the human situation may be transcended.

When I speak of democracy as in crisis, therefore, I am thinking of the inordinate strain which this particular historical situation places on our human resources. One of its grievous aspects is the low prestige of politics, especially in this country. It impelled Mr. Fulbright to say at the *Herald Tribune* Forum the other day that we have not found a way to bring into political life the best of our abilities and conscience in the service of the country. "Politics" in America is indeed a bad word. I once listened to a lecture by Harold Laski in which he said, "I never heard the word 'politics' used as an expletive until I came to America."

But a critique must be made in broader terms. Some very fundamental and disquieting criticisms have been made of democracy as empirical fact not only in the life of America but throughout the Western world. Let me read you a few paragraphs from what James Bryce said in *Modern Democracies,* published in 1921 (Macmillan Co.):

What then has democracy failed to accomplish? It has brought no nearer friendly feeling and the sense of human brotherhood among the peoples of the world toward one another.

Freedom has not been a reconciler.

Neither has it created good will and a sense of unity and civic fellowship within reach of these peoples. Though in earlier days strife between classes had arisen, it is only in these later days that what is called class war has become recognized as a serious menace to the peace of states and in some countries the dominant factor in political and economic conflicts.

Liberty and equality have not been followed by fraternity. Not even far off do we see her coming shine. Democracy has not enlisted in the service of the state nearly so much of the best practical capacity as each country possesses and every country needs for dealing with the domestic and international questions of the present age.

In some states corruption has been rife and the tone of public life no better than it was under the monarchies and oligarchies of the eighteenth century.

Lastly, democracy has not induced that satisfaction and contentment with itself as the best form of government which was expected and has not exorcised the spirit that seeks to attain its ends by revolution.

Well, we were warned long, long ago that democracy had within itself the seeds of dissolution if they should be allowed to germinate. Plato, through the mouth of Socrates, diagnosed the democratic situation in his day, in his time of disillusionment. I am reading now from *The Republic:*

The good which oligarchy proposed to itself and the means by which it was maintained was excess of wealth—am I not right?

Yes.

And the insatiable desire of wealth and the neglect of all other things for the sake of money-getting was also the ruin of oligarchy?

True.

And democracy has her own good, of which the insatiable desire brings her to dissolution?

What good?

Freedom, I replied; which, as they tell you in a democracy, is the glory of the state—and that therefore in a democracy alone will the freeman of nature deign to dwell. . . .

When a democracy which is thirsting for freedom has evil cup-bearers presiding over the feast, and has drunk too deeply of the strong wine of freedom, then, unless her rulers are very amenable and give a plentiful draft, she calls them to account and punishes them, and says they are cursed oligarchs.

To be sure, these words were written by a man whose disillusion had, as we believe, dulled his insight. Indeed, a much brighter picture can be drawn of the situation which prompted Plato to dismal foreboding. Yet if he could have read the words of Lord Bryce, he would surely have been tempted to say, "I told you so." And not without justification, for I verily believe that what he said is as pertinent in our day as it was in his, although we reject its finality.

As I was putting together the material for this address I recalled that serious doubts of democracy were not wanting among the Founding Fathers. You remember how Jefferson himself feared that democracy—although they didn't use the word in those days—that liberty and free government would perish if an urban civilization was superimposed upon an agrarian civilization. Alexander Hamilton, a man of different kidney, put the matter very crudely:

All communities divide themselves into the few and the many. The first are the rich and well-born, the other the mass of the people. The voice of the people has been said to be the voice of God and, however generally this maxim has been quoted and believed, it is not true in fact. The people are turbulent and changing, they seldom judge or determine right. Give, therefore, to the first class, the few, that is, a distinct permanent share in government. They will check the unsteadiness of the second, the multitude. As they cannot receive any advantage by the change, they therefore will maintain good government.

That, I am happy to say, has become heresy in American thinking. Moreover, it has been falsified by history; but there it stands, a part of our tradition. It is salutary to recall the forebodings of some of the early statesmen of the Republic, whether they reflect philosophic insight or class orientation. That a period marked by the enthusiasm and optimism of the Enlightenment, a period that produced the Declaration of Independence, should also have produced the Constitution, with its restraints and cautionary provisions, is an instructive fact. It reminds us that, "when our fathers brought forth upon this continent a new nation," they knew that it was peopled with very imperfect men. Their faith and hope have never been conclusively vindicated. They are still undergoing test. The finest things in life are always the most precariously held. And, paradoxically, we are safer with respect to those possessions which we realize we are in danger of losing. Democracy is one of those goods that we have in recent years taken altogether too much for granted.

Of course, the most startling thing in the contemporary situation is the attack on democracy from without, the rise of the totalitarian states. But about that I would say at this point only this: that we have not, I think, up to now, rightly interpreted the significance of that challenge or rightly assessed the situation with which it confronts us. Totalitarianism would never have gained the influence and power it has acquired throughout so much of the world if there were not serious faults in the armor of democracy. If the Western governments had been able with equal success to appeal to their citizenry for loyalty, for an all-consuming devotion to common ends, I think we should not have had to encounter on a global scale the totalitarian menace.

Let us consider some of the more conspicuous difficulties in the democratic situation so that we shall have them in mind as our course continues. Then I will raise what I regard as some fundamental questions concerning the philosophy of democracy.

At the moment we are all exposed to the ravages of a national political campaign. Increasingly, as the campaign goes on, I suppose we all are impressed that democracy in operation has its seamy side. I have, to be sure, found it to some extent a relief to note that there is nothing new about that in American life. Some of you have seen the Beards' recent book, *Basic History of the United States* by Charles and Mary Beard (copyright 1944 by Garden City Publishing Company Inc.). There are in it some interesting summaries and comments on political platforms of a few decades ago. In 1876 the Republican platform said, "We charge the Democratic Party with being the same in character and spirit as when it sympathized with treason," and then follows a choice assortment of epithets summarized by Mr. Beard thus: "Treason, incompetence, unworthiness, and incapacity." These were Republican words, supposed to describe the qualities of the Democratic Party in 1876.

The Democrats retaliated in kind. In 1884 they said, "The Republican Party, so far as principle is concerned, is a reminiscence. In practice it is an organization for enriching those who control its machinery." Mr. Beard summarizes: "Thievery, moral decay, corruption, incapacity." These were Democratic words supposed to describe the qualities of the Republican Party in 1884.

I suppose we in America have some capacity to disallow this sort of thing or to take it in our stride, so that we do not need to be too much depressed over it. Nevertheless, I shall be glad when the campaign is over.

Then there is the seeming hypocrisy in political platforms. The *New Republic* said recently, "Platforms are drafted by masters of generality and evasion. They aim first of all to be the greatest common denominator for conflicting interests within the party and next to attract as many votes as possible by promising everything to everyone regardless of whether the several promises are compatible with each other." This, of course, is characterizing politics at the bottom level.

The tendency to view party platforms cynically may after all be unrealistic in that it does not take account of the fact that politics is essentially an art, an art of persuasion on a huge scale. As such it involves the winning of support for a political movement from persons and groups whose motives are varied and are rooted largely in self-interest, individual or collective. To win an election, perhaps especially to win against the party in power, a maximum of persuasion directed to motives actually operating and a minimum of alienation must be achieved.

I think we have to be just as realistic about a political situation, and, unless we are prepared to find in the clash of interests, in the encounter of opposing groups, something ultimately socially constructive, then of course we shall have to give up the whole democratic situation as hopeless.

Again, there is the limitation upon the franchise—a black spot, indeed. We still have in eight states, as everybody knows, a poll tax, something which is as completely irreconcilable with the democratic ideal as anything one could suggest. I was interested, however, in reading some recent remarks of the Governor of North Carolina. As a southerner, he is opposed to Federal action in this matter, preferring to leave it with the states where he thinks it constitutionally rests. Nevertheless, he says that abolition of the poll tax in North Carolina has proved its validity, has proved that it is advantageous to the state. He believes that the goods of democracy will sell themselves. That gives one a little more hope; it always gives one more hope, I think, to get a historic perspective on any evil with which one has to deal.

The neglect of the franchise, however, is in some sense just as serious as its restriction. Think of the fact that in 1940 less than two thirds of the qualified voters went to the polls! This year, suppose that with the soldier vote it comes up fairly close to that figure; even so, it is disquieting that a democracy, in which the people have a choice every four years as to their national leaders, is able to muster no larger vote than that.

This is something to think about with very great seriousness, and I am inclined to think that Peter Drucker in his *Future of Industrial Man* (John Day Co.) has put his finger on the key to that situation. He says that, unless power is legitimate, it is corrupting and that in this country, since the full impact of the industrial revolution struck us, we have not achieved a really legitimate power. "Legitimate power," he writes, "stems from the same basic belief of society regarding man's nature and fulfillment on which the individual's social status and function rest." The average American, he says, still is "a Populist at heart." He is devoted to political ideals and forms quite outmoded in a day when power centers in great groups that are the locus of vested interests of one sort or another, and Mr. Drucker includes labor unions along with associations of capital.

This distribution of power has not been recognized in the political system. We are still holding our campaigns, making our speeches, writing our platforms, casting our ballots, on formulated issues which are not really expressive of the actual encounter of vital forces in society itself. I should hope that before this course is over we shall have more light on that aspect of our problem.

Then there is the matter of bureaucratic rule. The current Republican platform declares: "The national administration has become a sprawling, overlapping bureaucracy. It is undermined by executive abuse of power, confused lines of authority, duplication of effort, inadequate fiscal controls," and so on. There is, of course, another way to look at it. Max Lerner, writing in *PM* says, "Let us get one thing clear. There was no bickering to speak of under President Harding. . . ." He takes the charge of bureaucracy as really indicating a division of powers which occasions constant strife as to what policy shall be. We have in Washington a bureau here, a bureau there, and this bureau has to make up its mind, and that bureau, and then they perhaps have to clear, and there is all sorts of red tape, and consequently you have an administration that is always bickering with itself. Its bureaus cannot come to terms with each other. He says Mr. Harding's administration never bickered. "It was all so incredibly corrupt, and all the corruption was kept neatly inside the official family until the stench was too much to be contained even among the boys. There was no bickering under President Coolidge, because the government wasn't doing enough to add up to even half a bicker."

Take your choice. You have a situation here—I do not minimize the evil of competing bureaus, the uncertainty, the confusion, and the conflict and the bickering which that entails. The question is, is that a price which has to be paid in a free country for the exercise of increasing governmental functions? Mr. Lerner calls this editorial, "It bickers, but it works." The difficulty is that we still are unable to make government work well enough.

One might go on and speak of the corruption that exists in democratic governments. America is notorious for the corruption of city governments, as it is for the inefficiency of its county governments. Here again it is possible to be reckless in our judgments. Mr. Laski said one time, "I can destroy any case you can build up for democracy. I am sure I can knock it over in ten minutes. But I don't know any other kind of government that will last five." Yet to ignore our danger at this point is reckless indeed.

Now let me speak briefly of what I regard as underlying and insistent problems of democracy that we have to deal with in our time. The first is suggested by what I was saying about bureaucracy. What is government really for? The American people have not made up their minds. I think we see the emergence today of a new theory of government that is non-Jeffersonian; that is, it is not based on the police theory of state power. Interestingly enough, the police theory of government has theological roots in the idea that government exists because man in his nature is so prone to evil that some repository of force is necessary. Government is conceived as a dyke against the flood of man's iniquities. There is a pretty broad streak of that in Reformation doctrine, as some of you will recognize.

The emerging view to which I refer has affinities with classical doctrine. Aristotle declared that the function of the state is to serve the common good, to create the conditions of a good life. We are now trying to make up our minds to what extent we want government to be a positive force for public welfare instead of only an arbiter, an umpire. In other words, we are trying to make up our minds about the welfare state. Whether it will persist or not remains to be seen. It may be dangerous, as many of my colleagues believe, but the theory has to be evaluated. It has behind it a great weight of popular sanction. The issue has broad ethical and religious implications. The nature of man and his capacity for self-government are deeply involved.

Protestant Christianity has always maintained that man's condition is best described in terms of a "predicament." Man is in trouble and he needs to be saved. He is ignorant, to be sure, but this is declared to be not his main defect. He is selfish and prideful and his spirit is in need of regeneration. In recent years there has been renewed emphasis on this aspect of the human situation, not only in theological but in secular writings. Sometimes this "devaluation" of human nature seems to cast doubt upon man's capacity to be entrusted with self-government.

Interestingly enough, among the Puritans the notion that all men are sinners, that they are in a "fallen" state, supported democratic ideas by enabling the Puritan to insist that, since every man was a sinner, none was good enough to lord it over any other man. Macaulay in his *Essay on Milton* said that the Puritan "groveled in dust before his Maker, but he set his foot upon the neck of his king." Yet the question insistently arises whether such a view of man gives a sufficient basis for a philosophy of self-government. That I regard as one of the crucial issues in the theory of democracy today. Broadly speaking, the secular defenders of democracy resist the current devaluation of man and assert the progressive perfectibility of human nature. For us who stand in the Jewish-Christian tradition this is a problem of first rank. What do we really believe about the nature of man? I am not offering a solution. I should be gratified to secure recognition of the problem.

Then there is the effect of the collapse of liberalism as a political-economic philosophy—the *laissez-faire* tradition of free economic enterprise. As you well know, we do not hear much now about capitalism or the profit system. The current term is free enterprise. It is probably a more accurate term, and at any rate it sounds better. I am not saying that free enterprise has collapsed, but that the old idea—which had much theological support—that the welfare of the mass of the people was best served when everyone was looking out for himself, has been definitely outmoded in the thinking of vast numbers of the American people. The bearing of this change upon democracy is not sufficiently recognized. That it is relevant the intelligent businessman well knows. But I think he often misconceives the issue. Much has been said in business circles during recent years about our three liberties—the "tripod" of liberties, political, religious, and economic. By economic liberty is commonly meant the free-enterprise system. It is declared that, if any one of these liberties falls, the tripod falls. Hence, if free economic enterprise is destroyed, then there is no democracy left.

I am not going to debate that issue here. But I wish to say that no particular economic theory can today furnish a firm foundation on which to build a theory of government and a philosophy of life. The fact is that democracy in the Western world did develop in connection with the rise of the middle class, and the *laissez-faire* theory was intimately related to it. The spokesmen for business are historically right. But we are now at a stage of economic development where actual changes have forced a re-examination of theory. What the outcome will be no one knows. Doctrinaire views, whether "left" or "right" leave me unconvinced. The point is that we who cherish democracy must no longer bind it fast to the vicissitudes of economic theory. The conventional philosophy of democracy needs reconstruction in order to give it a more secure foundation.

Another critical factor is the growing difficulty in communication, in reaching a common mind, because of the increasing complexity and diversity of the common life: there are so many and such diverse groups, with different orientations, different ideologies, that unity continually eludes us.

We spent a great deal of time in the Conference on Science, Philosophy and Religion last summer discussing the problems of communication across the boundaries that separate groups, frequently antagonistic groups. This is not just a rational matter, it is not just a matter of reasoning one with another; it involves the problem of enabling one group to accommodate itself to a different frame of reference. It is, as Carl Becker said, moving from one climate of opinion to another. Do you remember what he said about modern man and Thomas Aquinas? "The one thing we cannot do with the *Summa* of St. Thomas is to meet its arguments on their own ground. We can neither assent to them nor refute them. It does not even occur to us to make the effort, since we instinctively feel that in the climate of opinion sustaining such arguments we could only gasp for breath."

I am quite unready to say that all this is true. It occurs to me that if we are totally unable to understand Aquinas, or Augustine, or Calvin, we had better see to our minds. But what Becker said illustrates a problem more aptly than he seemed to realize. For he seems to have overlooked the fact that millions of Americans, many of them among the most intellectually superior, do accept the philosophy of St. Thomas. Perhaps few of them fully understand it, but it does furnish a "frame of reference" within which they interpret life and make their moral judgments. The gulf between contemporary systems of thought defines a problem of democracy. Diversity is not a denial of unity, but a counterpart; yet this is true only to the extent that differences are rationally apprehended, appreciated, and respected. We encounter this problem of mutual incomprehensibility almost daily. Have you not talked with people of different political persuasion until you had a sense of frustration and hopelessness? I have done that again and again—and very recently, I may say.

This is one of our major problems, and it means that we have to think out the function in a democracy of that sustained tension between opposites which keeps them in precarious balance but in vital interrelationship. The democratic instrument of persuasion is always in danger of mounting to coercion, on the one hand, and falling to the level of appeasement, on the other.

But democracy has its own way of resorting to trial by political power, for that is what an election is. When an election is in the offing, we reason all we can and then we test it out, and the irreconcilables have to be governed by the vote of the majority. To what extent does the success of democracy depend on increasing the scope of the area where agreements can be reached without an actual trial of strength at the ballot box? The question is important, I think. For while ballots are better than bullets, after all, a vote on a bitterly contested issue results, in effect, in the imposition of the majority will. Often it leaves a very bad taste in the mouth of the defeated. To be sure, acceptance in good sportsmanship of a popular verdict is one of the most highly prized of democratic virtues. And undoubtedly a readiness not only to accept the verdict but to give great weight in mind and conscience to an adverse expression of the public will is an essential object of democratic discipline. But it is implicit in the functioning of a vital minority that it is not ready to say that the "voice of the [majority of the] people is the voice of God." There is a time dimension in popular sanction and a convinced minority looks to the future to correct current decisions believed to be wrong. And since a democracy lives continually in peril of the abuse of majority power, it is always desirable that conflicts shall be resolved to a maximum degree in the give and take of discussion before recourse is had to a counting of heads. Majority rule is an essential device, but it is not the essence of democratic process.

But the fact remains that important decisions have to be taken in critical times on issues which have given rise to bitter conflict, when all that can be done with a die-hard opposition is to "mow 'em down." There is a limit to the effectiveness of discussion and the potency of sweetness and light. Here I think organized religion in America has lagged. It has not learned that a rugged political realism is essential for the implementation of its ethical ideals.

Another problem that has not been solved is that of the merits of independent political action as compared with party action. Religious people tend to glorify independence. And undoubtedly if there were no independents and no ticket-scratchers the campaigns would be meaningless. But this is only a fraction of the matter. We need to think again about the significance of the slogan, "Vote for the man and not for the party." I am strongly inclined to think that though it sounds very virtuous, it has mischievous consequences. The reason is not that integrity is not of first importance, but that integrity does not register in a purely private way. Nor does it sustain itself in isolation. Again and again, when a person of high integrity is put in office, he becomes the instrumentality of the groups that make up a particular political following, and either he proves utterly inept or he becomes a compromiser and perhaps even a malefactor. Conversely, it frequently happens that a relatively weak person stands more firmly on a good party platform than a strong man on a defective platform.

Political realism requires that we understand that the important cleavages are not between individuals but between groups and movements. We must learn to make our decisions not just on the basis of the character and the personality of a man but on the basis of the alignment of forces which he represents as over against the alignment on the other side. If we would do that, we would less frequently end up in cynicism when we survey the results of our elections.

In short, we have to come to grips with the problem of power in the modern world, and I think that here our religious traditions have been exceedingly faulty. Has not the most vigorous expression in political terms of the Judeo-Christian faith in our time been a negative one, registering chiefly in sporadic opposition to particularly flagrant evils? This negativism has given rise to political ineptitude in facing a world in which ideals have to be vigorously and promptly implemented in order to preserve the equities in the human situation. This issue confronts us conspicuously in the international scene, but also in the domestic scene, in the balancing of group against group. The question is not one of having pressure groups or not having them; it is a question of how we are going to utilize the dynamic of inevitable pressure groups for the improvement of the democratic process.

One other thing I want to mention here. We have to consider whether we can continue to gauge the degree of democracy that a nation has achieved wholly in terms of political method. We have to face the challenge of the Soviet Union, which has not achieved much in democratic procedure as we define it, but which has achieved a great deal in terms of equalizing economic and ethnic status. I, for one, am not greatly impressed by the current efforts to rest the claim to democracy solely on freedom of discussion, of the ballot, and of the press. These are priceless goods, and no nation can permanently live without them and claim to be democratic. But the basic democratic principle is human dignity, and that is violated more grievously on the economic level than on any other under a system that continues to be subject to devastating depressions. To my mind the eradication of mass unemployment is a primary requirement of a democratic society.

Moreover, by our own professed criteria of political democracy we stand condemned because millions of our people are denied the franchise by means of an economic barrier in the form of a poll tax. The world is not going to be impressed very deeply or very long by our exaltation of individual liberty if we continue to be economically stratified and racially segregated.

There are other urgent problems that I can only mention today, some of which I hope will be illuminated in the course of these lectures. There is the vexing question of the relation of the expert to the mass of the people; also the question how much it is necessary for the common man to know and understand in a scientific and technological age. Since participation is a primary criterion of democracy, the conditions of effective participation in our kind of world are a matter of grave importance. Again, we have the problem of the relation between security and freedom, between social planning and individual initiative. This is becoming crucial. A question that presses for an answer within the religious community is that of the consistency of religious concepts of authority, of revelation, and of prophecy with democratic principles. Finally, in democratic education we are in urgent need of a clarification of the issue of indoctrination and the conscious inculcation of value attitudes.

Is it too much to say that all our major problems are in essence problems of democracy? Let me read as a final word these paragraphs from Charles A. Beard in the symposium, *Congress on Education for Democracy*—Proceedings of the Congress, August 15-17, 1939, Teachers College:

Universal suffrage, efficient government, material foundations, declarations of rights, and education alone cannot guarantee the safety of our civilization against the storms of passion and the lust of men for power. Behind all beneficent institutions of society, ever helping to sustain them, is that elusive but potent force known as the humane spirit. . . .

. . . Knowledge is not enough. Science is not enough. Both may be employed to kill as well as to heal. Accumulated facts, though high as mountains, give us no instruction in human values and the choices of application. It is the humane spirit that points the way to the good life. To reiterate the maxims of this spirit, to restate them in terms of new times, to spread them through education and daily intercourse, to exemplify them in private conduct, to incorporate them in public practice, to cling to them despite our known infirmities and hypocrisies—this too is a task of all who fain would make government by the people and for the people endure upon the earth.

II

CLASSICAL ORIGINS

BY

IRWIN EDMAN, Ph.D.

Professor of Philosophy, Columbia University

The theme of democracy is obviously of such great importance that I think one of the tragedies of our period is that the word has tended to become a cliché. We have come to think of it as something to which to give lip or even mind service, without using our minds to re-examine the term. And we have fallen into the fatal provincialism, I think, of remembering the origins of democracy chiefly in terms of those crises of our day which remind us of our own immediate history of democracy in this country, in France, and in England.

Now, the amazing fact about American democracy in its intellectual statements, in our own American classical tradition, is that it was given highly educated statement. If you examine, for example, the writings of Thomas Jefferson you will find that the documents to which I will presently refer really molded his thoughts, that the French and English origins of democracy, which molded our own early thinking on the subject, were themselves the product of what one may call intellectual classical education, an education in the political themes then available.

I am going to list these themes: first, the Greek city-state having once existed, there was Greek political philosophy, which was simply a rational and formal expression of Greek political practice; secondly, there was the theory of Roman law; and, thirdly, there was the early Christian idea of brotherhood, about which, if it were not treading on the province of Dr. Finkelstein, I should like to say a word or two with reference to its Jewish origins. However, I think it quite appropriate that each lecturer keep, at least officially, within the limits of his own province. And so, while I think I could say relevant and interesting things about the debt of the early Christian mystical political idea of brotherhood of the prophets, I do not want to steal any part of Dr. Finkelstein's thunder. So I shall leave that area to be illuminated by him next week.

But there is a fourth theme: the idea of individuality, of privacy, of solitude, of the protection of the individual against the commonwealth or society, which peculiarly grew up as a consequence of Stoic and Epicurean philosophy.

I am going to start with the first theme, of the Greek city-state, reminding you that, as in every generation there is one book that by a fusion of acumen and scholarship focuses an ideal, so in the past generation there has been one book about the Greek city-state that, I think, must be read if you wish to explore the idea at all. That book is *The Greek Commonwealth* by A. E. Zimmern.

In *The Greek Commonwealth* Professor Zimmern a quarter of a century ago pointed out that if you wish to understand the meaning of Greek ideas of democracy you must for the time being forget the notions of democracy that are current in modern British thought, beginning with Locke and Hobbe, ideas of rights and duties that go back certainly no farther than the Romans; these were not Greek ideas. You must forget the idea of representative democracy, that is, of democracy through representative government. You must forget our modern, complicated, industrial, internationally inter-related democracy. What you have to remember is the numerically small, the geographically provincial Greek city-state. You have to remember that it was taken as an axiom of biology, if I may so put it, that there were natural slaves in society and that the idea of a commonwealth applied only to free citizens. You must remember further that the line between the individual and society, between the individual and the state, was by no means even recognized in Greek thinking on the subject, or in Greek practice.

The summary and decisive statement, I think, is that of Aristotle in the *Nicomachean Ethics,* when he remarked that a beast or a god may live alone, but not a man. Man is a social animal, and the conception of the Greek commonwealth or the Greek city-state was that of individuals or free citizens abiding only in social relationships. So you find the notion of a group, a relatively small group of citizens, whose lives flowered and came to fruition only by their participation in the commonwealth, who were in two senses equal—and this is the first intimation of a genuinely democratic idea.

All men in a group were equal, first, in the sense that they all participated in all administration and in the legislation of the state. It was recognized that in the city-states of Greece, certainly Athens, one out of six persons at one time or another actually took part in the administration of the state. And every free citizen equally shared in the political decisions of the state.

But there was a deeper equality, and this was what Pericles, in his famous speech presented through Thucydides, boasted of, that Athenians and Greeks in general, as contrasted with barbarians, had equality under the law, that the government was operated by the consent of all, that is, of all the citizens. There was an almost mathematical conception of equality under the law. There was no private capriciousness as in tyranny, no violence as in anarchy or political chaos, but an orderly law established by equal participation and consent of all. Pericles's proudest boast was that Athenians lived not like barbarians under the violence and inequities of tyranny but under the law, equal for all and equally determined by all.

There is another trait, a less happy and amiable trait, of the Greek city-state that has provided ammunition, as an element of weakness, for every critic of democracy, including some very sympathetic ones like John Stuart Mill. It provided ammunition for Plato, who was profoundly suspicious of democracy, though it embodies at least two of his fundamental moral contentions, and for Aristotle, who, though he regarded democracy as the practically ideal or ideally practicable form of government, carefully limited democracy in a way somewhat equivalent to that of the framers of the American Constitution when they were careful to protect democracy against what they considered its possible danger, the hasty and precarious rule of an unthinking mob.

Plato and Aristotle, particularly Plato, sought to eliminate the vacillations of a commonwealth in which all could equally participate, particularly a commonwealth in which government was largely government by talk and persuasion. Plato was extremely suspicious of a democratic state because he had seen the internal corruption of democracy in Athens. Therefore, in the eighth and ninth books of the *Republic*, he makes democracy one of the lower forms of deviation from perfection in government, largely because the rule of an intelligent and knowledgable few has given place to the rule of the uninstructed man. And that is why it is often said, very glibly and I think falsely, that Plato's *Republic* is the first treatise on totalitarian government. It is the first treatise on the notion of a group of enlightened and responsible experts governing society not in their own interest.

Plato's criticism of democracy was a criticism of the failures and vacillations of a state that had not orderliness but a confusion of tongues. But Plato, for all his severity on democratic government, through Socrates states at least two notions that have become part of the democratic heritage, and the central part. I refer particularly to the idea stated by Socrates in the *Apology*, that the function of the enlightened moral philosopher was to be a free—a freely permitted and intellectually free—critic of the state, the noble gadfly, as he put it, of the lethargic noble steed which was the Athenian state. He asserted not only the right but the necessity of free political criticism.

Secondly, the important notion regarding any free commonwealth which is developed in the *Republic* itself, is that, if you wish to have health, psychical and physical in the individual, you need health in the state, and this is attained for both only when the state is so arranged that each member of the commonwealth is given the opportunity to fulfill his own native and characteristic capacity; or, as the Greek says in almost an equivalent of colloquial English, "where each member of the commonwealth does or minds his own business." This means a state which finds fulfillment for its members in their own characteristic virtues or excellences. It is a sound principle; you cannot have a healthy soul in a sick society. And a society is sick which does not provide for the natural appropriate functions of all its members in their characteristic capacities.

Plato had a notion that there were natural inequalities but he never quite thought of the free interchange or of the education to new capacity that modern democracy implies. Yet he does make provision for that in one place, where he says that among the workers a philosopher king may happen to be born, a king by nature. But, though Plato on the whole has a kind of caste system, his notion of a state as finding its fulfillment in the natural capacity and exercise of the capacities of members of the commonwealth is one that is woven into the very texture of all democratic thought.

Aristotle's notion of democracy comes nearer our own. It comes nearer, as a matter of fact, to something that it has become fashionable in certain advanced circles to smile at just a little. It comes very near resembling nineteenth-century bourgeois democracy.

Aristotle's contributions to the long tradition of democratic thought and also, for all his sobriety, to democratic feeling may be said, I think, to be these: first, a government, to be stable and effective, must rest on the consent of the governed; secondly, it must establish equitable law in the two senses in which I mentioned equality before; thirdly, it must be what Aristotle called a moderate democracy. By moderate he meant something, I think, very like what the founders, the leading influences, certainly, of the American Constitution meant.

He thought characteristically of a kind of golden mean, that a certain amount of wealth, but not too much—you will find this characteristic of the classicist—was the balance wheel in the functioning of the democratic society. The reason he thought a certain amount of wealth was necessary was that a certain amount of possessions freed those who had them from ambition to overturn the government in a violent desire for more wealth, and, on the other hand, a limitation of the amount of wealth was important, because complete possession of most of the wealth of the state would create the possibility of the violent use of power and also would cause a vast discontent in those who had no wealth at all.

A large central core of the commonwealth in the middle or moderate range of wealth was for Aristotle the ideal condition for a democratically functioning state. And within that society of moderate property holders he conceived that the consent of the governed and equality under the law defined the nature of a commonwealth which could be justified. Why? Critics of democracy, even favoring critics like de Tocqueville in writing about America or Bryce in *The American Commonwealth* or John Stuart Mill in *Representative Government,* have often raised the question of the justification of democratic government. And Aristotle, who always considered every art in terms of its total context in human action, also raised the question of the uses in human life of government, and he selected a moderate democracy of a section of the people stabilized by a certain amount of possessions without desire for more. What were the uses of such a government? I pointed out earlier that, in a sense, to ask what are the uses of government to individual life, is to phrase the question inaccurately, from the Greek point of view, for one only becomes an individual, a characteristically human being, in terms of one's social relationships, and a society, a commonwealth such as Aristotle describes, is justified as one of the instruments that bring characteristic human capacities to their fruition.

Aristotle conceived other societies within the state. There is the society of the family. There is also the liberal, unlegal or nonlegal society of friendship, described in the eighth and ninth books of the *Nicomachean Ethics.* But as long as men are bound together and involved with each other by economic necessity, as long as men are naturally social and gregarious, the state operating in terms of the consent of the governed who govern themselves under an equity of law is, for Aristotle, the characteristic instrument for the fulfillment or, better, for the liberation of human nature so that it can enjoy the liberal fruits of friendship and, ultimately, of art and poetry and contemplation.

Neither Plato nor Aristotle for a moment conceived a political theory in the abstract, or in cosmic or world terms. There is a pathos when we read them from this historical distance in the thought that political and social orientation was for them provincial. It happens that Athens was a special province, possibly one unequaled in the history of the world, but it was a province. And it never occurred to Plato or Aristotle, I think it is fair to say, that political speculation or analysis was possible except in terms of the city-state. It is characteristic and pathetic, and ironic in a way, that they should have thought that, because at the very time they wrote of the city-state—and they show signs of being aware of it, especially Plato—it was beginning to be erased from the world as a norm of political thought. And this for two reasons: one, the internal corruption of the city-states themselves, and, two, the fact of war, both civil war—the city-states quarreled with each other—and the threat from the empires to the east and west which ultimately destroyed the possibility of an independent city-state.

I do not want to draw too immediate a momentary, contemporary moral, but somebody ought to tell the editors of the *Daily News* and the *Chicago Tribune* about the most notable attempt at isolationism in the history of the world, namely, the city-state. The isolationism did not work, and the Greek city-state collapsed. As a result of its collapse democratic Roman thinking and Roman-Christian-Judaic thinking had to be almost completely transformed. By "transformed" I mean that the two schools of philosophy which began to develop political ideas in the Roman world simply ceased altogether to start with a city-state. It had become an anachronism, something perhaps looked back to with homesickness in a world in which people were not at home anywhere, in a vast, bleak, universal world, a world which, according to the Epicurean, could supply at best only precarious and private felicity.

And therefore, the Epicurean theory in politics is largely a negative one. Busy yourselves with politics as little as possible since there is no security in the political world. And since human beings, according to the Epicurean doctrine, are private sentients of private pleasures, its followers reluctantly counseled a strong government so that there should not be anarchy of competitive greeds and lusts. I think one may summarily say in a brief lecture that Epicurean political theory was a reluctant admission that there must be some sort of government against mutual depredation by the selfish beasts that human beings are. But any positive constructive political theory is not to be found among the Epicureans.

The opposite is true of the Stoics. Largely, our knowledge of Stoic political theory in one sense comes from a second-hand and second-rate source, namely, Cicero. I mean by second-rate and second-hand that while Cicero really was very good in political theory, he was much nearer Walter Lippmann than Aristotle. He was a good expositor to the semi-educated literate people of Rome, who today would be reading Walter Lippmann's expositions and feel that they had arrived at one of the fountainheads of political wisdom. Cicero is probably so understood because he is not an original philosopher, but he furnishes a wonderful, amiable, and urbane source book on the intellectual timbre of Roman political thought, especially Stoic thought, which is important here.

I am going to try very briefly to remind you what were the chief ideas among the Romans that have become absolutely the structure and texture of Western thought. First, the notion of individuals having equality not by being legal citizens of a given commonwealth but through sharing in the human distinction and the human identity of reason. Human beings, in so far as they were human, were reasonable, and therefore there was an intrinsic and inherent dignity in them all. Greek or barbarian, Roman or colonial, slave or free, a human being was instinct with the divine trait of reasoning. And this common reasonableness of humanity entitled them not only to be regarded as everywhere equally human and equal in their rights and obligations but enabled them to recognize what Cicero calls "natural law" and to judge all public laws by the degree to which they conformed to that natural law which was at once the incarnation of reasonableness and justice. The great idea was that there is an eternal and universal justice; that all laws derive their sanctions from the extent to which they incarnate that justice; and that all justice is identical with the reason operating in the universe and recognized by the minds of men in so far as they are human.

That sense of the eternal sanction of a reasonableness and equity in the universe itself, so that the edicts of any republic or commonwealth have a sanction just in so far as they conform to and incarnate that reasonable justness, is the great contribution that Roman thinking has made to the subject. What we call Roman law, which for so many centuries dominated the legal traditions of Europe, holds a political and moral ideal that was meant to be the application of natural justice in a universe of human relations, of which, ideally, the Roman Empire would be the expression and the fulfillment. Wedded to that idea of universal justice was another which, for all their severity and overrationalism, the Stoics borrowed from the early Christians, an idea that softened the notion of natural justice and mellowed it—the idea of universal brotherhood.

In the famous Hymn to Zeus of the Stoic Cleanthes, the poet speaks of the dear city of Cecrops, the dear city of Zeus, the dear city of God. The notion of the universality of natural law and justice was the rational expression of the brotherhood of man or of men, in the fact that they were children, as the Christians put it, or members, as Stoic philosophy put it, and as St. Paul put it, members of God. The notion of Christian love joined to the notion of Roman law and natural justice would seem to be more deeply woven into the texture of modern political and moral democracy than most current discussions remind us. We have become so accustomed to talking of the apparatus of democracy, its economic structure, that we forget that the form and contour of its human and moral meaning were set by these Greek and Roman thinkers whom I have had a chance only in the most summary way to describe to you today.

III

HEBREW SOURCES: SCRIPTURES AND TALMUD

BY

LOUIS FINKELSTEIN, Ph.D.

Rabbi (Jewish Theological Seminary); President and Solomon Schechter Professor of Theology, Jewish Theological Seminary of America; Director, Institute for Religious and Social Studies

The Scriptures and the Talmud contributed to the advancement of democracy in two ways. They include some of the basic principles of democracy; and they record the development of Jewish thought, as it adapted the institutions of life to an increasing awareness of democracy. It is from both of these points of view that the subject must be discussed if we are to understand the Scriptural and Talmudic sources of democracy.

The most significant contribution in literature to democratic thought is probably that in the early chapters of Genesis. In the first, we are told that God made man in His image. In the fifth, we are informed that the descendants of Adam were born in his image, and consequently in the image of God. This assertion that all men—all descendants of Adam—are alike the bearers of the image of God, are therefore possessors of supreme dignity, and that all are equal in this dignity, sets the goal toward which all democratic thinking must strive. It is not human equality nor human dignity alone which Scripture stresses. It is the combination of human equality and dignity.

This double basis of democracy is projected from the past into the future in the Pharisaic and Rabbinic concept of human immortality. The belief that man's soul is immortal, while not expressly enunciated in the Five Books of Moses, is in fact a corollary of the premise that all men bear God's image. Unless the term "God's image" is taken to refer to a physical appearance—a belief repugnant to ancient Pharisaism and the Talmud—it had to refer to man's spirit. But if man was created with the spirit of God within him, obviously that spirit does not perish with man's body, but survives it. The doctrine of immortality of the soul thus follows inevitably from the principle enunciated in the first chapters of Genesis, when these are interpreted in terms of a God Who is entirely spiritual and incorporeal. The doctrine of immortality, in turn, helps to reinforce the belief in human dignity and equality; for it asserts that we are not only equal in the reverence due us because of our Divine origin, but also because of our destined immortality.

Many years ago, when I first discussed the relation of the concept of immortality to democracy, I pointed to the contrast between the Palestinian idea and the Egyptian belief in the resurrection of the body, according to which only the bodies provided with special care and protection would be quickened. I indicated that this doctrine was essentially aristocratic; and that the Palestinian belief in immortality, according to which immortality was a reward to be won through a righteous life, was inherently democratic.

But even in Israel there developed two schools of thought with regard to the immortality of the soul. The School of Shammai, consisting of the conservative, priestly groups, held that immortality was limited to the righteous in Israel; while their opponents, the School of Hillel, taught that immortality can be obtained even by righteous pagans.

I believe it can be shown that the doctrine of the School of Hillel was the original Pharisaic teaching; for a passage of the Mishna enumerating the individuals who would not achieve immortality, mentions Balaam among them. This passage is described by the Talmud itself as having been formulated in the pre-Maccabean age; and there is good reason to believe that this is correct. The individuals who are described in the passage as having lost their immortality include various men whom the scholars of the days of Antiochus IV and his predecessors might have had special reason for excoriating. One was Balaam himself, who was of Syrian origin and might therefore be taken to personify the Syrian sages. But the fact that the early pre-Maccabean sages singled out Balaam as being unworthy of immortality implies that immortality was not a prerogative of Judaism, but of humanity.

Thus the Book of Daniel (12.2) reads: "And many of them that sleep in the dust of the earth shall awake." It does not say "many of the Hebrews sleeping in the dust of the earth," but "many of them"—of any people, whatsoever.

It is important to remark that the Biblical and Pharisaic doctrines that man is made in the image of God, and is therefore immortal, not only establish the dignity and equality of all men; but also the dignity of womanhood and the equality of the sexes. This profound truth is usually overlooked by historians of the emancipation of woman. It is generally held that this emancipation began with the teachings of the Greek philosophers and found its first effective expression in the teachings of St. Paul. But the verse in Genesis, to which I referred, specifically states: "And God created man in His own image; in the image of God created He him; male and female created He them" (Gen. 1.27). There can be no doubt that one of the purposes of this verse was to assert emphatically the doctrine of the dignity of womanhood and of the equality of the sexes. In the Rabbinic teaching women are recognized as immortal, together with men. In the future world, Sarah shares eternity with Abraham, and Rebecca with Isaac.

The theme of human equality recurs again and again in Scripture. "Are ye not as children of the Ethiopians unto Me, O children of Israel? saith the Lord," according to Amos (9.7). In several remarkable passages, the author of Job stresses human equality: "The small and the great are there; and the servant is free from his master" (3.19). "If I did despise the cause of my man-servant or of my maidservant when they contended with me, What then shall I do when God riseth up? And when He remembereth what shall I answer Him? Did not He that made me in the womb make him? And did not One fashion us in the womb?" (31.12–15).

In the light of these theoretical teachings, it may seem inconsistent that the Scriptures and the Rabbinic law tolerated the institution of slavery, and even that of plural marriage. But in this respect, as in others, the theological and philosophical insights of religion at their beginning affected but slowly the pagan institutions which they were ultimately to overwhelm. It is clear that the Scriptures inculcate monogamy. Thus Adam is created with one wife; Isaac, the patriarch who was offered as a whole-burnt offering to God, and therefore had a place of special esteem, likewise was monogamous. When Job's afflictions were removed, all that he had lost was returned to him doubly. But in his greatest afflictions, God spared him the loss of his wife. The suggestion occurs to one that the author deliberately avoids bestowing two wives on Job. Throughout Proverbs, Ecclesiastes, and the Song of Solomon, the theme of monogamy returns.

In the Pentateuch itself, God commands Abraham "in all that Sarah hath said unto thee, hearken unto her voice; for in Isaac shall thy seed be called to thee" (Gen. 21.12). This assertion of the rights of the first and principal wife as against those of second and later ones may seem elementary to us; but it was the first step in the destruction of the institution of plural marriage.

Similarly, the Pentateuch virtually abolishes Hebrew slavery. This was, likewise, a first and indispensable step in the abolition of slavery as an institution.

Even more important than the proclamation of the theoretical dignity and equality of men, and the weakening and ultimate abolition of institutions symbolizing inequality, was the emergence of a series of institutions destined to make democratic thinking effective. The first of these was that of the lay scholar, as opposed to the hereditary priest. In early times, the interpretation of the law and the ritual among Jews, as among other oriental peoples, was the prerogative of the hereditary priesthood. The development first of the Scribes and then of the Pharisaic scholars, whose authority derived not from ancestry, but from learning, opened the gates for a democratic interpretation of Scripture and of the law itself. The manner in which these lay scholars obtained the right to render decisions, and to instruct the priests themselves, is a saga of democratic achievement. Time came when the High Priest, before he entered the sacred shrine to perform the most sacred service of the year (that of the Day of Atonement), had to meet with the lay scholars, to obtain instruction from them, and to promise observation of the ritual as they taught it. Even the right to examine the diseased for the purpose of separating them from the community, given expressly to the priests in Leviticus, was ultimately exercised by lay scholars. The priest acted only as a mouthpiece for the scholar.

It is probably no exaggeration to assert that the whole history of western religion has been influenced by this emergence of the lay scholar as an authoritative expounder of the Torah. Both in Judaism, and in the religions akin to it, the authority of the hereditary priesthood was replaced by that of men called to the vocation of expounding the faith. Religion interpreted solely by a hereditary priestly caste might have become a force for reaction; but instead became in time the foundation stone of democratic thought and influence throughout the west.

Allied with the emergence of the scholar was that of the house of prayer, independent of the Temple in Jerusalem. The Temple in Jerusalem represented the authority of the priesthood; the synagogue was from the beginning an institution of democracy. Anyone could lead in the prayers; anyone could read the prescribed sections of the Law; anyone could become the head of the synagogue. The opening of the gates of heaven, as it were, to the masses of the people was a step of the utmost importance in the abolition of special privilege and the conceptions to which special privilege gave birth.

Old institutions, however, die slowly. Even after the Pharisees had established the principle that any scholar could interpret the Law, the Shammaitic group among them sought to limit the instruction in the Law to "those of good family." In reading the controversy between the School of Shammai and the School of Hillel on this point, one is reminded of the modern controversy about opening colleges and universities to all students, solely on the basis of relative ability. Like some modern leaders, the ancient Shammaites held that education should be the prerogative of the elect—the well-to-do who could devote all their time to study. But the House of Hillel insisted—and won its point—that "one should teach anyone," even the sinful, for many sinful in Israel were brought back to righteousness through study of the Torah.

In this instance, too, the School of Hillel rather than that of Shammai seems to have reflected the original Pharisaic teaching. Of the teachings of the Men of the Great Synagogue—the body of lay scholars who antedated the origin of Pharisaism and laid its foundations—only one has been preserved. "They used to say," we are told in Mishna Abot 1.2, "Be deliberate in judgment; raise many disciples; and make a hedge about the Law." For reasons which are too technical to discuss here, but which I outlined in *Journal of Biblical Literature* LIX, 1940, pp. 455-59, it seems probable that this maxim originally read, not "raise many disciples," but "appoint many scholars." In any event, the significance of the passage was that the teaching of the Law and its exposition was not to be limited either to the priesthood or to the "best" families. It was to become—as it did become—the prerogative of all who wished it.

These teachings and institutions were no more important as contributions by the ancient Jewish teachers to democracy than their development of the doctrine of freedom of opinion, and their respect for deviation from the accepted norm of the majority. Precisely because the exposition of the Law became a prerogative of an ever-increasing number of scholars, and because the meaning of the Law could be discovered only in free argument, the pre-Pharisaic and Pharisaic teachers arrived at the conclusion that even a rejected view may have sufficient merit to justify its being transmitted to posterity. Hence the Talmud contains on almost every page both the views which became the accepted norm and those which were rejected in its favor. The opposition's conceptions are immortalized together with those of the majority. Thus, though the School of Hillel ultimately prevailed in its arguments with the School of Shammai, hundreds of Shammaitic opinions have been preserved for us. More than that, the Hillelites taught that the School of Shammai was justified in following its own views on the Law and ought not to be urged, much less compelled, to adopt the view of the Hillelites; for the Hillelites maintained, "Both views are the words of the living God."

This extraordinary tolerance of deviation set the pattern for all later Jewish tradition. Many controversies arose regarding the interpretation of the Talmud itself. But Jewish tradition has uniformly held that no one can be asked to forsake the authentic and verified tradition of his fathers in the interpretation of Jewish law.

Perhaps the most powerful expression of this tolerance for opposition is that given by Rabban Gamaliel I, the grandson of Hillel, and preserved not in the Talmudic writings, but in the Book of Acts. When Peter and the other Apostles were brought before the Sanhedrin to stand trial on the charge of teaching an anti-Jewish doctrine, the Book of Acts records that Gamaliel "a doctor of the law, had in reputation among all the people," stood up and spoke on their behalf. The climax of his address, which cited precedents in favor of tolerance of deviation, is the verse: "And now I say unto you, refrain from these men, and let them alone; for if this counsel or this work be of men, it will come to nought; but if it be of God, ye cannot overthrow it, lest haply ye be found even to fight against God" (Acts 5.38–39).

The question of whether these were the precise words of Rabban Gamaliel on this occasion is not relevant; the important fact is that the Book of Acts, not otherwise friendly to the Pharisees, records that this great Pharisaic leader set down the principle that deviation from accepted or majority opinion is not a punishable offense. No matter how certain he and his colleagues might be that the teaching of the Apostles was erroneous, penalties could not be inflicted on them. On the contrary, it was assumed that if the teaching was entirely in error it would fail; and if it had a place in the Divine plan, to seek to crush it would be wrong.

With this background it is not at all surprising to find that the Jewish communities of Europe in the tenth and the eleventh centuries, surrounded by a feudal system which left little room for democratic thought and practice, remained islands of freedom and equality. The famous "ordinances of the communities," established by the Jewish settlements in the Rhineland, and later in France and in Germany generally, were models of legislation by will of the people. Under the leadership of the great scholar, Rabbenu Gershom, called "the Light of the Dispersion," these various communities even came together in the first part of the eleventh century and established a constitution limiting the authority of the community itself against its individual members. Among the rights reserved to the individual who believed himself wronged, yet could not obtain redress in the regularly constituted courts, was that of interrupting the service in the synagogue, until arrangements were made to hear him. This right of preventing the congregation from proceeding with worship until they were willing to see justice done, was one of the most formidable means of protecting the weak against the strong.

In this way the democratic tradition of Judaism, beginning with the very origins of the faith, continued right through the Middle Ages and even to our own time.

IV

MEDIAEVAL SOURCES

BY

GEORGE N. SHUSTER, M.A.

President, Hunter College of the City of New York

I shall confess to having accepted Dr. Johnson's kind invitation to discuss with you the mediaeval contribution to what is called democratic idealism with deep misgivings. My interest in the topic is genuine, but my competence to deal with it is very much open to question. You will no doubt pardon me for saying that I feel a bit like a Mississippi pilot steering a ship up the Amazon. It is fortunate that great scholars—Schnürer and Burdach, Boissier and Boissonade, Taylor and Pickman—are there for all of us to read. At least I may take credit for acknowledging my indebtedness to them before embarking upon the perilous waters of personal reflection.

It is obvious first of all that the man of the Middle Ages was not concerned, or at any rate was rarely concerned, with "democracy" in one specifically modern sense. He did not choose representatives who governed in accordance with the wishes of the majority for limited periods of time. True enough, during centuries he elected his bishops, and there was also in various parts of Europe a considerable amount of popular civil government. There was Jewish self-government, too, as Dr. Finkelstein has shown. But nobody objected to a fourth term. And though men were forever arguing and defending intellectual positions, they were never targets for consciously devised barrages of propaganda. The tribe, the folk, and the region accepted political solidarity to a far greater extent than does the nation or the "race" of the present time.

On the other hand, mediaeval man shared personally in the discovery of what may well be the only valid basis on which a democratic faith can rest. Man must be free because man is man—that was the proposition. It was derived from two premises. First, man is the image of God. True enough, his body was fashioned by nature, in accordance with great creative ideas or laws the evolutionary operation of which Augustine had described with remarkable intuitive insight into the process of cosmic becoming. But man's spirit, it was believed, came directly from God, and would return to Him again individual and entire, bearing the stamp of a history in part its own making and in part God's. There was in progress throughout each human life an august, inscrutable partnership between man and his Maker—a partnership of the giving of grace and its acceptance or rejection. And since things were so, one had to realize that in dealing with one's fellow man one was dealing also with God. Then there was likewise the possibility that in the existence to begin after death an astonishing revolution might be revealed. The masters of the here and now might occupy very modest mansions in the kingdom of God, while the slave in whom illustrious virtue had been made plain would walk in glory like unto an archangel's.

These truths were simple and complex as well. You could not easily cherish them without being compelled to alter your attitude toward your fellows in this life also. And as a matter of fact too well known to need stress, the movement toward community, even toward an egalitarian community of a sort, was deep and strong. Therewith the second premise was given. The community was willed by God and must consequently be all-embracing. Nobody could be excluded from it, and its government found its only sanction—as St. Thomas wrote—in the achieved well-being of all. There might be differing stations in life, but the differences were, above all, gradations of responsibility. It was because these social ideas had formed an integral part of early Christian faith that the miracle of the Christian triumph over antiquity could occur. Pickman is quite right, however, in reminding us that this victory was due not merely to the precept to love one's neighbor, but also to a great wisdom, a remarkable prudence, mustered by Christian leadership as it set about wrestling with the practical tasks involved in the building of a community which might be *sacrum imperium*, a holy empire, on the one hand, but was always a justly treated citizenry, on the other hand.

The problem of reconciling the religious demand for perfection with the imperfection latent in every compromise with earthly reality is beyond solution, of course. Thou shalt not kill, for example. Clearly that is the simplest demand of love. Yet the soldier must kill. Is the soldier's trade therefore forbidden to the Christian? If it is, how shall the community defend itself against aggression? These questions were not easy, and it was a long time before the Church could reply without seeming to violate its own confession. And if we look carefully we shall see that similar queries continue to arise out of the ever-existing antithesis between the democratic ideal and the social reality. All men are created equal, we say, and therefore the will of the majority of men must be preferable to the will of the minority. But as a matter of fact there is inequality, and the majority is often palpably wrong, so that democratic living is a constant endeavor by informed leaders to educate the majority and thus to render it less ineffectual than it would otherwise be. Perhaps then the doctrine of majority rule does not follow logically from the basic fact of equality. But we have only to ask ourselves, "If not the majority but a minority is right, who is to tell us about the matter?" in order to see that there is no possible way in which democracy can avoid committing its destiny to the majority. It is necessary and therefore prudent to be governed accordingly. Similarly, the wisdom of the early Middle Ages resulted from a commitment to ethical absolutes which refrained from dogmatism where the here-and-now relative was concerned. One was to practice the virtues of love and humility wherever possible. That this rule was never interpreted with laxity it would be absurd to claim. But certainly Ambrose and Jerome did not so interpret it.

The Christian attitude toward the community was further characterized by the separation of Church and State. Here the new religion differed radically from all the creeds of antiquity. Perhaps the fact was rooted more deeply in history than in doctrine. Certainly the Christian desired a State that was not secular. But his thinking reflects the gradual unfolding of the Trinitarian theology, in the formulation of which speculative Neo-Platonism had an important part. From the Father came all things that are, the world of nature and the human spirit, the gregariousness of man, the *materia*, matter, in which the Divine ideas are implanted. The Son, the Word Incarnate, was the Builder of the Church and the Exemplar. And the Holy Spirit was the guide, the fount of inspiration and of prudence, from whom the grace of wisdom was received. And yet these Three were not distinct but rather One. The Christian therefore faced the task of divining, in humility and in trembling, how the imitation of his Master was to be achieved in detail within the mysterious framework of the Divine plan. That obviously called for the perfect use of earthly things, as Augustine had taught, and also for the imperfect, necessarily imperfect, drawing out from evil of what good it contained. But the State it was which dealt with evil. Mediaeval man did not often go as far as did the extreme Augustinians, Luther, for example, toward repudiation of the nonspiritual State. Yet he almost never lost the tragic sense of life, recovered for us of today in a different form by such able thinkers as Reinhold Niebuhr and Theodore Haecker.

Granted such an attitude toward the State, the preservation of the integrity of the Church became a fateful question. If one believed that religious faith was the sole basis upon which a definition of man could be erected, one was inevitably driven to the attempt to make Christians of others. Even more essential and primitive was the urge to preserve the purity and holiness of the Church itself. But how were these things to be accomplished? So long as the surrounding world was hostile, the answer was comparatively simple. The example of saint and martyr persuaded the unbeliever, brought hope and solace to questioning minds and hearts. But as the opportunity to create a Christian community became real, it was only the dissident minority which barred the way. Often enough such minorities were what we should term subversive. The Manichean and the Paulician did not play fair, were the advocates of infiltration in those days. Could one then resort to the suppression of dissidents both within and without the Church?

It was a fearfully difficult problem. To have raised it at all was to have taken the greatest step forward in history toward the ultimate realization of the democratic ideal. I say "ultimate" because no answer has as yet been found. The democratic ideal is not so much a doctrine as an agreement to accept man as the social absolute. He is to be taken as he is—a creature who can be either good or evil, crafty or honest, foolish or wise. You affirm your faith in him because of what he is essentially, and of what he can potentially become. But you do not say that he is, here and now, either good or bad. You say that he is both; and you say further that collectively, in community, he can be good only when goodness shapes the common action. In making these decisions you are committing yourself not to static contentment but to ceaseless effort. Who, then, can be astonished that the Middle Ages found no solution for the problem which remains, in cognate form, the conundrum of a secular democracy? You will recall how Augustine, a great Christian if there ever was one, in the end replied. He said that he had always believed the Church must not use force to convert the heretic and the infidel. But it was proved that imperial edicts threatening the recalcitrant with penalties did win them over to orthodoxy. As a consequence, reasoned Augustine, God had demonstrated that force did bring men around to the truth. It is a pretty good argument, and one is not surprised that Augustine accepted it, in view of the parlous conditions under which he lived. A modern man can appreciate his difficulty. We have seen in our time that virulent antidemocratic forces can take advantage of the freedom conceded by democracy in order to bring about its destruction. And very few of us, I suppose, are not tempted to believe that German democrats should have banned Hitler and suppressed his doctrine. Today there is in this country a strong demand for legislation to curb those who preach and practice group discrimination, rightly held to be incompatible with the American view of life, and who advocate social revolution by force. Well, Christianity had become the formative influence in the European community. Was it going to tolerate those who sought to destroy it?

The astonishing fact is that the men of the Middle Ages struggled for so long a time to find a solution based on humility and love. Saint

Bernard, who represents his period so illustriously, continued to maintain that the heretic must be won over by argument and not by force of arms. And when he opposed the pogroms that marred the life of so many cities during the period of the Crusades, he did not of course talk like a modern humanitarian, but he did speak like a Christian. One may suppose that, if Christendom had spread less rapidly and more evenly, it might have more generally found the wisdom to approach the difficulty with the prudence of its first period. Unfortunately, it did not. Throughout all the dreary history of the Inquisition, churchmen resorted to a thoroughly un-Christian method of treating a Christian problem. And the end was a staggering *reductio ad absurdum* not merely because Galileo was taken into custody but primarily because two of the greatest Saints of the late Middle Ages, Savonarola and Jeanne d'Arc, were burned at the stake with benefit of clergy. To that dreary debacle many factors contributed. But it would be a mistake to conclude therefore that the Middle Ages had nothing to say to us on the subject. For they did produce both Francis and Thomas Aquinas. In the life of the one and in the teaching of the other the outlines of the ancient Christian wisdom are plain to see. For my part, I find them better guides to the study of the courtesy which is the major requisite of a good society in the pluralistic sense than are most of their successors, secularist or otherwise. Liberalism is well and good so long as nobody is kicking up a fuss. But liberalism does not answer our question because it has never honestly faced the problem of the human community. For what does it mean to be told that we all differ and yet all agree? The plain fact is that we do not. There would have been no persecution of Jews in Germany if Catholics and Protestants had been able to do something more constructive than distrust each other. Franco would have been out of Spain long ago if any two of the forces which oppose him could have joined hands. In short, if a resolution to seek social wisdom on the basis of a commitment to humility and love that are rooted in Divine command does not avail anything, despite Thomas and Francis, then what will?

At any rate, St. Thomas brings us immediately to mediaeval education, one of the most significant advances toward democracy in the history of the race. The popularity and the relative egalitarianism of the Schools have their lasting significance. But of the system of Scholasticism at its best I should like to speak in a kind of paraphrase of what Waldo Frank has written so beautifully about the Torah. That system was an endeavor to use discussion in order to make manifest the relevance of the manifold actions of daily life to religious faith. If you return to St. Thomas's *De Regimine Principuum* as a good example of Scholastic method, you will find it singularly lacking in generalizations. It is concrete, practical, even upon occasion fussy in a sort of comical way. But the author is serving a holy purpose. Persuaded that every action, indeed every thought, can take on religious meaning if the governing intent is Divine service, he deprives the commonplace of meanness and confers dignity upon routine. Who is not reminded at this point of Brother Juniper's cabbages planted upside down in order to reveal the rightness of obedience? Yet only so long as Torah and Scholastic treatise are inspired by an abiding commitment to God can either have value. In the Christian case it was not the university nor indeed education itself which mattered so much, but rather what some one has called *der heilige Geist des Mittelalters*—the sacral spirit of the Middle Ages.

And so the ideal did struggle to take on form. There had survived in the collapse of Rome only the priest, the soldier, and the boor. But slowly there developed in the cities a free citizenry of organized artisans. The guild was more than a labor union. It was more like what David Dubinsky is trying to make out of a labor union. To discern that of which it was capable, one has only to think of matters as diverse as the Cathedral of Notre Dame, the guild halls of Brussels and Danzig, and Shakespeare's Company. Europe has been haunted ever since by the memory of these organizations. You can trace the nostalgia for them in writers as diverse as Péguy and Bernanos, Ruskin and Rilke, Chesterton and Eric Gill. Government itself acquired in the better hours of mediaeval history some of the sense of community which characterized the guilds. We must not fancy that the guild citizenry did not know public opinion. Even as late as the Tudor period in English history, when the modern concept of autocracy had already blossomed, that citizenry had a mind of its own. Read only what it said openly and bravely about the beheading of Thomas More. No doubt it had been rebellious over the matter of Papal levies. But it was incensed at the conduct of the King.

Indeed, the more one reads of the period, the more certain one is that it was an age of democracy because it had all the faults of democracy. There was everywhere the disorder—the chicken bones and eggshells—of the mob. That mob did queer things in church. It staged theatre there. It slyly affixed farcical statues to the towers of cathedrals. It spoke its own language, and the subjects about which it conversed were not always refined. The Renaissance was to a far greater extent than most of us realize a sort of uplift movement sponsored by the intellectual aristocrat. If the nude figure then captivated Raphael and Michelangelo, it was not because there had been no nude figures previously. It was only because the people's nudity was obscene, even as its wives were coarse and its moral code superstitious, that the master struggled to reveal the Platonic loveliness of the human form. Erasmus, Colet, More, Pico, and the other great Italians, were not innovators but educators. They longed to restore the great dignity and sweep of ancient aristocratic Rome, as these qualities had been manifest in Augustine, Ambrose, and Jerome. When Petrarch repudiated Aristotle for Plato, he was quite evidently and undisguisedly in quest of the golden age.

But when one tries to find a single pose of mediaeval man that shows him as he truly was, one turns to his outings, which were the pilgrimages. They were often rollicking enough, Heaven knows. People exuding false piety sold trinkets at a usurious profit and dubbed them relics. There was no doubt too much of wine. But all these things were like the smudge of children's fingers on a white cloth, for the Holy Grail was really at the end of the journey. And together with the Saint whose shrine one eventually neared, one was joined with the living and the dead in an august commingling, called the Communion of Saints, but embracing, in all truth, sinners, too, of the here-and-now and of the purgatorial realm beyond, priests and people, men and women and children, the unwashed peasant and the burgher who knew the protective sweetness of balms and spices. Where, one wonders, does history afford such another pageant of hands woven together across time and eternity? Yes, you may say, if you like, that the finale was the dance of death which followed the remorseless plague. There was need in that democracy of reform and science, of urbanity, and even of a measure of incredulity. But surely the time did not lack a social ideal.

Therefore when Gilbert Chinard wrote the life of Thomas Jefferson he found the antecedents of the Declaration of Independence in old English law rather than in the writings of Rousseau and the Encyclopedists. There the inalienable rights of man had been arrayed in solemn juridical phrase ere the stone on Alfred's grave was dusty. Such was the Christian heritage. Perhaps we shall have to learn from the Middle Ages that the masses of men will always insist upon those rights for themselves but will not easily of their own accord concede them to others. Patently, the flagrant acts of prejudice in which the Middle Ages indulged were democratic enough. John Huss, let us remember, was tried by his peers and slain despite Emperor and Pope. Jews were put to torture even though the Councils had placed anathemas on pogroms. All of which means that democracy is a viable social method only so long as the commitment which underlies it is grasped and endorsed. That is why, I venture to say, Dante is great even as is Joachim of Flores, while Marsilius of Padua is not great. For Marsilius sought from debate and conference what they can never give—namely, certainty. But Dante sought to rest the freedom of debate upon certainty. Mankind is always having to choose between these two. Latterly, I believe, it has chosen wrong.

V

REFORMATION SOURCES

BY

JOHN T. McNEILL, Ph.D., D.D.

Professor of History of European Christianity, Divinity School, University of Chicago

I much regret that I have been prevented by unavoidable duties from hearing the earlier lectures in this series. The plan of the series is admirable, and the committee's choice of Richard Niebuhr as today's lecturer was a most happy one. In his regrettable illness I have been asked to take his place. This I can do only in the sense that I hold the floor and occupy the time assigned to him. While the program has my approval, I confess to a little minor disquiet of mind over its language at one point. I refer to the distinction between "origins" and "sources" in the titles employed. I do not quite know why the origins are classical and the sources Hebrew, mediaeval, etc. Perhaps, in fact, no distinction between *fons* and *origo* was intended; or perhaps it has been elucidated in earlier lectures. At any rate, I am assuming that no one who heard the other lectures has come to this one with any shred of belief that the Reformation is to be regarded as the *fons et origo* of democracy.

I

Great was the debt of the Reformation to democratic elements in the church and society of earlier ages. In ecclesiastical organization there have been elements of democracy at every stage. When the Apostles invited the Christian assembly at Jerusalem to elect from among themselves as relief officers "seven men of honest report full of the Holy Ghost and of wisdom," we learn, the proposal "pleased the whole multitude," and they proceeded to act upon it. From that day forward both direct and indirect, or representative, democracy has had a large place in church affairs. The rapid growth of the church and the establishment of large units of organization made it necessary either to employ undemocratic means of government or to practice representative democracy. In fact, both developments occurred; and often we find both elements in smoothly working combination. During the Patristic era when the so-called monarchical episcopate took shape, there was still a great deal that was not monarchical in church practice.

The mediaeval monks and friars were great makers of constitutions. These were, of course, plans of government not for the masses but for a select group. Generally they employed the principle of representative democracy, with a greater or less admixture of monarchical authority. From the twelfth century on, the acts of and discussions concerning the provincial and diocesan organizations of the church show a growing understanding and an increasing use of the principle of representation in church government.

Secular governments of the late Middle Ages exhibit similar phenomena. Many cities passed through a series of bold experiments in democratic government. The constitutions of Iceland and of Switzerland were from the first purely democratic. The rise of the parliaments of England and of Scotland, the functions of the *cortes* in the Hispanic kingdoms, the employment of assemblies for government in local areas of France and efforts to give to the Estates General of that country real and permanent power, are phenomena of a widespread trend toward democracy. Even though this trend was checked in some regions of Europe, it achieved permanent results in others. The parliament of England gained enough strength to depose a discredited king in 1327, and survived to check the absolutist ambitions of later rulers.

In the Middle Ages the advocacy of representative democracy reached its culmination in the Conciliar movement which attempted to reduce the Papacy to a limited monarchy, subordinating its authority to that of universal representative councils or parliaments ecclesiastical. The effort did not succeed. The Renaissance popes condemned

Conciliarism in no ambiguous terms. Nevertheless, between the Conciliarists and Luther the demand for a reforming council was frequently voiced. The Reformers were the heirs of the Conciliarists: but they adopted a more radical course.

It is thus evident that whatever the Reformation did to democracy, it did not give it birth, or even rebirth. In setting down such a topic as "Reformation Sources of Democracy," I assume that the committee, at least subconsciously, acknowledged that the Reformation helped to nourish democracy and to strengthen it for its modern conflicts; to this general view I would subscribe without reserve.

There are about four ways in which inquiry on the relations of the Reformation and democracy may proceed. We may first ask how the leading principles of the Reformation affect the spirit of democracy. Secondly, we may inquire in what respects and to what degree the church polities springing from the Reformation exhibit democratic principles. Thirdly, we may evaluate from the angle of democracy the political teachings of the Reformers. And fourthly, we may try to relate all these to the history of political action, asking in what, if in anything, political democracy has been enhanced by Protestant teaching and ecclesiastical practice. Obviously, more is demanded here than this lecture can supply. The field is wide, complicated, and controversial; and one lecture can provide no more than a scant introduction to it.

II

The principles of the Reformation cannot here be analyzed in the manner of Protestant scholastics and textbook writers. Everybody knows that these principles include a doctrine clumsily called "justification by faith." On examination we find that the justification is not forensic: it is not something that takes place concerning a man's status but within his soul. And we see that the faith associated with justification is not creedal and intellectual belief: it is the "heart's utter trust in Christ," or, to quote another phrase of Luther, it is "the soul throwing itself upon God." A man is not the author of his own faith; it is awakened in the heart by God. By this faith the believer is at once justified and regenerated and empowered to good works. It is a "living, busy, active, mighty thing." Before there is time to ask whether good works are to be done, it has done them.

Whatever may be thought of the validity of this by philosophers, psychologists, or theologians, it is a conception calculated to liberate and enhance personality. It gave to Luther and his fellow believers deep confidence in God and freedom from fear. Luther in the Wartburg used to sign some of his letters "Eleutherius"—the Liberator. A year earlier he had written *The Freedom of a Christian Man,* in which he discourses upon the liberation, enrichment, and fructifying of life that spring from faith. He thought he had discovered the spiritual way to freedom.

The sense of personal, direct, and constant dealing between God and the soul is so intense here that Luther has been charged with mere religious individualism. "Faith is a matter in which each one is responsible for himself," he remarked in 1523. But he is really very far from saying that no Christian can help another in the spiritual life. This is, in fact, what he most emphatically denies. The Reformation doctrine of the priesthood of all Christians must be noticed here. In my judgment this doctrine has been widely misinterpreted: it has been caricatured even by those who professed to be its advocates. It is glibly made the equivalent of a mere naked individualism in which every Christian is his own priest; and it is alleged to abolish priesthood itself. In fact, it extends priestly functions to all true Christians and makes every Christian his neighbor's priest. "By that priesthood," says Luther, in a typical statement, "we are able to appear before God, to pray for others, and to teach one another mutually the things that are of God." The priestly function of every Christian is to help others toward God. The whole conception is of fellowship arising in the religious sphere and extending to social and economic mutual service. It leads to the hallowing of the lay calling. "A cobbler, a smith, or a peasant" is a priest when he joins with the labor of others his own special service to the community. The priesthood becomes a ministry to others; and the special priesthood of the trained and ordained minister who leads the people in worship is an extension and specialization of the common priesthood. The minister is thus a representative of the Christian people. When a bishop is consecrated, one person is taken from the community of Christians who all share in the common spiritual power and is "commanded to exercise this power for the rest." All Christians are called to be priests but they are to select those who shall exercise the ministry in their behalf. This they have a right to exercise only with the consent of the whole body. (Luther's *Werke, Weimar Ausgabe,* XI, 412. XXI. 180–194. For other references see J. T. McNeill, *Unitive Protestantism,* pp. 36f., 122f.) Luther and his early followers did not always stress the implications of this doctrine with its spiritualizing of representation and its strong motivation for democratic fraternalism. But it was not without influence in German Lutheranism, and was more vigorously affirmed by action in the Reformed Church. Some leftist sects of the Reformation era employed the principle of the lay priesthood to the exclusion of any permanent distinctive ministry such as both Lutheran and Reformed churches maintained and defended.

While Zwingli and Calvin affirmed the doctrines we have referred to, they emphasized another doctrine for which Luther fought but which he never made so central as they did—the doctrine of predestination. Calvin's predestinarianism has usually been seen by historians of political thought in relation to his political republicanism. Professor Irwin Edman writes: "As Luther stressed liberty, Calvin stressed equality. . . . The elect are democratically equal." He adds that Calvin's church constitution was relatively democratic (*Fountainheads of Freedom,* p. 56, Reynal & Hitchcock). He justly sees these facts in relation. It would be easy to quote numerous older political writers who hold the same view. Buckle, contrasting the Calvinist with the Arminian position, goes so far as to say:

> The more any society tends to equality, the more likely it is that its theological opinions will be Calvinistic; while the more a society tends to inequality the greater the probability of these opinions being Arminian (*History of Civilization in England,* I, 612.3, Longmans, Green & Co.).

Bancroft has a different emphasis: he holds that the doctrine of predestination "inspires a resolute, almost defiant freedom in those who deem themselves the subjects of God's electing grace" (*History of the United States,* II. 461, D. Appleton & Co.).

Probably such writers are mainly trying to account for the trend toward the practice of democracy where a reformed church became active or dominant. This much is clear: man, whether poor or rich, weak or strong, obscure or eminent, was viewed as a sinner in desperate need of God's grace or the undeserving recipient thereof. There was no room for pride, great need for contrite obedience to God, and an awful sense of the duty of conducting one's daily affairs in complete accordance with God's will. The Christian must live in the knowledge that in all his life he has dealings with God—*"in toto vita negotium cum Deo"* (Calvin, *Institutes* III, vii, 2).

But this does not isolate him from society. Weber has laid a mistaken emphasis upon the isolation of the soul in Calvinism. Election is of the individual; but it is of individuals who, normally, have been exposed to grace through the communion of saints in the church. And the elect become at once co-operatively active in that divine society, the church of God, and in the social order. Their social life is activated and directed by their religion; mere isolation has no place in the Christian life. Calvin would have thought totally inadequate the *obiter dictum* of Whitehead: "Religion is what a man does with his solitariness." (I am not assuming that Whitehead thinks it adequate.) Religion is the basis of what a man thinks and does about everything in his experience, not least about his vocation. We are placed under the sternest obligation to hold our talents and possessions in stewardship to God for our neighbor. "Everyone should inwardly consider that no matter how great he is, he owes himself to his neighbors, nor should a limit be set to his beneficence short of the failure of his resources" (*Inst.* III, vii, 7).

Under this heading of the relation of democracy to the principles of the Reformation, much else might be taken into account. Many Protestants would want to throw the emphasis upon the doctrine of Scripture. I doubt whether we could gain very much light on our problem by pursuing that theme without much more extended notice than is here possible. There are two main difficulties. One is that everybody, whatever he set out to teach, quoted the Bible. It was in it that King James and Bishop Bossuet found divine-right absolutism and Filmer found his strange notion of the patriarch-monarchy. It was used by the Protestants of different schools both for and against democratic government. Secondly, its authority for the individual was channeled through confessions of faith which in many cases gave elementary direction to political thinking. The Bible was a great and constant inspiration to the Reformation: it was not so explicitly and simply, as often assumed, the directing authority for Reformation thought and action. But what has been said of faith, the common priesthood, and predestination is sufficient to suggest a positive relation to democracy in the body of Reformation principles.

III

We now turn to a brief consideration of the church polities that took shape in the Reformation. Amid all the varieties it is broadly true that Protestant polities are "conciliar," that is, they employ the principle of government not by individuals, but by representative councils. (Councils may of course be called by many names: assemblies, synods, colloquies, presbyteries, classes, boards, commissions, etc.) Where the episcopate has survived it has generally been subjected to a great deal of limitation or jurisdiction, as was already done in some degree before the Reformation. The Convocation of Canterbury (revived in 1861 after a long period of suppression through government encroachment upon the Church) received its essential character in the thirteenth century. It seems to owe something to the fact that its principal framers in that era, Kilwardby and Peckham, were trained respectively in the Dominican and Franciscan friar orders. Anglicanism during periods of its highest efficiency has relied a good deal also on diocesan synods; and in the present century it has developed a new and important organ of conciliar government, the National Assembly.

Like Anglicanism, German Lutheranism has suffered a good deal from political interference. It fell under the control of princes in many parts of Germany when Luther encouraged the rulers to take action for reform and reconstruction after the Peasant War. The result was to place German Lutheranism in a position in which its development was conditioned by political authority in an unfortunate degree. Partly through concessions made by Luther the development of church government in German Lutheranism was out of accord with the basic teaching of Luther and Melanchthon.

The Reformers inherited more of mediaeval modes of thought than they realized or were disposed to acknowledge. They were, as I said earlier, the heirs of the Conciliarists. It was natural that Luther, at an early stage in the controversy over Indulgences, and shortly after his appearance before Cardinal Caietanus at Augsburg, should appeal for a general council to hear the case. This he did on November 28, 1518, affirming (almost in the language of the decree *Sacrosancta* of the Council of Constance, 1415) that "a sacred council lawfully assembled in the Holy Spirit, representing the Holy Catholic Church, is above the pope in cases concerning the faith." The demand for a council was insistently voiced by Luther and the Lutheran element in the imperial diets for many years, and the Protest of Speyer (1529) from which Luther's party was called "Protestant," complains of the failure of the Emperor to bring about the "free general Christian council" which he had promised. In 1523 Luther defended the local system of representative government introduced at Leisnig in Saxony, a feature of which was the provision of a popular call of the pastor (Luther's *Werke,* W.A. XI, 400; Sehling, E. *Die evangelische Kirchenordnungen,* I, 596ff.). But in 1526 he rejected the synodical plan for Hesse drawn up by the ex-Franciscan François Lambert. After the Peasant Revolt, Luther was hesitant about permitting laymen of all ranks a voice in church government. He apparently felt that the lay folk were not yet ready for such responsibility rather than that they never would be ready for it. The prince, who was in his view the agent of God for government and at the same time the principal lay Christian, was in a different position, and was invited to take responsibility in reforming the parishes. Soon arose the system of appointing consistories instead of elective synods. Yet Luther favored synodical assemblies in the Schmalkald Articles of 1537, and it was written by Melanchthon into this authoritative document of Lutheranism that "the judgments of synods are rightly the judgments of the church." The American development of Lutheranism in all its branches exhibits its natural adherence to the synodical principle.

It is justifiable to argue with G. V. Lechler that a presbyterian constitution is in no way incompatible with the views of the Saxon Reformers (*Geschichte der Presbyterial und Synodalverfassung,* pp. 8f.).

It is not in early Lutheranism but in the Reformed or Calvinistic churches that we see the unhesitant adoption of representative constitutions.

In all the Reformed churches the conciliar type of organization has prevailed, and it has assumed similar structures in different national and territorial environments. It is ecclesiastical representative democracy (or conciliarism) with safeguards against radicalism. It involves a framework of elective governing bodies superior to that of the local church. The consistory or kirk-session which controls the local church is composed of the minister and a number of elders elected by the members of the congregation. In Geneva the elders were chosen by the Little Council, for their spiritual fitness, from among the politically elected governing councils of the city. This system assumed a theocratic conception of the city republic, and it gave high responsibilities to laymen of the church. A. Mitchell Hunter writes of Calvin in this connection:

> Consistent with his view regarding the common priesthood of believers . . . he restored to laymen a position in church government which they had not held since primitive days. He gave them seats of equal authority with the clergy in the church court which supervised and directed the religious life of the community (*The Teaching of Calvin,* p. 199, Maclehose, Jackson & Co.).

Elsewhere the elders were generally elected by the congregations. The minister and one elder, elected by his brethren, attend the next higher council (colloquy, classis, or presbytery). "The authority of the colloquies," says the French *Discipline,* "is subject to that of the provincial synods, as the authority of the consistories is to that of the colloquies." Over the provincial is the national synod, called in Scottish presbyterianism the general assembly. Since the Reformed churches did not regard themselves as merely national, and frequently sought unity beyond the ranks of the Reformed, it was natural that the

Westminster Assembly's *Book of Discipline* should refer to "ecumenical" assemblies.

In an ampler study one would be tempted to draw some comparisons between the Reformed polities and those of the mediaeval religious orders, and to test the hypothesis of an historical filiation, say, from the Cistercian, or the Premonstratensian or the Dominican constitution to the earliest Protestant experiments in polity to which the Reformed churches were indebted—those of Vallerand Poullain, François Lambert, and John à Lasco. There lies here an attractive invitation to research. The Reformed church orders claimed scriptural authority; but it would be folly to argue that they took origin from scriptural guidance alone. They accorded well with the Reformation doctrines of faith and justifying grace and of the priesthood of the laity, for which a scriptural basis is more justly claimed. It was with respect to the ministry—a ministry without prelacy—rather than to the whole tradition of government, that the scriptural claim was plausible. Modern studies of the primitive church have left us with at least some vestiges of the Reformed interpretation of the New Testament ministry, but he would be a bold and misguided Presbyterian who would claim today that the system as a whole is discoverable in Scripture. There went into its making a good deal of democratic feeling caught out of the atmosphere of the times, and a great deal of common sense.

I must omit consideration of the variant church orders of Independents and Anabaptists, Quakers and other groups, and of modern Baptist, Congregational, and Unitarian churches, all of which exhibit advanced democratic features, as well as of the highly interesting polities of the Methodist churches of Britain and America, which are also essentially democratic.

IV

There exists a certain correspondence between the political thought of the Reformers and the ecclesiastical polities they preferred or adopted, but this is not so close as to be at once and always obvious. They were not primarily political theorists, and their utterances in this field are incidental and unsystematic. The word "democracy" is not in favor in their vocabulary. Generally for them it bore suggestions of anarchy or sedition.

All the Reformers began with a basic respect for existing governments as coming under the scriptural commendation: "Let every soul be subject unto the higher powers . . . the powers that be are ordained of God" (Rom. 13.1). We may have difficulty in bringing ourselves to realize how far government for the Reformers was a thing given, like the sunshine or the tide or the plague. Nevertheless, the divinely ordained ruler was not above criticism. Luther did not much like the rulers God had chosen. A good prince, he said, was *rara avis*. He ventured to advise princes, somewhat in the manner of the many writers of the "mirror of princes" literature from Augustine to Erasmus, but with more vigor. When you advise princes (or presidents) in print, anyone may read what you say and put his own construction upon it. The peasants mistook Luther for a revolutionary ally, and, when he vehemently took the side of their enemies, they thought he had broken his word. Through all that is haphazard and extreme in his political thinking there is a basic consistency, and it adds up to a middle-of-the-road political philosophy, neither absolutist nor specifically democratic. It is absurd to equate Luther's ideas of the state with those of Machiavelli or to regard him as offering aid and comfort to Nazi totalitarianism. Yet he gave to political government a sanction more pronounced than it generally obtained in mediaeval thought. Government is freed from church control: in no respect is it freed from religious and moral obligation. The state is also given a cultural function: it is to institute the means of education. And where the church needs reformation, the emperor and princes should see that a council is called for reform. But the state has no authority in the realm of religious belief. Christians reply to a ruler who would tell them what to believe: "We will not obey you at all." God does not permit anybody but Himself to rule the souls of men. It is futile to try to compel belief. Heresy is a spiritual matter. "You cannot cut it with iron, nor burn it with fire, nor drown it in water." The sects should be allowed to preach: they will cancel one another. The magistrate must, however, take action to silence blasphemous attacks on the Gospel.

"For Luther," writes J. W. Allen, "rightful authority arose essentially from the nature of law." The authority of the ruler is "limited by the law of God; that is by the text of scripture and by natural law" (*Social and Political Ideas of Some Great Thinkers of the Renaissance and Reformation,* edited by F. G. C. Hearnshaw, pp. 181-183, G. G. Harrap & Co.). Mediaeval ideas of natural law in fact underlay the whole of Luther's political philosophy. He finally authorized resistance to the Emperor on the ground that by the law of nature the bond between superior and inferior is dissolved when the superior demands blasphemy and idolatry. "Whenever [Luther] uses a theoretical argument for a judgment or an attitude affecting secular politics, he confidently makes his appeal to this great traditional doctrine" ("Natural Law in Luther's Thought," *Church History,* X, 1941, p. 227). The Gospel does not cancel natural law, but accords with it.

We can say of all this that there are suggestions of democracy but that there is no espousal of it in Luther. He could not have foreseen what weight would be given to his hasty pamphlets called forth by stirring political events. Could he have known how we would wrangle about these matters in the twentieth century, he might have tried to put the fragments together into something like a systematic treatise.

It is well known that Calvinist scholars in the decade after the massacre of St. Bartholomew (1572) went to press with a series of treatises on politics in which tyranny is assailed and magistracy is based on popular rights. It is perhaps equally known that such British Protestant writers as Ponet, Goodman, and Knox in Calvin's own time wrote with similar radicalism. But you will read a good deal of Calvin before finding any comparable support of democracy. He enjoins patient obedience to the powers that be, which are instituted by God for the restraint of sin. He sharply disapproves of French projects for resistance to the king by force. Most emphatically he affirms the duty of submission even to bad rulers, of whom the world has many. The Christian's response is in obedience, suffering, and prayer. This, however, involves no concession to the worship of the state. The state and society are to be subjected to the sovereign majesty of God. As "the ministers of divine justice" rulers hold a sacred office, and those who despise their office insult God (*Inst.,* IV, xx, 6–7). Under necessity they may justly make war against destructive aggressors. While tyrants are generally to be suffered, God sometimes raises up liberators to overthrow them. God Himself casts down insolent and tyrannical rulers: "Let princes hear and fear" (*Inst.* IV, xx, 30–31). The state does not exist for itself, but as God's instrument for the peace and order of society and the protection and support of true religion.

This theocratic principle is fortified by a doctrine of natural law. Although Calvin regards men as morally unable to do anything for their own salvation, he holds with Cicero and all the Christian exponents of natural law that the moral law has been engraved by God (*a Deo insculpta est*) in the minds of men and provides them with a discernment, dimmed but not destroyed by sin, of what is right (Cf. *Inst.,* IV, xx, 14–16). Commenting on I Cor., 11.14 he refers to a bad law as an attempt to abolish the integrity of nature. If any legislator in tyrannical pride attempts to make vice not vice, "the suppressed light of nature will nevertheless break forth and will prevail" (*emerget tamen oppressum naturae lumen ac praevalebit*) (*Opera* XXIV, 662).

Very nearly related to this, if not, as Doumergue supposed, to be identified with it, is Calvin's teaching about *gratia generalis,* common grace—that general moral endowment by which even the non-elect contribute to the social good (H. Bavinck, "Calvin and Common Grace," in *Calvin and the Reformation,* by E. Doumergue and Others, 1901, pp. 99–130). It might have been expected that Calvin would have attempted to restrict citizenship on the basis of his view of election. This he never did; and in fact to have done so would have been inconsistent with his theory of common grace. Anyway, he made no profession of being able to discern between the elect and the reprobate.

Calvin went further than this in opening doors of escape from oppression. Passive resistance may be employed. When commands against God's will are given, the Christian will not obey. For Calvin, God alone is lord of the conscience. But active armed resistance is not wholly excluded. If there exists any popular magistracy set up as a constitutional check against tyranny, this agency is to direct resistance to the tyrant. By way of example he cites the Spartan ephors, Athenian demarchs, and Roman tribunes; and he adds, thinking of France and Germany, that a parallel may be found in the meetings of estates and diets. Evidently he thought that the condition for such orderly resistance existed generally in his day. The members of such magistracies would be guilty of perjury and of betraying the liberty of the people, if they should fail to resist the excesses of kings (*Inst.,* IV, xx, 31).

This was indeed a breach in the wall of absolute rule, and through it a phalanx of Reformed theologians and jurists presently issued— forerunners of those who were later to capture the citadel. But assuredly Calvin's guarded concession to the forces of revolt against tyranny is nothing original. Luther had come to the point of admitting the right of princes to resist the Emperor when the Emperor resisted evangelical reform. Hans Baron thinks Calvin's "Ephors" was suggested by Martin Bucer's advocacy of the authority of inferior magistrates at Strasburg. The Lutherans of Magdeburg, in conflict with Charles V about 1550, drew up a notable *Bekenntnis* asserting on the part of the "*untere Obrigkeit,*" or lower magistracy, the right of resistance for the defense not only of religion but of the "life, liberty, and property" of the people. John Ponet in his *Shorte Treatise on Politike Power* (1556) asserted on the basis of natural law the right of tyrannicide by private citizens "upon just occasion and common necessity" (W. S. Hudson, *John Ponet, Advocate of Limited Monarchy,* pp. 159ff). Tyrannicide had its advocates in antiquity and in the Middle Ages; Calvin does not countenance it, and he does not countenance irresponsible rebellion. But the concessions of an influential conservative have often been more liberating than the radical's trumpet.

Among the forms of government discussed to weariness by innumerable writers before him, Calvin, with most earlier wise men, votes for mixed rule. He views all from the standpoint of the desirability of maximum liberty, and he does not identify democracy with liberty. He would avoid the tyranny that is the corruption of monarchy and the anarchy that may arise from democracy. He thinks most favorably of "aristocracy or a mixture of aristocracy and democracy." By aristocracy he does not mean the control of an hereditary caste, but simply that of "the principal persons of the nation." An ordered liberty is his *sine qua non*. "I willingly confess," he remarks, "that no kind of government is happier than that in which liberty is regulated with becoming moderation and properly established on a durable basis." Those who are happy enough to enjoy such liberty ought to exert strenuous and constant efforts to preserve it; and magistrates who fail of an assigned obligation to maintain it are traitors to their country (*Inst.* IV, xx, 8).

There is some dynamite here, but it is not intended to be rashly exploded. Calvin had no grievance against the representative system of Geneva and he saw no justification for a party of revolt, even in France. During the struggles of the Protestant minority in France most Calvinists became much more radical than he. Beza, Calvin's successor, Hotman, who paid him a warm tribute of affection, and the Calvinist authors of the *Defence against Tyrants*, along with George Buchanan in Scotland, argued for political action to secure the liberties desired. There were many others. Most of these authors developed the so-called "Doctrine of the Ephors" to which Calvin had given one paragraph only. But it is questionable how far they were inspired by Calvin. George Buchanan is thought to have owed his ideas of the Scottish limited monarchy largely to John Major, a late laborious scholastic who wrote *The History of Greater Britain* in 1529. John Knox was probably somewhat indebted to the same source. Beza was a scholar of wide range. Hotman was versed in the lore of the law and in ancient political philosophy. The supposed authors of the *Vindiciae*, Languet and Mornay, were men of ample learning. Most of the material employed by these writers was not employed by Calvin, and their assertion of popular rights goes far beyond his. Moreover, they have much in common with certain Jesuit writers who, in countries where they found themselves, like the French Protestants, at political disadvantage, about the same period set forth doctrines of resistance. The fact ought to be recognized that political Calvinism as it moved with power into the modern era, fed upon much that was earlier than Calvin. It was represented by men who, basically loyal as they were to the Calvinist tradition, had the thought of the centuries at their command.

v

Our final question must be treated even more briefly. How far has the progress of democracy been affected by the teaching and practice of the Reformation? Here a contrast is often made between the Lutheran and the Reformed. In its baldest form the contrast is stated by a somewhat Nazified German scholar, G. Wünsch. The historical development of Calvinism, says Wünsch, has been toward a democracy Christian in its foundation; the historical development of Lutheranism toward an absolutism Christian in its foundation (*Evangelische Ethik des Politischen,* p. 182). This was written before the heroic testimony of the Lutheran church of Norway to the principles of liberty and human rights, a testimony given when none but the Lutheran clergy could find voice to condemn the tyrants. Some would argue that Lutheranism has no natural aversion to absolutism, and even that it invites tyranny. Let us remember that there is Calvinism also in Hitler's Reich, and that nearly half the population is traditionally Roman Catholic. Some of the greatest liberals and internationalists of modern times have been nourished in Lutheranism—such men as Oldendorp, Pufendorf, Thomasius, and Leibnitz. Bismarck was Lutheran, but not Hitler or Himmler. It is therefore, to say the least, indefensible to attribute Germany's unsocial international behavior to Lutheranism. It is truer to say that Lutheranism in Germany was overcautious and insufficiently activist in politics to affect the balance between absolutism and democracy. Lord Acton held that Lutheranism was "the bulwark of political stability." He adds:

Zwingli, who was a staunch republican, desired that all magistrates should be elected, and should be liable to be dismissed by their electors; but he died too soon, for his influence, and the permanent action of the Reformation on democracy was exercised through the presbyterian constitution of Calvin (*History of Freedom,* 1909, p. 81, The Macmillan Co.).

This may do for a broad justment of the matter. But it does not measure the extent of that Reformation influence which streams through Calvinist organization. Nobody can take the measure of it. But let us avoid the kind of generalization that excludes a whole province of fact. It must strike every reflective student of history that Germany was vastly less democratic than Switzerland before as well as after the Reformation. Perhaps in these countries the Reformation did not fundamentally alter the course of political development. Geneva had expelled almost everything that was undemocratic before Calvin saw the city. What he did to its democracy was to give it a new gravity and conservatism and therewith probably a greater durability. In the Netherlands it is certainly impressive to study the evolution of Reformed synods prior to and during the formation of the Republic, and to see community spirit being born in the community singing of the Psalms to Geneva tunes. In Scotland parliamentary government in the late Middle Ages resembled the system in England; the time came, however, when the Assembly of the Kirk was a more effective national voice than the Parliament. In that nation democratic sentiment ran high; it was best expressed in demands for a constitutional or covenanted king. The Covenanters broke into rebellion against Charles II on the ground that in violating the National (religious) Covenant he had forfeited the obedience of his subjects. These concepts flourished in the church of John Knox, who had appealed to the "commonalty" of Scotland and told his queen that as a subject born within the realm he had a right to criticize his government. But there is an old feudal basis, as well as a scriptural and Calvinist one, for the covenant theory.

The familiarity of John Locke and of Jefferson with Reformed thought; the praise of Ponet's treatise by John Adams in his *Defence of the Constitution,* and the rather indeterminate but intriguing evidence regarding the influence of Protestant leaders such as Witherspoon upon the foundation documents of this Republic, if there were no clocks or gongs, might crave our attention. But your craving is rather to hear my last word.

I have tried to say what in my judgment history is trying to say. The Reformers have been ignorantly blamed and inordinately praised for their political opinions. They were competent but not distinguished or original political thinkers. They did not do everything for democracy, but they did something for it. I think if they were living today they would, when duly initiated into its complexity, have a good deal of respect for the system of government under which we live. I am sure they would loathe and execrate Hitler who established tyranny and achieved this by revolt in defiance of law. But they would be shocked by the profane and secular views of government that prevail in our midst. Perhaps they would prophesy against us, saying: "Beware that thou forget not the Lord thy God, . . . lest . . . thine heart be lifted up . . . and thou say in thine heart, My power and the might of mine hand hath gotten me this wealth. . . ."

VI

HUMANISTIC SOURCES

BY

HORACE M. KALLEN, Ph.D.

Dean, Graduate Faculty Political and Social Science, New School for Social Research

I

Each of the three words in the theme assigned to me—*humanistic, source, democracy*—is a term of many meanings. Each is extremely ambiguous. In usage, each is rendered specific and singular by the business and desire of the user. The critical term of the three is *source*. What do we mean by *source*? A consensus of the dictionaries would give us *spring,* a locus of origination or spontaneity. When this meaning is transposed into a universe of discourse called philosophy or metaphysics or theology, *source* becomes an alternate for *first cause*. The empirical equivalent for a *first cause* least open to challenge is probably the biologist's *gene*. So far as our knowledge presently goes, the *gene* is the one item in nature which consistently repeats itself and on occasion alters itself. It not only reproduces itself in identical form but varies spontaneously and then reproduces the variant together with the variations in identical form. The *gene* as cause appears to be a self-reproducing identity capable of changing without self-liquidation. Although its alterings and mutations present themselves as discontinuous, they come as accretions to its own continuity; as accretions, that is, to a persistent identifiable nature and existence.

Now I shall take the term *source,* as applied to *humanism,* to mean a cause resembling a *gene*. I assume that what I am to do in this talk is to identify either a continuing or a recurrent cause, called *humanism,* in the generation and upkeep of an effect, called *democracy*.

Inquiry into causes is today *par excellence* the enterprise of the scientist. Identifying causes is his vocation, even when the field is theology. The use of scientific method in theology and the treating of theology as a field for the scientific vocation are, I know, not exactly popular in certain circles, but they have their friends, who are a growing company. They are a growing company because the method of science has proved itself to be of all methods the most fruitful in that basic phase of the human enterprise which seeks to sort out and define those events which invariably bring about certain other events that someone feels to be of great moment for the life of man.

An undertaking beset with hazards and doubts in all the sciences, the designation of causes is particularly such in the social sciences, where the variables are countless and the constants few, if not altogether lacking; and where a student may select any one or any group of the current components of an institution or an event, attribute to them causal efficacy, and support his attribution with rationalizations and with statistical tables whose mathematics are as infallible as anything. This can be done even if the elected components are in fact not at all sources or agents; it can be done with the greatest of ease wherever the uses of things, which are at once consequences and modifications of the natures of those things, are treated as origins, as the springs whence their natures have drawn or draw their existence. For example, it is well known that many great and influential democratic originals, such as Thomas Jefferson, made considerable use of certain classical writers whose productions are conventionally allocated to the humanities. But whether these humanities made a democrat of Jefferson and were causes of the beatitudes of democracy which we call the Declaration of Independence, cannot be decided on the basis of use or purpose. It is no more likely that Jefferson, having studied the humanities, became a democrat, than that Jefferson, being a democrat, chose from the humanities those texts which would nourish and sustain his democratic works and ways. But the disposition to call an event which preceded another event the cause of the succeeding event is inveterate, and the temptation to do so is particularly strong in history and the other social sciences; so that it is hard not to label certain of the humanities which figure in

Jefferson's spiritual history causes of his democracy, *post hoc propter hoc*. I shall try not to be led into this temptation, either with respect to Jefferson or with respect to any of the diverse sequences of humanistic and democratic ideas.

I shall also hope to by-pass a number of other temptations. One of these consists in declaring different meanings to be one and the same because they are communicated by means of a single term, word, or sign. It is as if oil and vinegar and water and wine and peroxide and quicksilver should be declared the same because they are carried in identical bottles. The identity of the vehicle contaminates the diversity of the passengers, and their variety and multitude are masked by its unity. One of the most significant instances of such contamination of meanings by symbols which usage provides is, of course, the familiar word *God*. It is a word employed by Plato, by Cleanthes, by Plotinus, by St. Augustine, by St. Thomas, by Spinoza, by Jefferson, by Calvin, by Edward Scribner Ames, by Mordecai M. Kaplan, by William James, by Sitting Bull, by Adolf Hitler and by countless other psychologists, metaphysicians, and theologians. However different the language of these men, the dictionaries make their words for *God* equal and interchangeable, and translate each as the alternate of any. But how could the men's meanings be made equal and interchangeable without terrible violence to the integrity of those separate meanings? Such violence can readily be done to the meanings of humanism and democracy when verbal illations mask fundamental divergences of intention. Those identifications are produced, as a rule, whenever we are passionately concerned with the survival and domination of one intention, regardless of the consequences to any and all others. For example, such a passionate concern is attributable to many who insist on deriving the democratic idea from Thomas Aquinas. As a matter of logic and history the derivation is, to say the least, highly debatable; as a postulate of passion, it is not debatable, nor is the passion debatable. Affirming itself, it involves the ignoring or the overriding of that which is different from itself or the identification of the different with itself. At its most likely, it confuses resemblance with sameness, analogy with identity.

This mode of mistakenly attributing causes is another one of the temptations into which the social scientist is all too often led. His sciences abound in analogical thinking, and a great deal of it is striking, and some of it is fruitful. There is no need to quarrel with it. But there is great need to be extremely cautious about employing it as a method of bringing to light sources, causes, or agencies, be they enduring and supporting, or transitory and lapsing. Transitory and lapsing causes occur in the social process at least as frequently as parents. Parents beget and get children, and not even the most intransigent theologian would hesitate to regard them as the sources or causes of at least the bodily being of their children. And so they are; they originate, they give rise to, and with this their parental efficacy consummates itself. It consists in a single act, largely contingent. It does not and cannot persist. After it has occurred parents are only the conditions and occasions of the being of their child, not its enduring and sustaining causes. Once a child is born its existence and survival are independent of its parentage. Its parentage—as of Jewish children in anti-Semitic societies—may render its existence precarious and its survival doubtful; or—as in all Nazidom—contribute causally to its torture and destruction. Once something has begun to exist, its survival and extinction are either functions of its own strength and weaknesses or of the strength and weaknesses of the enduring source of which it is an overflow and which sustains it. If its source is transitory and lapses, then, be it a man-child, an idea, a natural object or a human production, it survives or perishes as it goes and stops, on its own.

Beside these two meanings of the term *source* we must place another, which recurs frequently in certain types of scientific inquiry. This third meaning identifies source with *premise* or *ground*. When *source* is employed in this way, the connection between that which is spring and that which is flow is logical, not dynamic. Thus, if the relationship between *humanism* and *democracy* is considered dynamic, *democracy* will be an effect of *humanism,* not a conclusion from *humanism; humanism* will be a necessary antecedent of *democracy,* but *democracy* will not be a necessary consequence of *humanism*. If, on the other hand, the relationship between humanism and democracy be that of ground, or premise, to syllogistic conclusion, then humanism implies *democracy* and *democracy* is a necessary inference from *humanism*. For those who think of the term *source* in this way, *democracy* can exist only if and as *humanism* exists; the historic passage from humanism to democracy is incidental, is only an explication in time of an implication eternally present in the nature of human events. Many writers treat the relation between humanism and democracy as if it were of this character. As I read the record, the treatment is not an insight into the nature of the facts but the operation of a desire to conform the facts to a certain interest; it seems to me fundamentally debatable.

II

So much, then, for the term *source*. Let us now explore the terms *humanism, democracy*. Their meanings are too diverse and conflicting, and each is, especially in these times of ours, subject to too much variation, to make it possible to elicit, in the manner of a physicist or chemist or mathematician, the quality of cause, agency, or ground in their relations to one another. The most that I can honestly do is to choose one or more of these meanings, inspect their sequence, their similarities, their divergences, with a view to discovering what is cause and what is effect, and warn you that the choice cannot but express my own social passion and personal interest. Other people make other selections, as is their right. But mine is the only one about which I can speak with any degree of certainty and over which I hold such authority as it is decent to hold.

Since the task is to discern the nature of the relation between *humanism* and *democracy,* it is proper to seek first a meaning for *democracy*. The term appears early. Plato used it, Aristotle used it, Jefferson used it, and spokesmen of all sorts of interests and pretensions are using it today. The multitude of meanings are not reconcilable. That which I choose for discussion is Jefferson's. His meaning of democracy is unique. Its coming into existence as a fighting faith for all mankind can be variously dated but I accept a conventional date arbitrarily just as one accepts the date of an individual's birthday arbitrarily; arbitrarily, because as is well-known and well-ignored, an individual is begotten and goes through a long and not unadventurous process of gestation and development before he is born. His birth is but a new turn, a happy or a tragic turn as you will, in a biography already launched; and if you wanted to extrapolate backward you could set the birth of the individual at the beginning of the universe. This way of doing is not uncommon among philosophers of all sects, from theists and idealists to dialectical materialists and logical positivists.

Now the conventional birthday of democracy was July 4, 1776. On that day a conception was made flesh in an action, and the course of human events took a new turn. A war for independence and freedom was justified, its goals were defined, by the signing of the document known as the Declaration of Independence, for the support of which the signers mutually pledged each other their lives, their fortunes and their sacred honor. Seven propositions of this Declaration compose the unique beatitudes of the democratic faith of our times. Verse by verse, they read as follows:

1. We hold these truths to be self-evident (Jefferson had written "sacred and undeniable" but the phrase has been replaced with "self-evident");

2. that all men are created equal;

3. that they are endowed by their Creator with certain unalienable rights (Jefferson had written "inherent and unalienable," but the Congress struck out "inherent and" and stuck in "certain");

4. that among these are life, liberty and the pursuit of happiness;

5. that to secure these rights governments are instituted among men;

6. deriving their just powers from the consent of the governed;

7. that whenever any form of government becomes destructive of these ends, it is the right of the people to alter or abolish it, and to institute a new government, laying its foundations on such principles, and organizing its powers in such form, as to them shall seem most likely to effect their safety and happiness.

That is the all of the democratic faith, and a man can learn it, as a certain Gentile once wanted to learn Judaism, while standing on one leg. When, however, we come to the business of interpreting and implementing the articles of this faith in the works and ways of daily life, the case is different. A great deal of confusion obtains. One such confusion turns upon the meanings which different interpreters undertake to give to the term "equal" in the proposition "that all men are created equal." To some it is nonsense, a glittering generality flung obviously in the face of all experience. To others it expresses a metaphysical truth and is "self-evident" alone as such—namely, that the manifest differences between men are but appearances, unsubstantial and unimportant, that in truth and in reality men are identical and not different, each and every one being the same with each and every other and as interchangeable as machine parts.

The first interpretation, brought to action, leads to a struggle to perpetuate the modes of human association which the Declaration challenged and denied; it leads to the assertion and preservation of invidious distinctions; it divides the people into masters and servants on the basis of differences in faith, race, sex, birth, occupation, possessions and culture; it penalizes the different for being different by shutting them into the servant class and keeping them there.

The second interpretation, brought to action, leads to a struggle to bring out the hidden metaphysical equality or sameness by demanding of the different in faith, race, sex, birth, occupations, possessions, and culture that they shall liquidate their difference and conform their being to some type or standard defined by power and commanded with authority. Many *soi-disant* "Americanization" movements have been enterprises of this kind, purporting to transform the different into the same. In the actualities of daily life their methods and results have not been distinguishable from those of the interests that treat the idea that all men are created equal as a glittering generality. Both merely penalized the different for being different. Both made difference a ground of the invidious distinctions essential to setting up and maintaining a citizenship of the second class.

But it was precisely this invidiousness, this penalization of the different, against which the Declaration set the nation's will. When it was framed, men and women were being penalized for being what they were everywhere in the world. Women, being female and not male, had no rights that their male relatives needed to respect; Catholics penalized Protestants and Protestants penalized Catholics and each other—all but the Quakers who were penalized for being Quakers by all the other Christian denominations, while the Jews were penalized for not being Christians everywhere in the Christian world. Negroes were penalized for their color, poor men for their poverty, men who worked with their hands and were thus no gentlemen for working with their hands. With the proposition "that all men are created equal" the Declaration nullified all that. The men who wrote and signed the Declaration and the men and women who fought and suffered and died for it did not intend by this proposition either to abolish or to penalize differences. They intended to vindicate differences, to acknowledge and to defend their equal right to life, liberty, and the pursuit of happiness. They affirmed the right to be different and the parity of the different as different. They did not look to any hidden metaphysical equality; they looked to the overt experience that people who are different from each other can and do live together with each other on the basis of the equal title of each to the rights of life, liberty, and pursuit of happiness inherent and unalienable in each.

The authors, the signers, and the warriors of the Declaration neither were ignorant of nor ignored the historic and present fact that much of that living together consisted in mutual alienations of life and liberty and happiness. They knew that the family, the field, the workshop, the school, the playground, the hall of government, the battlefield, all too often show themselves to be, separately and together, very much like the jail and the gallows, techniques of such mutual alienations of these putative unalienable rights. But these men and women never meant by "unalienable" that human beings did not kill and maim and frustrate each other, fence each other in and fend each other off. They meant "unalienable" to be a synonym for "inherent," for constitutive. They meant that the nature of any and every human being, whatever his color, sex, race, faith, occupation, or social status, is constituted by these rights as a triangle is constituted by three sides and three angles; that life, liberty, and the pursuit of happiness make up the substance of human nature as the angles and sides of of a triangle make up the being of the triangle; that hence, so long as a man is alive he will struggle to go on living, to be free, and to seek happiness; that this, his characteristic mode of existing, may be attacked, may be multilated, may be destroyed, but that he cannot behave otherwise than so. Alienation of these unalienable rights, then, is like cutting off a limb or a head, an attack on the inward human essence, not the withdrawal of something called a right that can be put on and put off like a garment or granted and withheld like a gift.

If there is any humanism in the Declaration, it is enfolded in this, its affirmation that rights are inherent and unalienable, that they constitute the nature of men, each different from the others and each equal with the others; that as such they are both the spring and the goal of human societies. The proposition, "to secure these rights governments are instituted among men," retains today much of the revolutionary intent it had when it was announced. For those who hold the powers of government, often even in democracies, reveal an inveterate propensity to regard these powers as those of a master, not of a servant; and to treat government as an autonomous end and not a means to other ends. The rationalizations of this propensity are many, but the most ancient and respectable is that which names God as the source and sanction of any power, good or evil. Kings and popes, nobles and clergy rule over the common man by divine right; their authority may not be challenged nor their commandments disobeyed because they speak in God's name and as His delegates on earth. When the Declaration was made, all the political and ecclesiastical establishments of the world operated on a general assumption that men were made for governments, not governments for men; that man owes them obedience and service by God's will.

Against this prevailing assumption the Declaration set its principle—"to secure these rights governments are instituted among men." It declared the inherent and unalienable rights of man to be the end, government only a means; it made the people the master, government the servant; it made life, liberty, and the pursuit of happiness the purpose, government an instrument to attain this purpose.

Moreover, by setting the origin of the just powers of government in the consent of the governed, it rejected the claims of divine sanction for the powers of all monarchs, whether secular or ecclesiastical, as false claims contrary to the truths about human nature as the Declaration affirms these truths. It implies that only *just* powers can hold the sanction of the consent of the governed, and that powers not so sanctioned, whatever may be claimed for them, are unjust. And all forms of government are, by implication, unjust when they become "destructive of these ends." Then the people have the right to treat them as they would treat any other agency or instrument which they have devised and used for the purpose of life, liberty, and happiness. They may enlarge, contract, or reshape their tools so as to make them fitter for the purposes they should serve. They may invent new tools and throw the others aside. There is no supernal authority, no infallible doctrine and discipline by which to judge the works of state or church or economic establishment or any organization of interest you will. Doctrine and discipline are agencies which serve, not masters that rule; their only measure is how they serve to secure the equal rights of different people to life, liberty, and the pursuit of happiness.

III

Such, in sum, is the meaning which I find *democracy* to draw from the propositions of the Declaration of Independence. As I read the record, it involves a definite break with the entire tradition of the Western world, including much of what is usually regarded as *humanism*. Before the insurgence of this idea of *democracy* neither the ancients nor the moderns failed to penalize this or that section of their own community and all the members of every other community for being different. Let alone the fact that chattel slavery was universal and endemic, the Greeks drew invidious distinctions between themselves and those whom they called barbarians; the Jews between themselves and the Gentiles; the Romans between themselves and their subject peoples; the Christians between themselves and the Jews, the heretics, and the infidels. In each case the different must not be equal but subordinate, second-rate, worthy only of subject-status and servile occupation. Alike the pagan and the Judeo-Christian traditions affirmed some sort of supernatural sanction for their discriminations against other human beings. John Calvin brought it to the ultimate height of metaphysical authority. He made a dogma of the proposition that, as Jefferson wrote in 1822 to Benjamin Waterhouse, "God, from the beginning, elected certain individuals to be saved, and certain others to be damned; and that no crimes of the former can damn them; no virtues of the latter save."

The attitude which this consummates is a component of the Greek view of life no less than of the Jewish, but the irony of history made it with the Jews an automatic compensation for their frustrations as a people. It is to them that the tradition attributes, not wrongly, the pretension of being *the* Chosen People. Similar pretensions were and are operative among all the peoples of the world but their expressions have not received equal recognition. The Hellenes were not less elect to Plato and Aristotle than the Hebrews were to their prophets and rabbis, but the pagans did not erect this sentiment into a dogma of religion whence they might draw consolation and reassurance. The Jews did. Their God was God omnipotent and just, yet He was capable of playing favorites and choosing out of the infinite multitude of His creatures one group to be His particular people. However, He was to be their particular God without any fundamental detriment to other peoples, who were also this omnipotent God's creatures and care. If I understand the prophetic and Judaist view correctly, it was more psychological than logical. The election of Israel did not mean the rejection of the other nations; it meant, not that the nations were rejected but only that Israel was preferred. The Christian employment of this dogma of reassurance and consolation carries its logic to the limit. Christian dogma changes the status of the Jews from that of the Chosen People to that of the Rejected People. According to it, just and omnipotent God chooses only those human beings who believe in the Christ and rejects and condemns to eternal damnation those who do not believe in the Christ. Calvin modified this classical view by adding that our finite minds cannot know whom, in the Christ, infinite God's omniscience and omnipotence has elected and whom rejected. But, whether we think of divine election after the manner of the Jews or after the manner of the Christians, we see the dogma as exercising a dominating influence in Judeo-Christian culture. We see it as a means of making and supporting invidious distinctions between man and man, as a rule for penalizing the different because it is different. In the climate of opinion where this dogma figures, equality is the synonym for similarity or identity; difference is condemned and rejected. Although holders of this dogma have recently discoursed eloquently and at length about "the infinite value of the human personality," they have not really meant any and every personality, with all its differences on its head. They have really meant personality that agrees with them or that is persuaded or that is tortured into agreeing, and is thus become a member of God's elect who alone can be infinitely valuable; the otherwise-minded personality, being God's reject, is punished for its difference by being only infinitely valueless and damned.

But this is precisely what *democracy* negates. Democracy sanctions and encourages differences and confirms the equal right of each and all to life, liberty, and the pursuit of happiness. It alone affirms, without any fear of challenge or contradiction, the "infinite value of human personality." The practical working of its concept of equality may be best illustrated from the attitudes, opinions, and conduct of Thomas Jefferson, foremost of the builders of democracy into the works and ways of the American people. I say foremost, because Jefferson was not only the author of the Declaration of Independence and the creator of the Bill of Rights, he was the leader in the enactment of these ideals into law, in his own state of Virginia, by securing the abolition of entail and primogeniture, the disestablishment of churches, the promulgation of the world-famous Bill for Establishing Religious Freedom, and the bill for public education. As ambassador to France, as Washington's Secretary of State, as Vice-President with John Adams, as President for two terms, and as guide, philosopher, and friend of his disciples, James Madison and James Monroe, he labored for a longer period than any other single personality in power toward shaping the political, the religious, the economic, the educational and the cultural life of the United States at home and their foreign relations abroad to the ways of the Declaration of Independence. In the domain of religion, for example, he sought the definition by law that churches are voluntary societies to which no man is bound by nature. "No man," he wrote in his *Notes on Virginia,* "has power to let another prescribe his faith. Faith is not faith without belief." He held that no church can claim jurisdiction over any other nor be forced to pay for the upkeep of any other; that membership in a church cannot be a condition prior to receiving civil rights or a basis of withholding or withdrawing civil rights. The value of a religion, he contended, was to be judged neither by the origins claimed for it nor the powers it pretended to; the value of a religion was to be judged by its consequences to the liberties and happiness of men. Writing in 1803 to Dr. Benjamin Rush, he called attention with approval to a vote of the Pennsylvania legislature rejecting a proposal to make belief in God a necessary qualification for public office, "although there was not a single atheist among the voters." Such a law would violate democracy by penalizing citizens for not sharing the beliefs of the majority. He opposed successfully a ministerial undertaking to get the phrase, "Jesus Christ, author of our holy religion," inserted in the Virginia Statute of Religious Liberty—this not because he failed to appreciate Jesus, but because it would violate the very idea of the statute.

Jefferson's appreciation of Jesus was singular and unparalleled: its consequence is what is called "the Jefferson Bible," a document it would repay you and all Americans to study. This "Bible" is a democrat's re-creation of "the life and morals of Jesus of Nazareth" and cannot be correctly understood except in the frame of reference of democracy. Its author constructed it by taking together the Greek, Latin, French, and English versions of the gospels, and the gospels only. He cut parallel passages from each, in order to compare them for agreements and differences, and he pasted them accordingly in his notebook. The result was a text which he called "the philosophy of Jesus of Nazareth." What emerges as important in this text is not what is regarded as important in Christian dogma. Jefferson lays no emphasis on the death and resurrection of Jesus; he lays all his emphasis on the social teachings. And, significantly, he brings these teachings together with certain of the teachings of Epicurus. Rejecting all but the words of Jesus that he believes to be authentic, he writes to John Adams, "I am a real Christian . . . a disciple of the doctrines of Jesus." Elsewhere he speaks of himself as an Epicurean and sees only harmony in the real Christian and Epicurean faiths. His contemporaries, all the clergy and the Federalist laymen, denounced his views of Jesus as blasphemous and atheistic. But they were views alone consistent with the propositions of the Declaration of Independence, views which enabled him to contribute with equal generosity to the Episcopal and Presbyterian churches of Charlottesville, both bitterly inimical to him, and to an enterprise for the purchase and free distribution of Bibles. They were views which, though he held a low opinion of Judaism, enabled him to write to Mordecai Noah: "Your sect by sufferings has furnished a remarkable proof of the universal spirit of religious intolerance inherent in every sect, disclaimed by all when feeble, and practiced by all when in power. Our laws have applied the only antidote to this view, protecting our religious, as they do our civil rights, by putting all on an equal footing. . . . It is to be hoped that individual dispositions will at length mold themselves on the model of the law, and consider the model bases, on which all religions rest, as the rallying point which unites them in a common interest."

This rallying point was to Jefferson the unalienable right to be different. To be different! Therefore to doubt, to inquire, to study and compare alternatives! A right no less unalienable to minorities than to majorities, also when a minority consists of one person only! Jefferson's deepest commitment was to the "illimitable freedom of the human mind to explore and expose every subject susceptible of its contemplation"! He had sworn, he once declared, "upon the altar of God, hostility to every form of tyranny over the mind of man." Set this Jeffersonian conception of human relations beside that of an official of the city of Boston, commenting upon assaults made against Jews and Negroes in that sometime Athens of America. Said the official: "Democracy means majority rule, and Jews and Negroes are in the minority." The implication is that minorities have no rights that majorities need respect. A completer contravention of the democratic idea and the Jeffersonian faith could hardly have been expressed by a public official, nor an attitude more consistent with the tradition of privilege and authority.

The full, practical meaning of the democratic faith as a program of conduct is exemplified by nothing so much as its repudiation of slavery. Neither the classical world nor the Judeo-Christian ages of faith in fact rejected slavery. There were certain Stoic expressions against it, but no efficacious overt action. Thomas Aquinas, currently a much-cited authority in justification of democracy, was no more opposed to slavery than Aristotle or Luther or Calvin; the enslavement of the different was a testimony to the rightness and power of the elect. True, the history of the predemocratic world records many slave and serf uprisings—whether in Greece or Rome or Northern Europe or the Americas—uprisings in which the slaves fought for their own freedom; it does not record a single instance of free men fighting for the liberation of slaves. This does not occur until the democratic revolution. Jefferson had written a denunciation of slavery into the Declaration of Independence which powerful interests in the Continental Congress erased; and the same interests succeeded in writing safeguards of property in human beings into the Constitution. But there was not room in the same nation for both democracy and slavery. From democracy's first day in our United States free men waged a war against slavery by tongue and pen, by stratagem and force. The war finally became a great civil war in which free men staked their all to set slaves free and, having done so, wrote their victory into the fundamental law of the land as one more step toward the conversion of the ideals of the Declaration of Independence into realities of the American way of life.

IV

Now, given this meaning for *democracy*, what has *humanism* contributed to it? Replies to this question will depend, obviously, on which of the many meanings of *humanism* one chooses to consider among the sources of *democracy*. Current discussion gives the conventional meaning a factitious potency. The conventional meaning is the academic meaning. It designates as *humanism* a concern with the humanities, and the humanities as the secular literature and sometimes the graphic and plastic arts of the "pagan" Greeks and Romans. This literature is "classical." It is written in ancient Greek and Latin.[1] It bulks large among lists of "hundred best books," which as a rule do not include anything written in Hebrew. The emphasis falls on its being secular. Thereby it is opposed to the Greek and Latin religious texts of our Judeo-Christian cults. Humanism began as a cultivation

[1] Jefferson himself had a humanistic education in this sense. His regard for the classics was such that he made them the core of the curriculum that he proposed for the students of his University of Virginia. In view of these facts, it is worth while putting into the record his opinion of the relation of the Greeks and Romans to *democracy*. I quote from two letters, one written in 1816 to I. H. Tiffany about the Greeks in the time of Aristotle; the other in 1819 to John Adams about the Romans:

To Tiffany Jefferson wrote:
"But so different was the style of society then and with those people, from what it is now with us, that I think little edification can be obtained from their writings on the subject of government. They had just ideas of the value of personal liberty, but none at all of the structure of government best calculated to preserve it. They knew no medium between a democracy . . . and an abandonment of themselves to an aristocracy or a tyranny independent of the people. It seems not to have occurred to them that where the citizens cannot meet and transact their business in person, they alone have the right to choose the agents who shall transact it, and that in this way a republican, or popular government, of the second grade of parity, may be exercised over any extent of country.

"The full experiment of government, democratical but representative, was and still is reserved for us. . . . The introduction of this new principle of representative democracy has rendered useless almost everything written before on the structure of government; and in a great measure, relieves our regret, if the political writings of Aristotle, or of any other ancient, have been lost."

To Adams Jefferson wrote:
"And if Caesar had been as virtuous as he was daring and sagacious, what could he, even in the plenitude of his usurped power, have done to lead his fellow citizens into good government? I do not say to *restore it*, because they never had it, from the rape of the Sabines to the ravages of the Caesars. . . . But steeped in corruption, vice, and venality, as the whole nation was . . . what could even Cicero, Cato, Brutus have done, had it been referred to them to establish good government for their country? They had no ideas of government themselves, but of their degenerate Senate, nor the people of liberty, but of the factious opposition of their Tribunes. They had afterwards their Tituses, their Trajans, and Antoninuses, who had the will to make them happy, and the power to mould their government into a good and permanent form. But it would seem as if they could not see their way clearly to do it. No government can continue good, but under the control of the people; and their people were so demoralized and depraved as to be incapable of exercising a wholesome control."

of those works of pagan man in preference to what was offered as glosses upon the revelations of the Judeo-Christian God. It set those humanities against that divinity. It made secular society the peer, and better than the peer, of the churchly. It exalted *this* worldliness over otherworldliness, preferring the discourse of human reason to ukases concerning superhuman salvation. By and large, it was anticlerical, even in the church itself. Very many of the early humanists were ordained priests or monks. They were secretaries, librarians, prelates, popes. Others were officials, merchants, courtiers, princes. Their minds were first allured, then liberated, by the alternatives to the authoritarian tradition which they encountered in the undogmatic thinking, varied content, and perfect expression of such writers as Cicero, as Tacitus, as Ovid or Pliny or Varro, as Quintilian, as Plato, as Aristotle, whom they had come to read at first hand at last.

As, for the most part, the clergy were the literati, the making of *humanism* was first a churchly event. Petrarch was a churchman but like so many of his colleagues he was a churchman in the same way as a physician is a physician who does not need to practice medicine for a living and spends his days painting pictures. The liberation and delight which the humanities brought clerics like Petrarch, in the course of time carried the classical writers into the fanes and made of them themes of disputation in the academic halls. To be a grammarian was for a time as exciting a vocation as to be an admiral of the ocean sea. It was not long before the humanists' eagerness regarding the humanities reached out to the originals of divinity. They dared to read the Scriptures in Hebrew and in Greek.

That which the humanists found in the Scriptures of the original tongues was not what authority had drawn from them. An impulse which had first been simple curiosity developed quickly into free inquiry challenging authority. The perusal of the sources at first hand revealed difference and variation in the sources themselves. The discovery of difference and variation led automatically to comparison, and then to the exaltation of the free movements of reason over the conformities of faith. These free movements created in the course of time what is today known as Higher Criticism. Its techniques consisted in the direct observation, the watchful analysis, the careful comparisons and reorderings, the continuous over-all scrutiny, which pertain to the methods of science.

The classical instance of a humanist according to this meaning of *humanism* is, of course, Erasmus. His *In Praise of Folly* is a judgment upon all users of authority of his day—the soldiers, the priests, the philosophers, the rhetoricians, the pedants, the landlords. His sense of the humanities make him one of the great ironists of divinity, whose popes he regards as tyrants of the City of the World rather than servants of the City of God, whose friars sell salvation in the market place, whose scholastics find the choice between killing a thousand men and mending a beggar's shoe on Sunday a vital option; who regard letting a woman tell a lie a more momentous alternative than that the world should perish; who are so learned that the apostles could not understand them as they argue of how one body occupies two places—heaven and the cross—the right hand of God the Father and the consecrated wafer; as they expound that Mary escaped Adam's sin. Erasmus not only read the New Testament in Greek, he undertook to translate it for the uses of the common people. To make his translation, which in 1516 he dedicated to Leo X, the most accurate in his power, he collated the best available manuscripts, comparing them verse for verse and chapter for chapter, recognizing inconsistencies, seeking the true version instead of the authorized one. Willy nilly, he found himself raising questions concerning the Epistle to the Hebrews, the Epistle of James, The Revelation, the second and sixth chapters of John, the second of Peter, and so on. His concern, like Jefferson's, was the philosophy of Jesus. He prized the spirit, which is without price, more highly than the relics whose magic uses brought good prices. That in virtue of which he was a humanist as distinguished from the champions of divinity was not merely his delighted knowledge of the classics. It was his method of treating differences with respect, his readiness to accept the so-called unauthoritative on the same level as the authorized, to treat authority as a claim only that must make good by merit and not by rule, to exalt free inquiry and to cultivate the toleration which such inquiry postulates. Thus he gave Martin Luther sufficient cause to call him the "greatest enemy of Christ" and to proclaim that whoever crushed Erasmus would crush a bug that would stink even more when dead than when alive. Thus he gave the conformist churchmen sufficient cause to brand him as a heretic and to place all his works on the *Index*.

This sort of *humanism* is the antithesis of another kind which has had a certain vogue in the academic arcana of our time. Why its protagonists call it *humanism* has never been clear to me. I presume that they do so because their central concern continues to be the humaner letters of Greece and Rome which excited and liberated the humanists of the Renaissance; that they disregard the Hebraic originals of our Judeo-Christian tradition and fix their attention on Plato and pre-Christian platonism and to a lesser degree on Aristotle. Their spokesmen in the United States have been the late Paul Elmer More and Irving Babbitt. T. S. Eliot is a perverse half-English variant and I do not doubt that many would associate with them our charming and eloquent French colleague, Jacques Maritain. Although they call themselves humanists, their preoccupation, however, is not man nor the humanities, but God as conceived and defined by certain classical writers of whom the foremost is Plato. Their method, far from being that of the sciences of our day, is not even the over-all scrutiny, the careful observation, the free inquiry of Erasmus. Their method is authoritarian and dialectical. To them man's nature is dual and not one. It has a superior and an inferior part, a soul and a body, and the body is all animal impulse and unchecked desires, and the soul is a unitary principle of human nature inwardly harmonious to, if not a derivative of, the universal and eternal being of God. Over against the multiplicity, the variety, the this-worldliness, of the modern sciences of man, these *soi-disant* humanists set a hidden single, indivisible, eternal, universal human nature, which acts as an "inner check" on the phenomenal multiplicity and variety and holds them together and directs their ways by its infallible force.

Professor Werner Jaeger has written an illuminating and very sympathetic interpretation of the original of this species of humanism as it took form in the dialogues of Plato, with their antidemocratism, their racism, their doctrine and discipline of authority (stated firmly but somewhat gently in the *Republic,* fiercely in the *Laws*), drawn from the "divine order." This has recently been published in English translation as volumes II and III of *Paideia, the Ideals of Greek Culture.* They bring to us the authentic root of what Jacques Maritain opts to call "theocentric humanism." And no democrat could take exception to it if only it did not, in Plato, explicitly condemn and excommunicate democracy and serve, after Plato, as a sanction for all the ways of penalizing the different of which democracy is the rejection. Not only are the great religions of the world different from each other in countless specific ways, but each great religion is diversified into denominations, sects, and cults, each with its own characteristic singularity of imagining God and what He requires of man. There is the God of the trinitarians and the God of the Unitarians; there is the God of the theists and the God of the deists; there are the gods of the polytheists and the God of the pantheists; there is one God Who is all reason; another Who is all love; another Who is all will; there is a God Who is all spirit and a God Who is no less body than spirit. The *theos* of the theocentric humanist differs from sect to sect and man to man and land to land. The center of his *humanism* is not one but many.

If our humanist accepts this fact, if he does not presume to excommunicate all other centers but his own as false and evil; if he does not undertake to compel other men to center on his one as *the* One, laying upon them all the penalties of the record if they refuse; if he acknowledges the equal right of different men to think their gods in such a manner as shall to each seem best for enhancing his life, liberty, and pursuit of happiness, then his center is in fact not God but men. Then the *theos* is not invoked as the justification of coercion and tyranny but becomes the agency "to secure these rights"; the human being is set free by means of the *theos.* Then the idea or image or being of God is taken honestly and openly for that which in the history of civilization it actually is—a function of mankind's struggles for life, liberty, and happiness. The God upon Whom a man centers becomes then like the wife of his bosom, the hearth of a home of his own, instead of the noble lady whose beauty and virtue he compels other men to acknowledge by the force of his infallible sword. The fascist's state, the nazi race, the Japanazi's sun-goddess, the communist's dialectic of matter, cannot offer themselves as rivals and substitutes of this God. He is plural, not singular, multitudinous, not totalitarian; man is the measure of Him, not He the measure of man. He is the God of the tradition of Protagoras, not the God of the tradition of Plato. He is the figure of a *humanism* which stems from the *humanitas* that, during the second century before the Christian era, came to existence among certain Romans of sensibility and sense after their minds had been awakened and their hearts opened by the impact of the philosophy of Epicurus, with its social detachment, its charity, and its intellectual freedom. *Humanitas* was the humanism of the Scipionic Circle. It comes—altogether accidentally, perhaps—to its high place of expression in a comedy by a member of that circle, the African Terence, who had been a slave and had been manumitted. In this play, based on Menander's *Heauton Timoroumenes,* trivial in plot, for the most part trivial in utterance, a character pronounces lines that have become part of the wisdom of aspiration of our Western world. They are: *Homo sum, humani nihil a me alienum puto.*

Legend has it that the audience which first heard them rose in tumultuous applause. The line had stopped the show. But its meaning, which has haunted the hearts of men ever since, did not get beyond the show until the Democratic Revolution; nor has it advanced lightly, nor without blood and sweat and tears since. This meaning is at the center of still another conception of *humanism* which, being a consequence and function of democracy, knowingly prefers among the thinkers of classical antiquity Protagoras, the plebeian, to Plato, the aristocrat. This *humanism* is sometimes identified with the pragmatism of William James. Its spokesman is the late F. C. S. Schiller, one of William James's foremost and most original disciples. In his *Plato or Protagoras* he throws into a fresh perspective the debate between the former Asiatic self-taught porter and inventor, friend of Pericles and Euripides, butt of Aristophanes, and the embittered Athenian nobleman. The works of Protagoras are lost to us. Some were burned by the Athenians; others have perished. What remains are a few sentences which indicate why.

They point to a man-centered humanism, to *humanitas*. "Man," wrote Protagoras, "is the measure of all things, of things that are, that they are; of things that are not, that they are not." The idea of importance is that man is the *measure,* not the creator. Whatever a man's philosophy, he has to take things as experience brings them to him, and he has to value them in terms of their bearing on his life and liberty and pursuit of happiness. Before he can say that this does exist, and that does not exist, he must have some impression, some idea, of this and that. They must be present, somehow, to be declared nonexistent; even as they must be present, somehow, to be declared existent. The presence must make itself felt and, as felt, may be measured. This measurement is a human art; it is the all of the method and the content of science; the gene of the body of knowledge. Considering the gods as objects of measurement, Protagoras declares in another fragment, "With regard to the Gods, I cannot feel sure that they are or they are not, nor what they are like in figure. For there are many things that hinder sure knowledge; the obscurity of the subject, and the shortness of human life."

These are presumably passages from Protagoras's book, *On Truth*. He had read from it in the house of Euripides to a company of free minds of the Greek enlightenment. To some theocentric humanist there present it must have been blasphemy. Protagoras was denounced and condemned to death. He fled Athens, but the book was burned.

As I read the record, an ultimate statement of this meaning of *humanism* is to be found in the Book of Job, which is itself an assimilation of Greek form to Hebraic insight. There is a familiar, oft-repeated English verse, "Though He slay me yet will I trust in Him." The Hebrew original, correctly translated,[2] reads: "Behold, He will slay me; I shall not survive; nevertheless will I maintain my ways before Him." Another verse declares: "Mine integrity hold I fast and will not let it go; my heart shall not reproach me so long as I live." These are Job's reply to the words which the author puts in the mouth of Job's theocentric comforters, who argue that since their

---

[2] This is taken from a version somewhat different from the standard texts.—The Editor.

friend's torture must be from God he can be relieved of it only if he looks upon himself as God looks upon him, admits his sin and repents. But Job holds fast to his human dignity and affirms the integrity of his human essence against the inscrutable absoluteness of omnipotent God. Between him and that God there is no common measure. For what measure has man save his human passions and human values, and how can these be applied to omnipotence and omniscience without limiting and belittling it? In consequence, Job, the symbol of all men, must stand up on his own feet alone, working out his destiny by his own measure, recognizing that a just and omnipotent God cannot indulge in a chosen people, cannot elect a favorite, but must maintain all His creatures with an equal providence, thus vindicating the right of each to his different integrity. For the claimant to election by omnipotence also claims the rule of omnipotence; his claim becomes a pretension to mastery over all mankind and thus a threat of war and slavery to the different, and ultimately of disaster to the pretender himself, be he a single individual, a state, or a church.

Humanism in this meaning has a certain kinship with *democracy*. But it was elicited from the Book of Job after the Democratic Revolution. Before that Revolution Job was held to be a vindication and proof of the ways of God with the unelect.

v

I think we may now come to some conclusion concerning humanistic sources of democracy. Certain humanisms provide obvious analogies with democracy; others, no matter what is claimed for them or who claims it, are altogether incommensurable. Analogic humanisms are such because of certain techniques of attitudes or processes which occur also in the ways of democracy. But the authentic humanists of history to whom those pertained, such as Erasmus, had no inkling of modern democracy and in all likelihood would have been shocked by it. Their humanism was not a source of democracy because their end, their goal, their stopping place was this humanism, not democracy. Again, it was not a source because while democracy follows, it does not *follow from* this humanism. The latter is chronologically prior; only, however, in so far as certain of its aspects are a dynamic common to both itself and democracy may it be designated as a source. Those aspects, we have seen, are not the intellectual or aesthetic content of this humanism; they are the methods of the humanists, in the degree that the methods consist in observation, free inquiry, unrelaxing scrutiny of thoughts and things. The humanism which works by the methods of authority, which sets dogma above observation, rationalization above reason, and belief and obedience above security and free choice, cannot be said to contribute anything to democracy.

Lastly, there is also a humanism which may be taken as a synonym for democracy. But it would be as correct to hold that democracy is the source of this humanism as that this humanism is a source of democracy. For democracy is chronologically prior to this humanism. Even though it does employ Protagoras and Terence to support its vision, it comes to expression in a social atmosphere, a climate of culture, where the propositions of the Declaration of Independence are the gradients for human relations and the methods of science for human discourse. This humanism, hence, is pluralistic, empirical, and libertarian. Its spokesmen acknowledge, they respect, they endeavor sympathetically to understand, differences and the cooperation of differences. They hold with William James, in his *Will to Believe* (Longmans Green & Co.): "No one of us ought to issue vetoes to the other, nor should we bandy words of abuse. We ought, on the contrary, delicately and profoundly to respect one another's mental freedom." Instead of demanding or exacting conformity, they endeavor to live and let live, to live and help live. God, some of them argue, is, on the record, either a name for companies of many "divine" beings struggling for survival as human beings struggle and forming their associations with other species, not the human only, according to its role in this survival; or else God is a name for an all-powerful entity, differently imagined by different men, that brings forth impartially all the infinite diversities of experience, not men only nor what men find good and what men find evil, and that just as impartially sustains and destroys them all. God so conceived, these humanists hold, cannot favor man over any other species; nor any race or cult of man over any other; nor any human doctrine and discipline over any other. All maintain themselves or perish, under such a God, not by favor, but by their own dispositions and abilities and relationships. According to these humanists each form of existence, has, under such a God, its own different type of life, liberty, and happiness; each has an equal right with every other to achieve its type. Among men, each comes together with others to form societies—churches, states, economies, civilizations—because by these means each can "secure these rights" more aptly, more abundantly, than he could alone. The ends are the Many. The means become the One, generated by the Many. Institutions and governments are at their best when their oneness is thought of and treated not as organism but as organization; when they express not unity but union; when they consist not in integration but orchestration; when they are modes of the free association of the different organizations of liberty whose just powers are the hearts and the heads of all the human beings whose organizations they are.

There may be others, and as apt, orchestrations of *humanism,* with *democracy*. If there are, I must regretfully declare that I have missed them. But I do not think there are; for when humanism is taken thus humanly, democracy is humanism, humanism is democracy.

VII

LITERARY SOURCES

BY

AMOS N. WILDER, Ph.D., D.D.

Professor of New Testament Interpretation, Chicago Theological Seminary, and Federated Theological Faculty of the University of Chicago

This course wisely includes a scrutiny of the relation of imaginative literature to freedom. Realities as fundamental as freedom are not fully grasped nor are they adequately transmitted apart from literature and the arts. In the understanding of freedom "conscious intellectual conceptions and dogmas are not to be exaggerated in their influence as against unconscious processes," says Whitehead. Here, too, "intellectual activity is apt to flourish at the expense of wisdom." ("Aspects of Freedom" in *Freedom, Its Meaning,* ed. by R. N. Anshen, New York, 1940, p. 47, Harcourt, Brace & Co.) The important unconscious processes of which Whitehead speaks are just that experience which imaginative literature can most fully mediate. And such literature can serve as a source of freedom not only in the sense of a valuable documentation but also in the sense that these classic utterances of freedom serve as a leading factor in the diffusion of its ideals and values.

There is indeed some tendency to disparage the significance of literature in the achievement and maintenance of freedom. In fact the depreciation of writers at this point takes two contradictory forms. On the one hand, they are accused of irresponsibility (*Le Trahison des Clercs;* "The Irresponsibles," etc.)—a charge which assumes their importance and influence in public questions; on the other, their contribution of whatever kind is counted insignificant.

At the International Congress of the P.E.N. Society held in wartime London in 1940, a Polish writer raised the question pointedly:

The freedom of the world!—millions of copies of books by Remarque, Barbusse, R. Rolland, H. G. Wells, Hasek, T. Mann, B. Russell, prepared the road for a better, finer world. But what have we achieved? . . . I have lost everything. I come from a country of libraries thrown into the bonfire, a country of ravaged laboratories, of pillaged museums. We have been defeated on our own terms. . . . The words of the great writers have had less influence in the shaping of reality than the rubbish of the one scribbler, Adolf Hitler.

A somewhat similar analysis was made by Aldous Huxley in a paper prepared for the Conference on Science, Philosophy and Religion in 1943, in this case bearing on the influence of writers for peace. After the early years of the First World War writers and artists proceeded to represent war realistically, as something senseless and criminal, he pointed out.

The same mood persisted for some years after the close of the conflict. Books such as *All Quiet on the Western Front* achieved a fabulous circulation in every part of the civilized world. The causes of war were investigated and exhaustively set forth by scores of writers, blueprints for a better world appeared by the hundred, and a whole literature of uplift, tinged by sociology and political economy, crystallized round such peacemaking institutions as the League of Nations. In all history no generation of men has been more fully or more effectively informed about war and its consequences than was the generation which flourished between 1918 and 1939. Never, at any rate during the earlier part of this period, have there been fewer chauvinistic writers of talent, or more brilliant advocates of internationalism. Never has so much learning and industry been expended upon the analysis of war's causes and the elaboration of preventives. It was with their eyes wide open and with the warning voices of their favourite authors ringing in their ears, that the peoples of Europe marched once again over the precipice.

It is such considerations that lead to a disenchantment with the influence of the writer or the view that in the last analysis the writer and artist are only mirrors of society rather than leaders or legislators. Thus Dos Passos:

I cannot see how even the most immortal writer is more than the best possible type of moving-picture machine constructed to focus the present moment on the screen of the future. The present is people and the future is people. The good writer is like a sponge that sops up the lives of the people he lives with. (P.E.N. Congress Report, London, 1941.)

But such negative conclusions are unnecessary. The writer does have, has had, and will have a significant influence for freedom, though it should not be exaggerated. Distinction must be made. Some writers have little influence because their ultimate sanctions for freedom are superficial. Some writers have a great influence because their sanctions are profound. We propose the thesis that the literary defense of freedom must be rooted in religious faith to be historically significant. The modern literature of freedom and of peace has been ineffective in good part because it has not laid hold of or challenged the deeper level of human responsibility. Particular historical freedom will not be won save where transcendental freedom is achieved.

Misunderstanding of the significance of literature for freedom arises, however, at another point. It is one aspect of modern educational psychology to depreciate the transmission of values through the written word. Emphasis is placed on action and participation. It is with patriotism and social ideals here as it is with the religious heritage: Scripture and written tradition are heavily discounted as against life-situation activities. We must teach children by immediate contemporary group experience rather than by the Bible. So we must teach democracy by projects, by doing rather than by reading, by practice and not by indoctrination.

Now such a proper emphasis on action has only this danger, that it misconceives the power of literature and of Scripture. Some of our friends among the psychologists and educationists—we do not speak of the judicious—have failed to make some important distinctions. Surely the weight of their attack falls not on imaginative literature but on discursive writings. It is not poetry, drama and fiction, not painting and sculpture, not Scripture and mythology, that they rightly attack, but rather abstract exposition. The indoctrination that they rightly depreciate is of the dogmatic, not the symbolic kind. Symbolic indoctrination is, alas, only too effective, as we know to our cost in connection with Nazism and Shinto. Religion *can* be transmitted by Scripture; patriotism *can* be transmitted by the printed page; the meaning of freedom *can* be transmitted by the spiritual incendiarism of literature. A boy of fifteen lying on a rug and reading *Les Misérables* or the life of Lincoln or *Scottish Chiefs* can be infected with democratic ideals and enthusiasm, and living experiences in democratic living will thereby take on deeper significance. Life offers countless opportunities for moral experience. What is important is that the individual when such opportunities come—whether manufactured or not—should have had his ardors and charities aroused. The seals of isolation, insensitiveness, and blindness must have been removed.

For the potent effect of literature on men one can instance the influence of Plutarch's *Lives*. Black print on a white page read by the individual in his secret chamber can shape the ideals of youth, can suddenly kindle a man to action, can cause the scales to fall from a man's eyes. A notable testimony here is that of Frederick Douglas, the Negro slave, regarded by many as the greatest leader of his people. He tells in *My Bondage and My Freedom* of how his "curiosity in respect to this *mystery* of reading" was aroused by hearing his mistress read from the Bible. She agreed to teach him. His master bore unconscious witness to the potency of literature in quoting the axiom, "Learning will spoil the best nigger in the world. If he learns to read the Bible, it will forever unfit him to be a slave." Douglas later got hold of a popular schoolbook, the *Columbian Orator,* containing "one of Sheridan's mighty speeches on the subject of Catholic Emancipation, Lord Chatham's speech on the American War, and speeches by the great William Pitt, and by Fox." Hereafter he wavered no longer in his nascent conviction. "Light had penetrated the moral dungeon where I had lain." (See citation in Bernard Smith [ed.], *The Democratic Spirit,* New York, 1941, pp. 379, 380, A. A. Knopf.)

The misunderstanding with regard to the value of literature and art arises partly from a failure to recognize their dramatic aspects. Men fail to recognize that the reading of imaginative literature *is* participation in action; it *is* what they rightly insist on: contemporary experience—yes, though what they read may refer to 1776 or to the resistance of the Maccabees. For it is of the essence of great literature that we are drawn into vicarious experience in such reading. It is a moral exercise. We are participants.

We shall center our attention on the nineteenth and twentieth centuries as most immediately suggestive of the contribution that literature can make today in the cause of freedom. But we must see this period in its historical background and have in mind the story of liberty since the sixteenth century as it has found literary expression. Moreover, we are desirous of finding a central theme for our presentation so that it will not be a mere miscellany of quotations. To find such a central theme we must go farther back than the eighteenth century. And as soon as we begin to enumerate the countless writers—poets, dramatists, novelists, essayists—who have written in the defense of one or another type of freedom, we see not only how necessary it is to set limits to our undertaking and to find a central theme about which we can order our reflections and our instances, but also how important it is to establish a criterion by which to distinguish the more from the less significant.

As we look back, then, from Emerson and Whitman to Wordsworth and Shelley, and behind these last to the poets of the eighteenth century, and behind these to Milton, we find ourselves led to inquire into the presence or absence of religious influences in the literature of freedom and into the character of such religious influences as may be found. The aim of this whole series of lectures and the basic concern of the Institute for Religious and Social Studies make it appropriate that we consider especially the religious relations of our topic.

Indeed we propose as our unifying theme the following hypothesis: the most significant literature of freedom in the modern world has had its roots more or less immediately in the Hebraic-Christian faith, and the most notable figures, despite appearances, reveal a significant, if indirect, relation to it. We recognize that important writers appear to speak out of nonreligious persuasions, particularly rationalist or utilitarian or romantic. Part of the interest of our approach will be to identify the value of such other inspirations or outlooks and to note the complex way in which they are found combined with traditional religious concern. But it is our thesis that true religious sanctions will be found in the most significant literature of freedom and democracy and that, contrary to what is often maintained, many vociferous and rhetorical and highly esteemed sponsors of liberty have not made as significant a contribution as is often supposed.

My own interests have led me to explore the religious motivation of the literature of freedom in respect to the Protestant and especially Puritan tradition. What I have to say here no doubt could be correspondingly documented in writers under immediate Jewish or Catholic influence. Indeed, it might be said that as between these three faiths I have undertaken the hardest assignment. The Protestant, especially one who would find his illustrations in the Calvinist background, seems to enter the lists with a formidable handicap. Can the democratic faith grow in the soil of original sin and predestination! Father Hecker plausibly argued that Calvin's doctrine of the enslaved will was incompatible with the Declaration of Independence and the concept of natural rights. What concord is there between democracy and determinism? Democracy, he taught, is the fundamental denial of the tenets of Luther and Calvin. Nevertheless, we believe it can be shown that Reformation impulses underlie some of the most powerful literature of freedom.

But it should not be necessary to apologize in a course like this for the attention we give to the subject of religious inspiration and content. Indeed, to deal with the literary sources of freedom at a strictly literary level would amount to little more than making an anthology of purple passages.

After all it is a commonplace that we owe our liberties in America to two main sources, the Biblical tradition and the Enlightenment. What is, however, immediately imperative is to assess their respective contributions and to identify their respective expressions in literature.

Now with respect to Protestantism and the Reformation I would sketch in the background for much of the literature with which we are concerned. The relation of Protestantism to Anglo-Saxon culture shows two chief phases, and each of them has enormous significance for the conception of freedom and each of them has inspired major literary activity.

Primary Protestantism, the Protestantism of the sixteenth century, was concerned with time and eternity, with the perpendicular dimension, with transcendental freedom. It interpreted life in terms of pilgrimage, spiritual warfare, and the Biblical drama. When it found expression in literature, as it did for instance in Bunyan, it had a great world-picture and body of symbol to work with, and a great dynamic for its conception of the soul. But it was when it entered into fruitful union with the humanism of the Renaissance, as it did in the case of Milton, that we find its supreme literary expression. And the prominence of the cause of freedom in Milton's life and writing derives from his religious faith. We do not intend to delay with Milton, but we draw attention briefly to his work as a classical instance in the matter of the literary sources of freedom. It is true that many questions immediately arise with regard to Milton in this connection. It is true, on the one hand, that he was by no means a "leveller" and, on the other, that he was by no means orthodox in his Reformation theology. One might also ask where in his poetry, as distinct from his tracts, we are to find literary sources of freedom as modern writers define freedom.[1]

Surely at this hour it is not necessary to defend the great republican who devoted the best twenty years of his life to the Commonwealth and to the cause of civil, cultural, and spiritual liberty. Professor Douglas Bush of Harvard, in a discussion of the "Irresponsibles" before the Conference on Science, Philosophy and Religion, in 1941, paid a unique tribute to Milton as one in the great tradition of the artist who is first of all a citizen: the tradition of Aeschylus, Cicero, and Dante. (See *Science, Philosophy and Religion: Second Symposium*, New York, 1941, pp. 307-335, Harper & Bros.)

What should be said is that in *Paradise Lost* and in *Samson Ago-*

---

[1] We need not linger over such an extreme indictment of Milton as we get in Hilaire Belloc's portrait (*Milton*, Phila., 1935). Note also Whitehead: "The pursuit of freedom with an intolerant mentality is self-defeating. For all his equipment of imagination, learning, and literary magic in defense of freedom, the example of Milton's life probably does as much to retard the cause as to advance it. He promotes a frame of mind of which the issue is intolerance. "Aspects of Freedom," in R. N. Anshen, ed., p. 51, Harcourt, Brace & Co., *op. cit.*

nistes, Milton's animating impulse is his disappointment and indignation at the miscarriage of freedom. The epic is a study in the theme that man cannot be politically free if he is the slave of passion. Nor is the freedom at issue here a mere partisan or even patriotic freedom. It is a spiritual freedom, the ideal of the Kingdom of Saints, with all its overtones of the Biblical drama of human destiny. Milton's theology may not be that of Luther or Calvin. The Reformation faith is richly wedded to the classics and to Renaissance rationalism. Professor Bush summarizes Milton's outlook as follows:

> Milton has been claimed as an ancestor by irresponsible libertarians, but he himself always maintained that one who loves liberty must first be wise and good. His dynamic conception of Christian liberty, which freed the regenerate man from external restraints and made him, under Christ, the pilot of his own ship, was both Christian and classical. For Milton, as for the contemporary Cambridge Platonists, and for the long line of Christian humanists before them, the spirit of man was the candle of the Lord; they conceived of right reason, the divine faculty of the moral judgment and the moral will, as fused with the light of revelation. These principles of rational faith and ethics kept men like Milton from Calvinistic determinism on the one hand and from the mechanistic determinism of Hobbes on the other.

Yet it must be said that the gravity and dimensions of *Paradise Lost* as indeed the power of the *Areopagitica* spring out of the moods of primary Protestantism with its fresh sense of the august issues that gather about the human soul and the human lot. No example could better illustrate the significance of religious sanction for the literature of freedom. In comparison with political and moral eloquence of this kind the familiar odes and poems to liberty of the eighteenth century and the Romantic period are like the college chants of school boys or the patriotic effusions in a village newspaper.

One point that Professor Bush makes about Milton bears on what we shall say later about rationalism as an ingredient in the literature of freedom. The mature Milton, though far from disowning reason, attacked intellectual pride and self-sufficiency.

> One conspicuous illustration . . . is found in Milton's changing atti-

tude toward the Baconian . . . vision of man as the potential conqueror of nature; in the tract on education he stressed science far more than most humanists had; and he glorified Galileo, without suspecting that the study of things might come to supersede the study of right and wrong. Yet the earnest Christian and Platonist was more typical of himself when he explicitly ranked scientific knowledge below the knowledge of God and the true end of human life. Experience only deepened his sense of that distinction, and in *Paradise Lost* he insists that science, knowledge of the external universe, does not and cannot illuminate the moral problems of everyday life.

In this connection Dr. Bush draws the contrast of Shelley who was less circumspect, and whose defense of freedom, we may add, was thereby weakened.

Let us now briefly survey the role of religious influences in English literature from the time of Milton down to the present. There is a connection between the increasing secularization of the modern world and the limitations of the literature of freedom. In this period the prestige of the Christian world-view and the Biblical world-drama receded. By the time of Wordsworth and Shelley it was hardly possible for a writer to present an ambitious work to a wide public in terms of either the Protestant or Catholic world-assumptions or with controlling use of Christian symbolism. (See Basil Willey, *The Seventeenth Century Background,* New York, 1942; and compare H. N. Fairchild, *Religious Trends in English Poetry,* New York, Vol. I, 1939; Vol. II, 1942.) For a time men were content with a divorce of reason and faith, but this segregation of religion meant its ultimate withering away before the claims and exuberance of reason. This process carried with it the decay of classical symbolism as well. These two great "mythologies" by varying stages lost their power over men's lives and imaginations and could be used only as ornament rather than sanction. And if this be true of the eighteenth century how much further has it gone in the nineteenth and twentieth centuries! As it bears on our particular interest, it would mean that the literature of freedom in the Romantic writers and in modern writers has therewith been deprived increasingly of those supreme sanctions which would have made it most effective. The matter is of course complex, and continuing religious sanctions manifest themselves often in disguised form. We recognize that magnificent expressions of the ideals of liberty appear in modern literature. It still remains to identify the role of religious assumptions, however depleted. One outcome of such an analysis will be instruction and challenge to present-day writers as to the most effective defense of freedom today and in the future.

In this period it is "secondary" Protestantism which makes its impact on culture, taking form in the latter seventeenth century. This type is marked by a present realization of grace and present personal fulfillment, and is therefore inclined to world affirmation and to mystical and ethical rather than metaphysical issues. The accent falls on subjective experience, emotional release, and leads to individualism and sectarian associations. This type of Protestantism was able to marry itself in complex ways with eighteenth-century rationalism, with German idealism and with Romanticism, and thus both to leaven these movements and to be influenced by them. Thence come the most interesting literary productions of this type of Protestantism. The motifs of primary Protestantism could still reappear in it often in a desiccated form. Secondary Protestantism, indeed, had its own unfortunate offshoots of eccentricity and emotionalism. Such phenomena hastened the divorce of significant elements of the modern world from the Christian tradition, and writers like Blake, Shelley, Emerson, and Whitman are found in strong reaction against the religious heritage, and their defense of freedom proceeds therefore on the surface, largely from secularizing assumptions. But it is our thesis that the influence of the religious tradition remains powerful in some of the chief writers of the Romantic movement and the nineteenth century and accounts for the most significant contribution they made to the defense of freedom.

In studying the continued operation of this tradition under the disguises of Romanticism, of bourgeois values, and later of naturalism and Marxism, we can easily fall into error. Because of its intimate identification with such movements, we can lose sight of it and conclude that it has ceased to act. Another error is to suppose that such general movements themselves are essentially pagan. The supreme problem of modern culture is the judicious evaluation of its component traditions and the identification of its greater and lesser values. Here more truly than in overtly pagan days is it imperative to "test the spirits whether they be of God." Such delicacy of diagnosis is nowhere more important than in connection with secondary Protestantism and the congenial allies it has found in the past century and a half.

The ambiguity of many modern figures may be illustrated by Rousseau, whose influence has been so great on later liberal writers. Traditional religious influences are not absent in his case; indeed, they are accountable for much of the best in his work, and this appears when we contrast him with the deists and the philosophers. Rousseau had Calvinist as well as Quaker influences in his background and education. He wrestled desperately with moral questions and was moved passionately against injustice and oppression. He called himself a theist as against the deists and pointed out the superficiality of the latter. In the *Nouvelle Héloise* moral autonomy and mastery take an important place with him as conditions of liberty, both in the individual and the state. The "general will" is a religious conception, since it is a means by which the universal moral law finds expression in man's collective life. The supreme end of the free state lies in its offering to men opportunity for full moral and spiritual development. Further, Rousseau in contradistinction from the philosophes had grasped the more sobering lessons that Montesquieu had to teach. And he rejected the materialism and the psychology of the English school, the individualism of Locke, hasty enthusiasms as to the perfectibility of man, and excessive confidence in the scientific economics of the day.

Thus in Rousseau we find an example of the combination of secondary Protestantism with Romanticism. The operation of the Christian tradition upon him is seen at those points where he differs from the main group of the Encyclopedists. They are more superficial, more fascinated by science and rationalism, overconfident as to what they can do for man, reacting in an oversimple way against what they see as priestcraft and superstition, and blind to man's deeper religious nature. They also were passionate for liberty, equality, and fraternity, but more superficially. They, too, exalted Reason and Nature, but more naïvely. These distinctions are to be observed and applied in the cases of men like Tom Paine and Jefferson, or men like Wordsworth, Byron, and Shelley, or later patriots and liberators. Rousseau like Wordsworth (as we shall see below) may lack much of a thoroughgoing Christian sanction for his idea of freedom but he no doubt was a prophetic voice of the modern world's aspirations.

The work of the English Romantic poets offers us similarly a significant body of material for those interested in the literature of freedom. Here, too, we have to discern and distinguish various influences, diverse inspirations at work. Here, too, the appeal to freedom rests upon differing sanctions, natural and supernatural, pagan and Christian. In this age the Christian world-picture had lost its hold. The eighteenth century bequeathed to the poet at most a sense of the divinity of nature and of man, and he must erect his own house of faith out of materials borrowed from many directions. Under these handicaps Blake and Shelley and Byron nevertheless speak, each in his own way, for freedom. The great enemy, as they see it, is the ancient régime in whatever aspect, tyranny, priestcraft, superstition, privilege. In their outlook, science, rationalism, benevolence, and Romanticism combine in various patterns. The classical and the Christian traditions appear in a minor way as ornament and illustration, and in a disguised way as an unconscious shaping influence. Thus Shelley is in such reaction against Christian dogma and authority that it is only in his later work that he includes Christ among the martyrs of liberty. Nevertheless, with Shelley and even more with Blake the aspiration to freedom has profound overtones and perspectives. Much of the poetry and eloquence inspired by the struggles with despotism in this period of the French and the American Revolution seems today dated. Its roots are not deep. But in *Prometheus Unbound* and in other work like the songs in *Hellas,* Shelley has become a voice of that which concerns our whole epoch and which Croce calls "the moral liberation and transcendence of modern man."

Wordsworth is the most revealing case here. In his origin among the independent freeholder population of the Lake District he is a good representative of the type produced by secondary Protestantism, a type which in this period had entered into fruitful if secularizing combination with eighteenth-century influences and Romanticism. Nevertheless, the basic Christian cast and temper is there in its English Protestant form, manifesting itself in a dynamic personalism and a particular conception of duty. No doubt the special form that his early experience with nature took and his consequent Romantic view of the soul evidence influences which in many men of the period led to pagan extremes. But such outcomes were checked in him by his Christian heritage. Thus when in his youth he was exposed to the full force of the ideas and emotions of the French Revolution, he was powerfully swayed, and his period of disillusion was a dangerous one. But he found his balance, and in his creative period he wrote poetry dealing with freedom that stands with the greatest. The sonnets dedicated to national independence and liberty and the sections in the *Prelude* that touch on the same themes rise above the work of Shelley or Byron or Heine or Victor Hugo or Swinburne in considerable part because they have a further dimension given to them by his latent Christianity. Here is his ultimate sanction. It is to this he appeals, to

> our fearful innocence,
> And pure religion breathing household laws.

He speaks of those who

> the faith and morals hold
> Which Milton held.

And there is a passage in the tenth book of the *Prelude* where Wordsworth relates his own experience of the fortunes of France to that of the Hebrew prophets and speaks of "sublime behests" and "glimpses of retribution." This is not the language of a Romantic poet. And he goes on:

> When a taunt
> Was taken up by scoffers in their pride,
> Saying, "Behold the harvest that we reap
> From popular government and equality,"
> I clearly saw that neither these nor aught
> Of wild belief engrafted on their names
> By false philosophy had caused the woe,

> But a terrible reservoir of guilt
> And ignorance filled up from age to age,
> That could no longer hold its loathsome charge,
> But burst and spread in deluge through the land.

Surely a poet defends freedom better when he tells men of their compounded abuses and the righteous sentence of heaven that falls upon them than when he flatters their passions.

Robert Will said of the Reformation that it gave to the aspirations of the Renaissance and of Humanism, as it were, a breath of eternity. We may transpose this and apply it to Wordsworth and say that Wordsworth's, however diffused, Protestant heritage gave to the aspirations in him of the Romantic movement a breath of eternity, and thus deepened and generalized the purport of his themes.

As we turn now to some of the American writers, we shall concern ourselves here, too, with the religious and especially the Puritan influence in their work. There were writers like Hawthorne and Melville who show still a strong Puritan influence just as there were writers like Emerson and Thoreau and Whitman who are anti-Puritan but who nonetheless betray the influence of that tradition. It is our conviction here again that the most effective American literature of freedom had religious sanctions, conscious or unconscious, and Puritanism surely is one of the forms of such sanctions which has had particular importance with American writers and readers. There are paradoxes here, indeed. It is a curious thing, for example, that some of those writers who are most clearly Puritan in their conscious outlook are sometimes found on the undemocratic side. For Puritanism could combine its incomparable transcendental sanctions for the worth of the human soul with a healthy fear of public passions and mobocracy. It was their theology that gave the Puritans their scorn for earthly dignities whether temporal or ecclesiastical. But it was their theology that gave them also their disabused sense of men's potentialities for evil. Let us recall here a classic passage from Macaulay:

> The Puritans were men whose minds had derived a peculiar character from the daily contemplation of superior beings and eternal interests. . . .

Instead of catching occasional glimpses of the Deity through an obscuring veil, they aspired to gaze full on his intolerable brightness, and to commune with him face to face. Hence originated their contempt for terrestrial distinctions. The difference between the greatest and the meanest of mankind seems to vanish. . . . The very meanest of them was a being to whose fate a mysterious and terrible importance belonged. . . . (From the essay on Milton)

It is our conviction that such potent faiths whether Puritan, Jewish, Evangelical, Catholic, are ultimately of supreme significance for freedom. It is no argument against this to point out that writers of Puritan background are not always correct if judged by the shibboleths of the French Revolution or of Jacksonian democracy. The point is that historical liberties will never be won where transcendental liberties are unrecognized. St. Paul was not "correct" on the matter of slavery, but slavery and other social tyrannies of the ancient world were overcome later because of the transcendental freedom taught by St. Paul.

Now it is particularly Hawthorne and Melville that come into view when we ask about conscious Puritan influence on American writers of the great period. Hawthorne is apparently found on the undemocratic side when he attacks the social reformers of his time. Yet Professor Curti points out that "this faithful follower of the Jackson men in politics had no illusions about American aristocrats, and that his sympathy with the exploited, whether on the plantation or in the mill, found expression. At the same time he was unable to pin his faith to mere reform. . . .

"The heart, the heart!—there was the little, yet boundless sphere wherein existed the original wrong of which the crime and misery of this outward world were merely types. Purify that inward sphere, and the many shapes of evil that haunt the outward, and which now seem our only realities, will turn to shadowy phantoms and vanish of their own accord." (*The Growth of American Thought,* New York, 1943, p. 393, Harper & Bros. The Hawthorne citation is from *Mosses from an Old Manse,* Houghton, Mifflin, 1882).

Hawthorne could be accused here of an irresponsible religious individualism, did we not know of his basic sympathies. His recognition of original sin is by no means incompatible with his commitment to freedom, indeed quite the contrary.

The case of Melville is even more clear. Again we borrow Curti's words to describe Melville's distrust of democracy, both "more theoretical and more profound," he says, than that of Cooper:

> He observed in one of his allegorical novels, *Mardi* (1849), that, after all, political freedom was not a prime and chief blessing; it was good only as a means to personal freedom, uprightness, justice, and felicity. . . . However loudly the thrall yelled out his liberty, he still remained a slave. . . . That all men should govern themselves as nations, needs that all men be better, and wiser, than the wisest of one-man rulers (pp. 395, 6).

But Hawthorne and Melville both had things they could teach to writers more ostensibly democratic. Their insights came to them as a legacy from the Puritan outlook. Melville indicates it when he finds the essence of Hawthorne's greatness in the fact that he breathed "that unshackled democratic spirit of Christianity in all things."

F. O. Matthiessen in his study of the age of Emerson and Whitman, *American Renaissance*, recurs constantly to this theme of the greater profundity and wisdom of Melville and Hawthorne as compared with Emerson and other writers (*American Renaissance*, London and New York, 1941, p. 270, Oxford University Press). Apropos of the transcendentalists and their ambiguous cult of perfection and cult of the future, he shows that Hawthorne gave it its most searching contemporary analysis:

> He sensed that Emerson's exaltation of the divinity in man had obliterated the distinctions between man and God, between time and eternity. Although no theologian, Hawthorne did not relax his grip on the Christian conception of time. This had been obscured by Thoreau and Whitman no less than by Emerson in their exhilaration over the fullness of the moment (p. 652).

Thus Hawthorne safeguarded the sense of man's limitations as a creature in time and the consequent tragic character of life. For him man's eternal relationships were better understood because he had not lost sight of man's temporal realities. Matthiessen grants that Whitman and Thoreau offer a more compelling image of the rising common man than Hawthorne, but Whitman's romantic view of the poet as his own Messiah and Thoreau's occasional sour or self-confident individualism both show the dangerous slope on which these writers lived. In fact the individualism of an Emerson, a Thoreau, and a Whitman can lead on insensibly to that of a Nietzsche of the first phase, and that of the Nietzsche of the last phase, and then the irrationalism of the prophet can become the irrationalism of the Führer (p. 546). The "green wine" of Emerson and the Messianism of Whitman—like that of D. H. Lawrence—illustrate the ambiguous forms that the love of freedom can take when it gets away from the restraints of religious insight. And woe be to such modern prophets if some pseudo religion, some idolatry of instinct or power or reason, flatters our antinomianism rather than restrains it.

In no person more than in Emerson do the contradictions of these varying sanctions and inspirations appear. There were naïve and dangerous aspects even of his mature thought, and there were deep sympathies and wise and prophetic discernments for which he was ready to pay a high price of devotion. Some of the criticism of Emerson by his contemporaries, gathered by Mr. Matthiessen, serves to localize the most suspect areas of his outlook. Henry James, Sr., speaks of him as "my unfallen friend" and says that he "had no conscience, in fact, and lived by perception . . . , an altogether lower and less spiritual faculty . . . and was fundamentally treacherous to civilization." Father Taylor said: "Mr. Emerson is one of the sweetest creatures God ever made; there is a screw loose somewhere in the machinery, yet I cannot tell where it is, for I never heard it jar. . . . He knows no more of the religion of the New Testament than Balaam's ass did of the principles of the Hebrew grammar." Charles Eliot Norton wrote: "His optimism becomes a bigotry, and, though of a nobler type than the common American conceit of the pre-eminent excellence of American things as they are, has hardly less the quality of fatalism. . . . He refuses to believe in disorder or evil." Apropos of Emerson's view of evil as negative, etc., Herman Melville made a marginal notation: "To annihilate all this nonsense read the Sermon on the Mount, and consider what it implies." And the statement that "the first lesson of history is the good of evil" Melville derided: "He still bethinks himself of his optimism—he must make that good somehow against the eternal hell itself." And further: "His gross and astonishing errors and illusions spring from a self-conceit so intensely intellectual and calm that at first one hesitates to call it by its right name. Another species of Mr. Emerson's errors, or rather, blindness, proceeds from a defect in the region of the heart." Finally we cite two phrases of William James apropos of the uprooted character of much of Emerson's thinking; he speaks of "the anaesthetic revelation" and "the tasteless water of souls."

However unjust it is to marshal these adverse judgments, they do nevertheless suggest why Emerson's defense of freedom was imperfect. Concepts like that of the "infinitude of the private man" (compare: "the divine pride of man in himself"—Whitman) are not congenial to moral seriousness. They lead on to pretension, intoxication, and anarchy. Like other forms of mysticism, transcendentalism is "numb to the intricacies of human feeling," to use a phrase of Mr. Yvor Winters spoken apropos of the mysticism of some recent poets. Disregard of the Biblical realism leaves all such immanentists with an insufficient sense of the tragic in life. And such immanentism invaded American thought in many forms in the period we are considering, and still continues. These sectarians and illuminati and deists serve freedom and other causes nobly out of motives of sentiment—patriotic and humanitarian—but they do not assail the ultimate bastilles nor destroy the works of the devil.

But there was another and magnificent side to Emerson and we presume to assign credit for it to the Puritan tradition behind him. He represents the human type, the cast of man produced by secondary Protestantism, and this appears in him. The specific Puritan strain is no doubt compounded with and overlaid by the cultural influences of the time but it cannot be silenced. It appears particularly in the insistence on autonomy, however confused; in the quest for present fulfillment and emotional release, indeed for ecstasy—and it was here that the temptation to an irrational romanticism was so strong in all Protestantism of this period; in the aggressive moralism and the moral-prophetic vocation, which under idealist influence could take the form of identifying poet with seer.

Stuart P. Sherman, in an essay on Emerson that today appears curiously dated (*Americans,* New York, 1922, ch. IV, "The Emersonian Liberation," Chas. Scribner's Sons) well says that the new movement of the young American idealists led by Emerson was "genuinely Puritan by its inwardness, by its earnest passion for cleansing the inside of the cup, by its protest against external powers which thwarted or retarded the efforts of the individual soul to move forward and upward by light from within." His chief theme is that Emerson transmits in new and revitalized form "the vital forces of the great moral traditions while at the same time he emancipates them from the dead hand of the past." We have in him "a fresh flowering of the ancient passion for self-perfection." Sherman indeed does here confuse Puritanism and Platonism, but he is fundamentally right about the Puritan lineage in Emerson, however obscured, and it is to this that we assign his best service to freedom. It appears in the radical protestantism of his discounting of old authorities in all realms and his readiness to question and revise all existing valuations, in his essentially moral concern with life, in his sound instincts and courage in the matter of the abolition movement, in his personal integrity and freedom from contamination by prevailing false values, and in his dedication to the disinterested life of thinker, poet, and artist. His defense of freedom falls short of the fundamental character of Melville's or the whole-souled immediacy of Walt Whitman. But in varying ways all these men, together with Thoreau, gave to America the initial formulation of its democratic symbols, its master myths, its types, heroes, demi-gods, fables, and poems. As Newton Arvin says of Whitman: he was "something more than the orator or lyrist of democracy"; he was "its biographer, its image maker" (*Whitman,* New York, Macmillan, 1938).

Brief attention to Whitman will clarify further some of the issues raised above. The following lines from *By Blue Ontario's Shore* will introduce our observations.

Are you he that would assume a place to teach or be a poet here in the States?
The place is august, the terms obdurate . . .
. . . Are you really of the whole people?

Are you not of some coterie? Some school or mere religion?
Are you done with reviews and criticisms of life? animating now to life itself?
Have you vivified yourself from the maternity of these States?

Here the poet is imperiously summoning the poets of the future, the poets of democracy, and indicates to them their curriculum. Like himself they are to make America their study, its origins, its people, their livelihood, the war between the states, its mountains, and its rivers. They are to vivify themselves from "the maternity of these states." They are to learn fraternity and individualism and freedom. They are to become aware of that which alone "holds men together," "which aggregates all in a living principle"; they are to become prophets of "the great idea, the idea of perfect and free individuals," by this kind of initiation. And in contrast he repudiates those who would aspire to such a role who may be of some coterie, indeed of some school or "mere religion."

Here then is an excellent utterance to bring into relief the peculiar vision of Whitman, both its merits and whatever restatement it requires. Indeed, this utterance may be taken as indicative of a basic and all but irreconcilable difference of outlook in the celebration and defense of freedom from that we have so far defended; yet each has enormous justification. Their reconciliation is all important to the defense of freedom today. One school would defend and further freedom on empirical and contemporary grounds almost alone. Another would do so on traditionalistic and historical grounds, not to say on grounds of revelation and Scripture. Surely both are right but the partisans of the one misunderstand and ill appreciate those of the other.

Whitman writes out of a passionate vision, a secular revelation, whose overwhelming force for him and his disciples can only be compared to that with which the early impulses of the French Revolution and the Bolshevist Revolution gripped their adherents. This is nothing less in his case than a magnificent irrationalism such as history occasionally brings forth under propitious circumstances—if not a religion, yet like a religion. And, though we may term it irrational, it is not therefore to be depreciated, however much we may wish to scrutinize and to assess it. For such formidable waves of faith, whether they grip an individual chiefly or a school or a people, must have some real relevance to reality, must have partial validity, must be grounded in real needs and real satisfactions, however much they outrun their due limits.

What we are saying about Walt Whitman's democratic faith and his blindness toward older faiths is true also of other kindred utterances for freedom in and before his period and indeed in many derivative and imitative voices for freedom that have arisen since and down to our own day. They appear to have it in common that they find the nourishment of their eloquence in the empirical experience of the greatness of men, whether known within or known by observation without. No sanction for their exaltation of man in ancient record or religious classic appears to be needed. The present occasion, the present demonstration, the observed heroism in the great or common instance, the subjective intoxication—these persuade by themselves and come with such force as to disqualify older testimonies. Indeed, older testimonies in the nature of the case seem to be compounded with negations or qualifications or, having gone to seed in church or state, have thereby come into disesteem. The present elation, therefore, does scant justice to older instances which nevertheless may represent wider truth and rest on surer foundations. The dusty page of the classic or even of ancient scripture—how much more of old-time prophet: Luther, Knox, Milton—is suspect as dogma. So the nascent dogma is unjust to the older dogma. And the new prophet sees the old as dying with the past, while limitless horizons open up before the new. As Whitman writes:

Others take finish, but the Republic is ever constructive and ever keeps vista.

So it is with the faith in the "democratic vistas." Yet all the time the present ardor draws its deepest force from the older faiths. The present stream, conscious only of its own flood, ignores the fountains and the wells from which it has sprung.

We are in a position now where we can briefly apply our conclusions to the present situation. The writer today has a great opportunity and a great responsibility. Authors should recognize that their work is not inconsiderable, whether for good or for evil. The reading public should assign a high value to the true artist, poet, and writer as shapers of public ideals and transmitters of the democratic faith.

The years straying toward infidelity he withholds by his steady faith.

Of course it is the rare and great writer whose work reaches many and endures to touch many generations that we first of all desire. But we should not underestimate the contribution to democratic ideals made by the large number of less-gifted authors. Their countless poems, stories, novels, plays, nay, columns, editorials, addresses, sermons, if they state the principle and values of freedom with some pungency, with some particularity, with countless special applications —these can indeed render a service that the great cannot render. Because of their ubiquity and iteration men and women are not permitted to forget or become insensible to the ideals that we cherish. The general concepts are not allowed to become hackneyed or to lose their compelling force.

But whether great or small, the only truly decisive or momentous service of freedom will be wrought by those who address themselves to the ultimate responsibilities of men in terms of the grander religious faiths. Only so will writer and reader transcend the specious ideals of liberty ambiguously identified with self-interest, class interest, national interest, which in the outcome engender slavery rather than freedom and passion rather than magnanimity. Only so will they transcend a barren eloquence drowned out by the hoarse voices of appetite and envy, or a rhetorical liberalism impotent before the chaotic tides of social impulse. Only so will they use the grave words, freedom and liberty, not as banners of schism and torches of destruction but with accents that can touch the universal soul of man.

VIII

THE FOUNDING FATHERS

BY

MOORHOUSE F. X. MILLAR, S.J., Ph.D.

Professor of Political Philosophy and Head of the Department, Fordham University

It seems to me the time has come for us to reappraise our history as a people. In the light of our present achievements in the world, now that we have become the greatest of the leading nations, we can see things in a perspective which was not given to those who were engaged in the earlier processes of our development. There is a good deal to be corrected in the way our history has been written, and a good deal to be done to gain a closer insight into the principles that really underlie our history as a nation.

We are one of the youngest of the nations. We can boast of only about three hundred years against the thousands of years of European peoples and the several thousands of years of China and India. And during that time we have been hampered to a certain extent by what might be considered an inferiority complex in relation to other peoples.

We, I think, have achieved one of the most constructive developments in the line of government that can be pointed to anywhere in history. Our Constitution is singular and unique and the form of government which was established under that Constitution is quite peculiar to ourselves, so much so that when we are forced to take into consideration other people's affairs, we find it very hard to understand their lack of some of the great benefits which we enjoy, as is clear from the problems with which our State Department is now confronted.

Owing to the fact that we are so young, we naturally inclined in the beginning to look to other people for precedents or for principles, and the assumption among our historians to a very large extent has been that we derived our principles from the French—the French Revolution, and the French philosophy of the eighteenth century.

Now, it is true that after the Constitution was adopted there was a good deal of borrowing from the French. We looked to France as having achieved the greatest innovation in the way of a revolution against tradition ever accomplished, and we failed to realize what we actually had achieved in our own revolution. To my mind our own revolution is by far a more important event, for the simple reason that it was from the very first moment constructive in its tendencies. There was at the beginning a desire for unity, first unity with England and then unity among the colonies. The leaders—and I am talking particularly about the leaders, not about the popular opinion of the day—were bent upon a definite constructive effort as far as the building up of the future of this country was concerned. You can see it in Otis's declaration of the rights of Englishmen, and you can see it all through the revolution itself, until finally you come to the achievement, the final achievement, namely, the framing and ratification of our Constitution.

As I have said, there was a French declaration which was assumed to have furnished us with the principles for this great effort. There are still those who write and talk as if the French Declaration of the Rights of Man were much more important than our Declaration of Independence. Some seem even to assume that we derived our Declaration of Independence from the French Declaration of the Rights of Man, though the French declaration was flashed upon the world some thirteen years later. That is a peculiar kind of anachronism which one sometimes meets with.

Then, later on, our university professors, particularly, and some of our great lawyers, went to Germany and learned the German philosophy of law and government, especially that of Kant and of Hegel, which was contradictory to the fundamentals of our Constitution. The theory developed that we derived all our democratic institutions from some place in the backwoods of Germany. That was the Teutonic myth. In time, of course, the people began to learn more about the Middle Ages and there was greater insight into mediaeval developments. They began to see that, after all, our democratic institutions are indebted, essentially for such things as constitutional limitation of government, chiefly to the Middle Ages, beginning with Magna Charta and continuing down through the centuries of English history, and that our tradition is definitely an Anglo-American tradition.

But with this came a kind of mythical interpretation of our history. There was a mythical view of Jefferson, a mythical view of Hamilton—and he was more or less assumed to be the villain in the piece—and there was a mythical Washington.

After the First World War we had the debunkers. They reacted against this mythical approach to our history and began to depreciate and devaluate these great men. Just at present there seems to be a definite movement for a reappraisal along sane and objective lines. As an instance, I would refer to Charles Beard's book on *The Republic,* also his *Basic History of the United States.* They show a new perspective, a new appreciation of the past and a much saner and sounder one.

As we look back to the Founders, I will take particular notice of Washington, Hamilton, Jefferson, Madison, and of James Wilson, about whom very little is known, though he was one of the most important, especially in the convention and, later, as Justice of the Supreme Court. These men had ideas and principles which are a little strange to us now, especially as a result of the influence of the debunkers and the confusion of these principles with the French revolutionary principles.

To begin with, they had a clear idea of the distinction between natural law and positive law, and a definite understanding of how positive law must necessarily depend upon natural law. You can see that during the trend of the revolution itself. First, they laid claim to the rights of Englishmen according to the constitutional setup of England, and, when they were denied these rights, when the English refused to accede to this claim, they fell back upon natural law because in natural law they had a right to these positive legal rights. That is a matter of the definite relation between natural law and positive law.

Today there are not many who believe in natural law because they do not understand what is meant by it. Natural law is nothing but the exigencies of human nature, the sound exigencies of human nature which antedate any activity on the part of man. Natural law is the practical evaluation of human experience both individual and collective in the light of a sound concept of man.

The Founders had this sound concept of man. It was a Christian concept, and it was a traditional concept that goes back to the Middle Ages. They got it to a very large extent from a man who was very popular throughout the whole period of the revolution, but of whom the historians have practically nothing to say, and that was Jean Jacques Burlamaqui. His treatment of man, ethics, natural law, and of positive law in relation to natural law, is practically the doctrine of St. Thomas. He was a Protestant, a Swiss of Italian descent, and he wrote this work of his about 1737. It was rapidly translated into English and became a textbook in both the English universities and in our colleges here in the colonies. There was scarcely a man who could boast of being intelligent who had not read the book. It is from this book that the principle laid down in the Declaration of Independence, that we have a natural right to the pursuit of happiness, was taken. And you will not find it in any of the other sources acclaimed by our historians.

By "pursuit of happiness" the Founders meant, in accord with Burlamaqui, not only temporal happiness, but ultimate happiness; that is to say, happiness in the next world. Having the duty to pursue our final happiness we have the inalienable right to all the necessary means to the attainment of that end. That gave them a sound ethical foundation, because even Aristotle was deficient in his ethics in so far as he did not allow for the immortality of man, and St. Thomas pointed out that for that reason he was not able to lay a solid foundation for ethics or politics.

The idea of positive law was definitely assumed to be something demanded by human nature. There were those, even in the Middle Ages, and there are plenty today, who consider law and government as a necessary evil. To the Founders law and government are a necessary good for men. Men cannot live and develop as human beings except in a well-ordered society, which is a means for their developing as persons. This notion was very definite in the minds of the Founders.

With regard to Washington, as Beard has pointed out, Washington could very easily, had he been overambitious, have become a dictator. Conditions in the colonies were so anarchical after the revolution, and even during the period of the revolution, that the army and many of the wealthier people would gladly have supported Washington in any claim to dictatorship he might have made. On the other hand, there were those who deprecated any idea of a strong government, either in the States or under the Articles of Confederation. They were opposed to any vigorous reform. And it was because of the disinterestedness of Washington, because he really did think in terms of what would be considered the good of the country, that we were saved from a monarchical form of government or dictatorship. He had only to say the word, and he would have found plenty of support.

With regard to Hamilton, as I have said, the tendency in the past has been to look upon him more or less as the villain in the piece, that is to say, to assume that he wanted a monarchy, that he was overambitious, and that he despised the people. The actual facts in that regard are astoundingly contrary to this more or less traditional assumption.

A book has appeared recently which is a splendid example of what I consider the present trend toward re-evaluating our history. It is called *The Administrative Theories of Hamilton and Jefferson*, by Lincoln K. Caldwell, and it is a fairly objective work. The author has taken both these men and showed how they developed a certain administrative philosophy apart from their general philosophy, and that this was vastly important for the success of the Constitution. And the more important of the two, of course, even in Caldwell's appraisal, is Hamilton. He did want a strong union, a strong central government. And he adopted every available measure to achieve this end. But far from being a monarchist, he was in some respects very far in advance of the others in his democratic emphasis.

I will read a rather striking passage:

Madison noted that in the Constitutional Convention of 1787, Hamilton, though avowing himself a friend of vigorous government, declared it essential that the popular branch should rest on a broad foundation. In the constitutional scheme that he drafted during the Convention, Hamilton proposed that the House of Representatives be elected by the free male citizens and inhabitants of the several States comprehended in the Union, all of whom to the age of 21 and upwards shall be entitled to an equal vote.

At a time when the property qualification for electors was almost universally accepted, Hamilton's proposal was drastic indeed. One need only recall that Republicans as orthodox as Madison and Monroe, as late as 1830, were opposed to the abolition of the property qualification for the electors of Virginia. Defending the Constitution in the New York Ratifying Convention of 1788, Hamilton again declared "that there should be a broad democratic branch in the national Legislature." Explaining its political principles to Colonel Edward Carrington of Virginia, he maintained that he was "affectionately attached to the Republican theory." He expressed a "desire above all things to see that the equality of political rights, exclusive of all hereditary distinction, be firmly established by a practical demonstration of its being consistent with the order and happiness of society."

And yet at that time Hamilton was being accused of being a monarchist. That was very largely due to the jealousies of Jefferson, who, though he was decidedly a great man, was tremendously sensitive regarding anything like opposition. At the time when it was a question of each finding his proper function in the government, he assumed that Hamilton was constantly inclined to interfere with his department, that is to say, the Department of State. Also, he objected to many of the measures that Hamilton adopted in the Treasury Department. It is true that Hamilton was a bit imperious in character but the fact that they did not get on was not any fault of his. On the contrary, he tried very hard to come to an agreement with Jefferson, but Jefferson was just a bit too touchy.

Also, the two men differed very radically in their philosophy. Hamilton was very much more consistent, and the measures he advocated were in keeping with the principles that he propounded. That is not the case with Jefferson. Jefferson was very wise as an administrator, after he became President, and he thought of the best interests of the country. He was more democratic in spirit in that he wanted greater decentralization. But as time went on we find him advocating measures very similar to those that Hamilton had stood for. At the same time, he was all the while propounding principles of government which were unsound, shallow, and in many ways impracticable. And it is in these principles that he has shown himself largely responsible for the *laissez-faire* doctrine and policies that developed during the nineteenth century.

With regard to James Wilson, it was he who in the Convention, at the time of the deadlock between the small and the larger states, suggested the idea—an entirely novel idea—of divided sovereignty. He showed how there might be a double allegiance on the part of each citizen, an allegiance to the state and the state government, and another allegiance to the central government. And on that basis you could divide sovereignty between a central national government and the states, conferring certain definite powers upon the former while retaining the sovereignty of the latter.

That is one of the greatest innovations in political history. It rests on a notion of the state which again is soundly ethical, and we were the first people in history to found our Constitution directly and explicitly on a sound ethical idea of the state. In the Middle Ages there was no idea of the state, but rather the idea of a personal relationship between the overlord and the vassals. This did in a fashion hold society together for a while but it deteriorated because it was not adequate to the demands of human nature against the background of mediaeval tradition. The English by the time of our Revolution had developed an idea of the commonwealth that had been gradually and slowly taking shape since before the time of the Reformation. And against that background we explicitly and with full intent built our Constitution on a sound ethical foundation.

That the Founders were aware that they were attempting something entirely new, entirely in advance of anything that had been achieved before this time, is clear from the statements of men like Hamilton and Washington. In the first number of the *Federalist* Hamilton said:

It has been frequently remarked that it seems to have been reserved to the people of this country by their conduct and example to decide the important question whether societies of men are really capable or not of establishing good government from reflection and choice, or whether they are forever destined to depend for their political constitutions on accident and force.

Washington in his first inaugural address has the same idea: "The preservation of the sacred fire of liberty and the destiny of the republican model of government are justly considered as deeply, perhaps as finally staked, on the experiment entrusted to the hand of the American people." That is to say, looking at the conditions as they were in Europe, with constant warfare and people living under despotic forms of government—the despotic French monarchy and perhaps less despotic but certainly not less ambitious rule of George III—they determined to set up a new form of government, a republican form of government democratically controlled, basing the Constitution in the definite will and consent of all the people.

As Beard in his *Basic History* says very well, pointing out the issues that confronted them, "How to set up a government strong enough to serve the purposes of the Union and still not too strong for the maintenance of the liberties of the people?—That was the prime issue in the Convention."

We have to confine ourselves to certain definite aspects of the subject because of the time; so I will take up the question of the meaning of the word "people," as used in the Constitution, as the Founders use the word—with the exception of Jefferson. I do not think Jefferson really understood the constitutional meaning of the word "people," and he was not at the Convention. But those in the Convention, and the other great leaders, were very clear in their minds as to what the word "people," meant, or should mean, if they were to have a solid ethical foundation for the new establishment.

As I said a moment ago, it was Wilson who suggested the division of sovereignty and the possibility of such an achievement. In the first decision of the Supreme Court, in Chisholm *v.* Georgia, it was called upon to decide this matter of the relation of the State to the individual and of the States among themselves and each of the six judges delivered a separate opinion. The most important of all those six opinions was that of Wilson, though his opinion is not the one usually given in the case books.

James Wilson said in the case of Chisholm *v.* Georgia,

By a State I mean a complete body of free persons, united together for their common benefit, to enjoy peaceably what is their own, and to do justice to others. It is an *artificial* person. It has its affairs and its interests. It has its rules, it has its rights, and it has its obligations. It may acquire property distinct from that of its members. It may incur debts to be discharged out of the public stock, not out of the private fortunes of individuals. It may be **bound by contracts and for damages arising from** the breach of those contracts. In all our contemplations, however, concerning this feigned and artificial person, we should never forget that in truth and nature those who think and speak and act are *men*.

That is a definition of the state, of corporate personality, which avoids very many errors. Wilson clearly points out that the only substantial realities that you have in this situation are the individual men who compose the state. But then there are actual or existential relations, and that makes the state a corporate moral entity, something distinct though not separate from its members, and that is a sound Scholastic view.

Suárez, in the seventeenth century, had already defined the state as a corporate moral entity in this sense. You will also find the same definition of the state in this sense in Burke's *Appeal from the New to the Old Whigs*. But these are about the only three places that I know of where the state is thus defined. You have, on the one hand, those who maintain that the only realities at all in the state are the individual members, that the state has no existential reality of its own; it is just a sort of nominalistic term to designate an aggregate of individuals. That is utterly inadequate for the purposes of law and government. On the other hand, you have those who incline to make the state something separate and distinct from the individual members, as Hegel did, and as the Fascists and Nazis have been doing of late. But here you have a perfectly sound and common-sense view of the state as a real entity, as having personality, but it is a conventional thing.

Insight into the relation of nature to convention was part of their clear understanding of this problem. Human nature demands that we live in a state; we are social and political by nature. Aristotle saw that long ago. And it was maintained by the Scholastics throughout the Middle Ages pretty thoroughly, and especially by the great theologians of the sixteenth and seventeenth centuries in Spain; also in England the idea had become fairly clear in the light of English experience.

Without this idea of the state as a corporate moral personality we never could have had our Constitution. The leaders could not have figured out the possibility of dividing sovereignty. You see, it is the people themselves—Wilson says nothing of government here—who are considered as an entity, as a juridical whole; the juridical actuation of demands of natural law gives you the state as a legal thing, a juridical thing. There is the juridical bond. The state is based thus upon consent, but that consent implies obligations in justice. Once you have entered into the state there are certain consequences that follow in applying the virtue of justice and you owe it to the state as a whole to maintain and promote the common good.

Within that whole the people determine and delegate their sovereignty, the sovereignty of the whole, to certain individuals who will function for them, who have the duty to provide for the common good. When we elect a President we impose upon him the duty to provide for the common good. If he has this duty he has the right to our obedience in respect to those measures that are necessary to the maintenance and promotion of the common good.

The people constitute a corporate moral personality before they actually set up their government. As a matter of concrete historical fact, the two seem to be more or less synonymous. This is the meaning of the word "people" in the Constitution. The word "state" is used in a twofold sense, the people establishing their own governments, and the people acting under their governments, and you have to observe the context to see what the meaning of the word "state" is in the particular setting.

That would hold, you see, for a monarchy or for an aristocracy, because democracy is not the only sound form of government. Of course, for a people that is highly cultured and developed a Republic is undoubtedly the best form of government if it is properly organized. But the emphasis on democracy or republic, the word they used in order to differentiate a representative democracy from a pure democracy—which we find in the Founding Fathers—was entirely novel. And the fact that they set up this democracy was a departure from historical practice. Certain democratic tendencies marked the Middle Ages and there was a democracy in ancient Athens. An approximation of democracy is found in the Roman republic. But there had never been such a democracy as these men conceived when they laid the foundations for our Constitution.

Of all the members of the Convention and all the Founding Fathers the most democratic in spirit was James Wilson. He went even further than Jefferson and he was much sounder. In the Ratifying Convention of Pennsylvania, he pointed out what the Constitution really aimed at in this matter of democracy. He said:

> The advantages of democracy are liberty, equal, cautious, and salutary laws, public spirit, frugality, peace, opportunities of exciting and producing abilities of the best citizens. Its disadvantages are dissensions, the delay and disclosure of public counsels, the imbecility of public measures, retarded by the necessity of numerous consent. A government may be composed of two or more of the simple forms, . . . such is the British Government. It would be an improper government for the United States. . . . What is the nature and kind of that government, which has been proposed for the United States by the late Convention? In its principles it is purely democratical, but that principle is applied in different forms in order to obtain the advantages and eschew the inconvenience of the simple mode of government. If we take an extended accurate view of it . . . we shall discover that they all originally flow from one abundant fountain. In this constitution all authority is derived from the people.

There was a reason, of course, why he should be rather emphatic on the matter of democracy, because Pennsylvania was the most democratic of all the colonies, and rather radically so. And so he invited them to accept this new form of democracy in keeping with their predilection.

Now the question is how to carry on within a democracy thus constituted as a corporate moral whole, how to make decisions so as to express the will of the people. When the Founders speak of a people, they mean a civilized people, a people with its traditional law, with its juridical organization, with its government, and the methods of procedure to which it is traditionally accustomed. So in order to express the will of the people, they did not assume that the people had to act by way of plebiscites, which is a very unsound nonjuridical way of doing things, but that the will of the people might be expressed through the methods of procedure to which they were habituated. And it is in keeping with these methods of procedure that sovereignty was actually divided among the states, where the people acting through conventions ratified the Constitution, not acting through their Legislatures. That again was an innovation. The conventions were elected to determine that one point, whether they would accept the Constitution or reject it. And, as we know, several rejected it at first.

Notice that they acted through conventions, not directly. Why? Because they were accustomed to acting through representatives. They accepted this method of procedure. And they considered themselves as bound by the result, which is normal and I think in accordance with sound legal views.

But it implied also another principle which is vitally bound up with the notion of democracy, and that is the principle of majority decision, the binding force of a majority. Here there has been an enormous amount of confusion, chiefly because there are two traditions with regard to majority rule. You have the Anglo-American tradition—if you look at it from the point of view of tradition, not from the point of view of what people think nowadays—which goes back to the canon law of the Middle Ages. Canon law provided for the decision of the majority by reason of the majority being the greater and the more reasonable part. That is a mere assumption. You can always go behind an assumption. But it was embodied in the canon law and mediaeval practice. We find the canon-law principle taken over in Magna Charta. It is a method of procedure and a measure of patience, and it presupposes the consent of the people to adopt this method of procedure. It is on the basis of consent that the decision of a majority is valid. On that basis the decision of a majority is as binding as the decision of a judge in a court. It has a juridical effect and you accept the juridical effect. And that is our practice, and it is very exceptional.

Continental peoples in Europe do not understand majority decision in this sense, and that is why they cannot settle things. They cannot get ahead. They are unwilling to accept the decision of the majority if they do not like the results, and they are constantly rebelling against it or they are constantly being oppressed by the majority. Why? Because the continental view of majority goes back to Roman law, that the minority ought to submit; otherwise they would get knocked on the head, they would be coerced. It is a substitute for a fight, a battle. And it is not very pleasant for a minority to be reduced to that state, feeling that they have to accept or go to war about it.

And in the Middle Ages the continental peoples resented this view because it conflicted with their notion of equality; that is, the mediaeval notion of equality, which we have inherited, that men are specifically equal and that no man *of* himself, or no body of men *of* themselves, have any right to impose their will upon another. They must have a rightful juridical claim to do so. In other words, they must have proper authority. That is one of the greater obstacles to be met in trying to establish peace in Europe, to get the people to understand the sound meaning of majority decision.

To show how the framers thought about it we have a letter from Monroe to Madison stating the right principle. He says:

> There is no maxim in my opinion which is more liable to be misapplied and which therefore more needs elucidation than the current one that the interest of the majority is the political standard of right and wrong. Taking the word "interest" as synonymous with "ultimate happiness," in which sense it *is* qualified with every necessary moral ingredient, the proposition is no doubt true. But taking it in the popular sense as referring to immediate augmentation of property and wealth, nothing can be more false. In the latter, it would be the interest of the majority in every community to despoil and enslave the minority of individuals.

As I said, when people have consented to accept this method of procedure, the assumption is that the majority is more likely to be right than the minority. It is an assumption. It is a matter of practical judgment, and has to do mainly with the realm of opinion, where nobody can be so certain of his position that he is sure that the other fellow is wrong, and where things have to be settled tentatively, letting experience be the test.

You see, if the majority makes a decision, there is always the possibility, if it is wrong, for the minority to build itself up into a majority and reverse the decision. But that requires patience. It requires social and political virtues which are acquired only in the long run, and which are rather rare among countries of the world today.

The next point is the question of representative government. The Founders' idea again was not so original because it was the common idea of the English at the time, but it was peculiarly in contrast to our present-day view of the function of the representative. The present-day assumption is that a representative should more or less confine himself to the interests of his constituents, and he does not think much about his real function of trying to reconcile their interests with the interests of the country as a whole, the common good. People are beginning to insist upon that point. There have been several editorials in the *Times* and *Herald Tribune* where the point has been made. But it has not sunk in very deeply, at least as far as the politicians are concerned.

In the first Congress, when they were debating the question of the amendments to the Constitution, a certain Mr. Tucker moved to insert into the first amendment these words, "to instruct their representatives." That is to say, he wanted to tie the representative down to the function of being instructed by the constituents and considering that as a mandate. That was rejected very vigorously. There was a considerable amount of debate. But it was the sense of the House certainly that that was not in keeping with the sound traditional representative idea.

In answer to Mr. Tucker's proposal Mr. Hartly said in part:

> It appears to my mind that the principle of representation is distinct from any agency which may require written instructions. The great end of

meeting is to consult for the common good; but can the common good be discerned without the object is reflected and shown in every light? A local or partial view does not necessarily enable any man to comprehend it clearly; this can only result from an inspection into the aggregate. Instructions viewed in this light will be found to embarrass the best and wisest men. And were all the members to take their seats in order to obey instructions and those instructions were as various as it is probable they would be, what possibility would there exist of so accommodating each to the other as to produce any act whatever?

Edmund Burke has stated the thing very effectively in his Speech to the Electors of Bristol:

Parliament is not a *congress* of ambassadors from different and hostile interests, which interests each must maintain as an agent and advocate against other agents and advocates, but parliament is a *deliberative* assembly of *one* nation, with *one* interest, and that of the whole, where not local purposes, not local prejudices are to guide, but the general good, resulting from the general reason of the whole. You choose a member indeed; but when you have chosen him, he is not a member of Bristol, but he is a member of *parliament.* If the local constituent should have an interest or should form a hasty opinion, evidently opposite to the real good of the rest of the community, the member for that place ought to be as far as any other from any endeavor to give it effect.

More recently Miss M. V. Clarke, an Oxford scholar and author of a book entitled *Medieval Representation and Consent,* states:

If the main business of the Commons in early Parliaments had been no more than to push local petitions, their work could have no claim to be called political. No activity can properly be styled political which does not help directly to create or to modify public law. When this task is undertaken by a group of persons, a state of friction, due to the chafing of mind against mind, ought to be set up. This friction alone can throw off the spark that makes co-operation dynamic and, if representatives are to contribute to it, they must be charged under certain conditions. They must have a mandate to act for their constituencies, which is both temporary and general; it must be acknowledged that they owe to their electors not obedience, but judgment; that judgment must be exercised in co-operation with other representatives, in like manner empowered.

Were it not for our insulated attitude toward what is traditional and the failure of our educational system to fit us as a people to discern objectively, on the basis of the sounder American conception of man, between what was right or wrong in the past, we would be in a very much better position to assume the leadership that is now thrust upon us. A thorough and convinced understanding of the principles underlying our own system of government would be a corrective of Soviet Russia's ambitions. It would not only be an antidote but a corrective because it is not only more humane but decidedly much more dynamically human.

IX

DEMOCRACY AND ECONOMIC LIBERALISM

BY

GEORGE H. HOUSTON, ESQ.

I have been asked to talk today about Democracy and Economic Liberalism. Discussion of a subject so fraught with potentialities for progress in America or for conflict and retrogression cannot be undertaken casually but, to be effective, must be focused carefully and include a definition of the elements of our subject so that it may be considered with a minimum of the ambiguity and confusion of thought which all too frequently are found in discussions of this character. With your indulgence, therefore, I shall take a few moments for consideration of what is meant by democracy, by economics, and by liberalism.

Some years ago Columbia University organized in the City of New York an international congress to consider future education for democracy. As a member of the planning committee of this congress I participated in extended discussions as to what was meant by democracy for which education was to be provided, and it was surprising to me to note the divergence of viewpoint that existed as to the meaning of democracy. When the congress convened, a seminar was appointed, charged with the specific task of defining "democracy" for which education was to be provided. Its report set out at considerable length the widely differing views on this subject of those attending the conference. This divergence of view and confusion of thought still exist in almost every phase of American life into which the concept of democracy finds its way. Some think of democracy as the rule of the majority. Others speak of it as a way of life in which every individual has a part and in which the dignity of the individual is emphasized. Still others hold it is a form of social organization in which the individual has certain rights—not just privileges—of which not even the majority acting through the state can deprive him without just cause and due process.

The unhampered rule of the majority first found expression in modern Europe during the French Revolution. The first French Republic anticipated practically all of the characteristic features of modern totalitarianism. This régime has been aptly described as including:

(a) the dictatorship of a party in the name of a community;

(b) the use of propaganda and appeals to mass emotion, as well as violence and terrorism;

(c) the conception of revolutionary justice as a social weapon;

(d) the regulation of economic life in order to realize revolutionary ideals; and

(e) above all, the attempt to impose a uniform ideology on the whole people and the proscription of every other form of political thought.

This concept of democracy is illustrated also in the provision of the National Labor Relations Act by which a bargaining agency for the employees of a given employer is determined by the majority of such employees, with no voice in subsequent bargaining given to any minority portion of the group, classified as a bargaining unit.

If democracy is to be considered merely as the rule of the majority, I, for one, wish to record my opinion that no such thing as economic liberalism is possible, as no tyranny can or is likely to exist in the economic field, or in any other area of man's interests, greater than the tyranny of the many over the few, and over the individual who chooses to diverge from the majority.

If democracy is to be considered solely as a way of life in which each individual has a part but in which the individual is not clearly protected in his right to differ from his fellow beings and to diverge from the mass, I would want to know a great deal more about that way of life, the premises upon which it is based, and the safeguards that protect the individual from the tyrannies of majorities before I would wish to depend upon it as a sound basis for developing true liberalism in the field of economic activity. In the final analysis a way of life is largely an effect of cause and what we must consider are the underlying causes that generate the conditions we require for the development of true liberalism in the economic field.

I prefer to define democracy as a form of social organization in which the individual has clearly defined rights of which not even the majority, acting through the state or otherwise, can deprive him without just cause and due process. Its true name is individualism and it is opposed to all forms of collectivism or communitarianism. This is a very different concept from the ideas of democracy we find prevailing in continental Europe, where what the individual thinks of as his rights are actually privileges granted to him by the state, which retains the right and the power to recall them, in its sole discretion. They are in no sense inherent in his being. For the origin in the modern world of this concept of individualism, we must look to the island of Britain and particularly to England, where it has existed for a very long time, subject, however, to many vicissitudes. This concept of democracy in England has resulted in several important contributions to the social philosophy and judicial procedure of the Anglo-Saxon world including: the principle that the individual is the supreme unit of society, governments being created by and with the consent of the governed; the common law; and equity in judicial procedure. During several centuries of English life this concept of democracy has impressed itself upon many phases of social and political existence but nowhere more clearly than in the recognition of the right of the individual to life, to liberty, and to property.

It was upon this tradition that the United States was founded. It became manifest more and more clearly in the colonial constitutions and legislation and stands out with startling clarity in the second sentence of the Declaration of Independence, except that Thomas Jefferson saw fit to step away from it somewhat by the substitution of the term "pursuit of happiness" for "property." This Declaration was followed in a few years by the drafting of the Constitution which remained silent with respect to the protection of these "rights" of the individual. In fact it gave considerable emphasis to the domination of the majority over the minority and over the divergent individual, through the rule of the majority within each state and by states within the congress, always, however, with representation of minorities. In the instance of the construction of the Senate, particular emphasis was given to equality of representation of small states. Fortunately for the ensuing social development of America, certain of the states were not willing to assume that the silence of the Constitution with respect to the rights of the individual meant acceptance of the English tradition. As a result, the Bill of Rights wrote into the Constitution safeguards for the individual against the tyrannical domination of majorities, as they had never before in the world's history been spelled out, in a constitutional sense. For one hundred and fifty years thereafter these safeguards withstood all pressures, although from time to time they were amplified in various ways. During all this period they were considered to be of permanent and vital import to the American people. During recent years, however, not only has their virtue been questioned, but their effectiveness has been eroded to a place where it is a serious question as to whether we have not already passed over to the acceptance of the rule of the majority as the American concept of democracy, with the devil taking the hindmost individual, stripped of the rights long considered to be inherent in his being. In my discussion of economic liberalism I shall deal with the kind of economic life that can and should exist under a form of social organization in which the rights of the individual are recognized and effectively protected, in this American tradition.

Economics is an area of human interest also characterized by much confused thinking. I believe it is generally considered to be a fairly well-segregated portion of the social sciences, but it has always seemed to me to be about the most fragmentized, unorganized, conglomeration of alleged but unprovable facts, causes, effects, ideas, and theories that have ever been brought together in the name of science. By economics as I shall use the term I mean man's interest in the satisfaction of his physical wants. While I recognize that physical wants extend probably into every phase of man's existence, I wish to exclude from our area of economic interest man's interest in a Supreme Being as expressed in organized religion and otherwise, except to the extent that the activities of religious groups, through church organizations or otherwise, consume personal services, render personal services, acquire and use property or otherwise carry on activities that are inherently utilitarian. I also wish to exclude consideration of man's relation to his fellow being of a purely nonutilitarian aspect, if there can be any such; as well as man's interest in the material world of a nonutilitarian character, to the extent that there are any such interests.

The field of economics, as I understand it, is inherently utilitarian. I would define it as consisting of the production of goods and the rendering of services; their exchange and distribution among the people available to consume them; the acquisition, ownership, and use of property; and the organization and administration of government with respect to production, distribution, and property.

The activities of government which have to do with the exercise of the sovereign functions of foreign relations, national defense, administration of justice, the safeguarding of the rights of the people, and similar functions, have economic aspects, but they also have aspects that are not economic. In discussing the possibilities of economic liberalism today I wish to limit our consideration of the functions of government to those activities which affect directly the utilitarian aspects of the lives of the people.

When we come to the meaning of liberalism, we again find a variety of uses of the term, which tends to generate more heat than light. Some define liberalism as the orderly evolution from what is to what ought to be, in the carrying on of the lives of the people, with care always to preserve what is, until something better has been achieved and proved.

I prefer, however, to consider liberalism in relation to our economic life as that condition of existence under which man is released from the shackles of poverty, ignorance, and depressing environment; is made free to achieve the highest degree of personal accomplishment for which he is equipped by his talents, his industry, and his aspirations; but by which he is also at liberty to do directly the converse if he so chooses for his own reasons, or without reason. It is that quality of human organization which facilitates, as far as may be possible, the achievement by each individual of the type and quality of existence he chooses for himself, and is willing to work for. It is the implementation of the concept of personal liberty without license.

An inherent essential of economic liberalism, as I propose to use the term, is that each individual shall, to the greatest extent possible, by the exercise of his own free will, determine the character and direction of his own economic destiny. This concept, of course, must always be conditioned by a corresponding recognition of the rights of others —in other words, the freedom of the individual to live his own life must of necessity be conditioned by a corresponding recognition of the equal right of every other individual to do likewise. Each must limit his individual right thus to live to the extent necessary not to interfere with the enjoyment of the like right on the part of every other individual. This concept of liberalism is unalterably opposed to the so-called liberal doctrine we have listened to throughout the length and breadth of this country during recent years—that government can and is under obligation to do more and better for the individual than the individual can do for himself. This doctrine may be paternalism; it may be collectivism; it may be many things, but it is not liberalism.

With this background of preliminary consideration, the question lies before us as to opportunities in the America of the future for the application of the principles of liberalism in the economic life of the country—that is, in the production of goods and services; in their exchange and distribution; and in the acquisition, ownership, and use of property.

In the field of modern economic existence, the perpetuation and safeguarding of life is fairly well looked after. Standards of health, hygiene, and sanitation are in general far more advanced than like standards in other fields of economic interest. While, in some areas of industry and in some congested living areas, there still is far too great a spread between accepted standards of right practice and existing conditions, yet in this area of human interest there is little, if any, real conflict between differing theories of what ought to be. In general, steady progress is being made in conforming practice to sound theory. In fact, the right of the individual to life is recognized far more generally in our economic existence than is his right to liberty or to the true ownership of property.

The safeguarding of personal liberty in the economic aspects of life in our intricately organized and highly mechanized present-day society is very difficult, and our progress toward this objective has been discouragingly slow. There are many who seriously question whether we have been progressing or retrogressing, during the past generation or more, in the enjoyment of personal liberty. Its preservation in the economic field would appear to be dependent upon the application of a few fundamental principles that seem to be clear, even though their effective application may be difficult, if not impossible, at the present moment and, as all thinking people must admit, has never yet been fully accomplished. These prerequisites would include the following:

(1) Every individual should be able freely to obtain employment at all times and at any time, under working conditions that will maintain health and vigor and at wages that will permit of existence ranging upward from the minimum standards fixed by society for its own protection, in proportion to the expenditure of effort, industry, and ability on the part of the individual worker. Put another way, in a truly liberal economy and subject to a floor to the standard of living, to be fixed by society for its own good, each individual should be able by work to contribute to the common hoard of things required by the people at any time and almost at any place, and simultaneously should be able to take from the common hoard, by virtue of his earnings for work thus performed, an amount in goods and services which is equal to the genuine net value of his own contribution to the common hoard, taking into consideration all things contributing to his ability to produce, including the tools of production contributed by others, the cost of government, and the many other factors without which his accomplishment would be impossible. By the same token and with due consideration to his obligation to society not to become a burden upon it for his support or for the support of his dependents, each individual should be entitled freely to choose between working in order to acquire and possess things, and refraining from work in order to enjoy or waste his leisure.

(2) Every individual should have opportunity in his childhood and youth to qualify by education to make the greatest contribution of which he is inherently capable to the life and times in which he lives.

(3) Every individual should have the right to spend the proceeds of his work with the greatest possible freedom and the least interference as to

what he acquires, why he acquires it, what he does with it, what he does with the proceeds of its use, whether he consumes it or accumulates it—subject always to his recognition of the rights of others and to his obligation to support his dependents and not to become ultimately a burden upon society through improvidence during the productive years of his life.

While I have used the masculine pronoun in these statements I want particularly to emphasize that they apply equally to the feminine portion of our people.

The right of the individual to acquire and own property is an essential and inevitable concomitant of the right to work, to earn and to spend one's earnings. This is not merely the right of the individual to possess things, but is much broader. It includes of necessity the right of the individual freely to acquire things, to enjoy their use, to enjoy the fruits of their use, and to dispose of them. Any conditioning of these rights is a conditioning of the institution of private property and can only be countenanced in an economy of true liberalism when it can be clearly shown that the individual ownership of such property constitutes a specific obstruction to the mass use of that particular property and that such use is truly essential to mass progress.

The relation of government to the economic activity of the people should be one of active and sympathetic co-operation, with government remaining, however, the servant of the people and not their master. Government should not penetrate any further into the economic life of the community than is essential to the safeguarding of the rights of all individuals against the selfish tyrannies that otherwise would be imposed upon them by the few. Government should undertake specific projects in the economic field only when individuals acting by themselves or in groups cannot accomplish them effectively and then only to the extent that each such project is essential to genuine economic progress.

Let us consider each of these requirements for economic liberalism in more detail and compare them with the conditions we find existing today and in the recent past. Let us then endeavor to determine whether we are tending toward economic liberalism or away from it, possibly toward economic coercion and dictatorship, and what, if any, changes in current trends are necessary to put us on the road to true economic liberalism.

Freedom of employment involves two basic aspects, (1) the ability to find a job, and (2) freedom to take and keep or to leave a job.

As to ability to find a job, prosperity has been defined as a state of economic activity in which anyone wishing to find gainful employment at reasonable wages, as I have defined them, can do so. Depressions have been defined as the converse of this condition—in which freedom of job procurement does not exist. I believe it is now generally accepted as an observable fact that depressional unemployment manifests itself first and most intensely in the processes of building and rebuilding the durable facilities of the country, from the streets under our feet to the tops of the highest structures in the land, including the structural and mechanical equipment for production, transportation, communication, and commerce. It is also, I believe, generally agreed that, as mechanization of our modern life proceeds, the impact of these fluctuations upon the economic life of the nation tends to become more severe except as these fluctuations are dealt with by foresight and intelligent policies in business and in government.

There can never be any true and lasting liberalism in our economic life so long as the vicissitudes of world affairs, regardless of causes, destroy our economic balance at intervals with resulting deep pools of depressional unemployment. In our search for individual liberty, ability to find employment must ever be one of our most important problems.

There has been and still is a school of thought that finds the solution to this problem in America in economic planning by the state—that is, in the making of plans for the balancing of production and distribution with consumption demand, coupled with the enforcement of such plans by the coercive powers of government. Economic planning substitutes the judgment of a few, functioning through centralized authority, for the judgment of the many, functioning through the law of averages. When such centralized judgment is right, it may be nearly perfect, but, when it is wrong, its errors may be catastrophic in the breadth and generality of their application. The history of authoritarian governments in recent years in Europe has demonstrated this characteristic, together with the fact that authoritarian decisions are erroneous about as frequently as individualistic decision, although errors are better disguised for a time. I am deeply convinced that economic planning, as I have defined it, is not the answer to assuring jobs for all and freedom of action for the worker. I am very sure that over the long period government cannot do for the individual through economic planning as much as, or as well as the individual can do for himself, protected in his enjoyment of his rights, in the American tradition. Economic planning in its logical and rational development of necessity must control employment through allocation exactly as it must control consumption through allocation, rationing, and similar devices. Also it would be utterly destructive of the freedom of the individual in all other fields of human interest, as it can exist only by the coercion of all to a single, predetermined pattern of behavior. It leaves no room for the diverging individual or group. No open switches can be permitted to side lines on its road to mass destiny.

I am forced to the conviction, however, that in our modern, highly mechanized society we cannot leave solely to individual initiative the generation of continuous employment in certain of the durable-goods industries. Stabilization of employment in these areas of production must of necessity be based upon stabilization of demand for their products. The history of demand for certain types of new durable goods indicates fluctuations from valleys of a small fraction of long-time normal to peaks of double or more. Capital goods cannot be created to any great degree in advance of specific requirements. The causes of these sharp fluctuations in demand are as deeply imbedded in our existence as are the causes of our great depressions, many of which are only remotely related to our own internal economy. Stabilization in all other areas of employment, I believe, is fairly well assured if these deep, concentrated pools of depressional unemployment can be avoided. We cannot hope to achieve this stabilization very quickly by correcting effectively and immediately the underlying causes for these sharp fluctuations in demand. Even if we had the wisdom to do so, many of these causes lie, in part at least, outside our effective control. Our only hope is to prevent their destructive effect upon our existence while we grope slowly and carefully toward their ultimate correction.

I have long believed that in this field of production of certain classes of durable goods there is an area where the powers of government should be brought into play at times, to encourage and generate sound demand for such goods when such demand from private sources becomes acutely subnormal. Such government-generated demand should be curtailed to the disappearing point as demand from private sources again becomes normal or greater. Economic areas in which government can function effectively in this manner include the building of structures for government use, of highways, of river and harbor improvements, municipal services, sewage disposal, and the orderly and continuing replenishment and enlargement of the national store of goods engaged in such quasi-public services as national communications, national railroad transportation and the generation and distribution of electrical energy. The export of certain types of capital goods is also an area of activity in which government assistance can be of constructive value.

These opportunities for leveling out the peaks and valleys of employment were considered extensively during the great depression following the First World War but never were used effectively because of a general lack of understanding of the nature of the problems involved, lack of willingness on the part of private business to cooperate with government in the carrying out of broadly made plans for such undertakings, and lack of effectiveness on the part of government in the making of such plans and in their application, while safeguarding at the same time the liberties of the individual, the rights of private property, and the preservation of our economic system of free private enterprise.

I question whether private enterprise, left entirely to itself, can ever effectively stabilize employment in these areas of durable-goods production against the impacts of depressional unemployment. The Soviet Union has demonstrated that collectivism can stabilize such employment through national planning, coupled with coerced production, coerced distribution, and coerced employment. America does not believe coercion is either necessary or desirable. On the contrary, America believes deeply and generally in the principles of free private enterprise, voluntarily initiated and carried on—that is, in the carrying on of the economic activities of the country by the use of property owned by individuals or groups of individuals and controlled by its owners, subject only to equitable, uniform, and external regulation by government which does not penetrate into or interfere with the exercise of discretionary judgment on the part of ownership and management.

There are, however, vast areas of enterprise carried on in America today by the use of property that is not privately owned in the sense in which I have defined the ownership of property. One of these areas is in the field of natural monopolies, which are still nominally owned by groups of individuals, but the control of which is so dominated by government as substantially to condition and qualify the private character of the ownership of the property so employed. When the use of private property for a given purpose depends upon the possession of a franchise granted by government to use the public highways or to exercise the right of eminent domain, government has the right to subject such undertakings, as a condition of such use, to such conditions as in its judgment seem wise and necessary for the protection of the public interest. Such property truly is vested with a public interest. When, however, the owners of a particular piece of property cannot, by its use, initiate a new service, or, once initiated, stop it, or change its capital structure, or make substantial capital investments, or change rates charged for services rendered, without government approval in each instance, it cannot be said that the property so used and subject to such limited control by its owners is any longer genuinely private property.

Another large area of enterprise in America is carried on by the use of property owned outright by government—federal, state, or municipal—or by agencies of government, and is fully controlled by its owner. Such enterprise has passed entirely out of the category of private enterprise and is really government enterprise, although completely different in function from the essential activities of a sovereign government. Such enterprise is engaged directly in satisfying the physical wants of the people. Property so used is truly economic property, and, to the extent that enterprise is so carried on, the economy of the country has become truly socialized.

The time has passed when free private enterprise can be said to be the only medium used in America for carrying on its economic activities. A very substantial segment of the entire economy of the country is carried on by what is truly government-controlled enterprise, and a steadily growing segment is carried on by government-owned enterprise. Whether we like it or not, we must face the fact that, in the future, private enterprise as it has existed in the past in America must compete for public acceptance with these other forms of enterprise. The success attained by private enterprise in this competitive seeking for public acceptance will determine the character of American economic life of the future. One of the serious aspects of this situation has been the unwillingness of our people generally to face these facts. Another has been the secrecy, lack of real information, and legerdemain thrown around much of the government-owned enterprise that has been undertaken to date, including the shifting of the tax burden from government-owned enterprise, which usually is tax free, to a constantly diminishing area of free private enterprise, and of government-controlled enterprise.

These conditions have brought about a creeping socialization of our economic life, of which most people are not very conscious. If this country is ultimately fully socialized, it will not be because the majority of the American people truly desired such socialization but rather because they were not kept informed of what was occurring. Private enterprise, taxed to support government and to finance the losses of government-owned enterprise operating without taxation and under other forms of subsidy, frequently unknown to the public, cannot compete with such government-owned enterprise and will be destroyed wherever such competition occurs. I am confident that, if government-owned enterprise is required (a) to operate within areas, fixed clearly by statute in each instance to geographical, product, or functional metes and bounds as the case may be; (b) within each such area to absorb at the outset all private enterprise coming into competition with it; (c) to carry at all times its fair portion of the tax burden of the community in which it operates and of the country as a whole; and (d) to conform to the same standards of accounting accuracy and public disclosure of factual information as is required by government of private enterprise, the American people will be able to decide soundly, over a period, what portion of the enterprise of the country it wishes to have operated as government-owned enterprise. If the creeping socialization of the past decade and more continues without clearly defining and fixing the areas of public enterprise, without the effective disclosure of underlying facts and conditions, and without burdening socialized enterprise with its part in carrying the cost of government, complete socialization of our economic life is only a question of time and circumstance.

The real solution of these conditions lies, I believe, in an orderly classification of enterprise in which certain areas are clearly defined as those to be occupied by government-owned enterprise subject to the conditions I have outlined, others as areas of government-controlled enterprise, each fixed specifically as to its metes and bounds, with all of the remaining economic activity of the country carried on by free private enterprise.

I have no question but that the American genius for organization and administration in the field of free private enterprise can and will, if given the opportunity, successfully hold its own in genuine competition for public acceptance with government-owned and government-controlled enterprise and will contribute effectively to the solution of the problem of stable and increasing employment, at a living wage and better. This can be accomplished, however, only if and to the extent that the ownership of private enterprise, its management, and its labor, each deals effectively with the problems facing private enterprise in their respective spheres of activity and if government assists by removing some of the obstacles that now exist to the generation and development of new and venturesome private enterprise.

Private enterprise is not eleemosynary and should not be so considered, at any time. It exists by virtue of the profit motive, which is the most potent motivating impulse yet found for the stimulation of man's efforts to satisfy the wants of others. Recognition must be given to the legitimacy of profit and to the necessity for constantly hazarding capital in new and venturesome enterprise in search of profit, if private enterprise is to continue and to prosper. Speculation has come to have a disreputable connotation, and yet genuine speculation in the sense of hazarding capital in the hope of gain, is the essential keystone in the continuing existence of private enterprise. Too much thought has been given by both government and the capitalist in recent years to the preservation of capital already accumulated and invested, and too little thought has been given to the accumulation of new capital and to its use in new and venturesome ways. Genuine private capitalism should not and cannot protect the capitalist from loss arising from changes in techniques, styles, markets, or economic conditions, nor should the capitalist seek such protection from government or through monopoly or conspiracy in restraint of trade. On the other hand, the capitalist must be free to move quickly from one area of activity to another in response to changing techniques and conditions. The capital invested in the early days in the construction of canals was destroyed by new capital invested in railroads. Capital so invested has in turn been and will be increasingly injured by capital invested, first, in automotive equipment and, secondly, in aeronautical equipment. Any effort to perpetuate such earlier investments by discouraging the speculative development of new, competitive types of product or service will not contribute to the health of the economic life of the country as a whole, nor to the preservation of free private enterprise, but will constitute a fascistic type of control of the freedom of enterprise which is fatal to genuine private enterprise.

The capitalist and the business executive must be willing to look beyond the confines of an individual enterprise and participate, to the extent of their abilities, in the larger and broader aspects of the enterprise of the community and of the country as a whole. This should not be done, however, by attempting to put enterprise in a straitjacket as under the codes called for by the National Industrial Recovery Act, or by the avoidance of free competition, which is an inherent and essential quality of private enterprise.

There are many areas of the economic life of the country, however, where capitalists and managers in their individual capacities and in groups have very real and important functions to perform if the private enterprise of the country is to be carried on effectively and in constructive co-operation with established public policy. American business has yet to learn much of the art of effectively organizing itself into larger groups of enterprise than that represented by the individual corporation, without entering into conspiracies to avoid competition or operating in restraint of trade.

One of the very serious problems facing private enterprise is the erosion going on in the area of small enterprise and the tendency for the business of the country to be conducted by fewer and larger enterprises. This condition cannot be overcome by placing restrictions upon the size of enterprises but must be dealt with by making more favorable the circumstances and conditions under which small enterprises can be generated and can carry on. The trends of recent years, including the conditions generated by the war, have, almost without exception, been in the opposite direction.

The right of the individual to spend freely the proceeds of his labor in the acquisition of what he wants, means inherently free markets and competition of the sellers for the buyer's dollars. Such competition tends to generate ingenuity in the development of products that will attract the buyer's dollar, as well as ingenuity in reducing costs of production and distribution so that each buyer's dollar will yield him greater satisfaction of his wants. There has been a great deal of debate and public discussion in recent years about the high cost of distribution in a free market, including the cost of sales promotion, solicitation, advertising, retail distribution, and similar aspects of a free market in a capitalistic economy, as compared with the apparent economies arising from distribution by use of various methods of allocation or rationing of goods. Most of these discussions ignore the real value of free markets and induced buying; namely, competition in price, quality, and variety for the consumer's dollar. There is no place in a liberal economy for the rationing or allocation of goods to the consumer, except as an emergency measure in times of unusual and temporary crisis of the first order. Our experience with these devices during the present war and in the growth of black markets and similar channels of special privilege, which have developed because of them, cannot encourage us in the belief that they are devices of permanent value to economic liberalism. The capitalistic methods of distribution by inducement and of active competition for the consumer's dollar, voluntarily spent, possess advantages to the consumer in net cost and over-all satisfaction that cannot be equaled by any method of coerced distribution yet devised.

In addition to the owner of property and his manager, the industrial executive, the individual worker and his organization for collective action, the trade-union, are going to have to look the facts of economic life squarely in the face in a way they have not been willing to do heretofore in America and to deal with these facts of life candidly and effectively if the potentialities for worth-while employment that we have been discussing are ever to be realized. In seeking the optimum of employment we must recognize the fluctuating value, measured in money, of the products of employment. Just as surely as prices go up, so in the long run must prices go down. Wages cannot forever be a one-way street. They cannot forever go up regardless of the movement of prices. Bitter unemployment has been the only way at times in the past in which wages have been made to move in the direction of prices. American workers must come to recognize that, while they are entitled to take from the common hoard, through the buying power of their wages, the equal of their actual net contribution to the common hoard, by the same token they are not entitled to take more. By so doing they make the objective of universal free employment impracticable of attainment.

If trade-unionism in America is to constitute a monopoly in industrial employment into which monopoly each individual must be submerged before he can find employment in organized enterprise, whether it be industry or commerce, whether it be privately owned or government owned, then we cannot hope to have genuine economic liberalism. Vast changes have been effected in the relations of employees to employers in America during recent years. All these changes, however, have not been in the direction of liberalism. Some of them, on the contrary, have been in the direction of tyranny and of group conflict in which particular working groups have endeavored to extract from the common hoard of the national income substantially more than they have contributed to it. Some of these changes are in effect a reaction toward the mediaeval monopolism of the guilds. An instance of this character was the agreement recently forced by James Petrillo for the collection of a royalty for the account of the Musicians Union upon all phonograph records produced. Actions of this character are not in the direction of economic liberalism but are in the direction of the protection of what is at the expense of what might be and the creation of monopolies and the accumulation of vast resources for their unwarranted preservation.

Not the least of these reactionary trends of the present day is the extreme form of seniority preference demanded by certain groups of organized labor. Looked at superficially, seniority is plausible and rational—a sort of first-come-first-served arrangement. Looked at critically, however, it is being carried to an extreme which is becoming one of the anti-liberal forces now at work in this country and tending to convert the dynamism that made America great in the nineteenth century to a condition of stagnation. Its only justification is acceptance of the theory of the mature economy and the resulting limitations upon opportunity. It has no real place in an economy of true liberalism seeking to develop freedom of action for the individual.

It is well established, I believe, that human progress is made by the individual achieving the unusual, reaching out into the unknown to accomplish something new, and by the mass slowly, painfully pulling itself up to the new level fixed by such exceptional individuals. In any condition of true economic liberalism the exceptional individual must have freedom to achieve to the utmost of his capacity. Consider for a moment the effect of seniority restrictions upon such exceptional individuals in industry. They should have opportunity for rapid advancement; they should move, upon occasion, into new fields having greater opportunity for their particular talents. But in the face of seniority, they cannot move into such new undertakings upon their merits. Instead, in each instance they must start again at the foot of the ladder and climb step by step, following all the mediocrity which is senior only by the incident of the time of employment. Matthew Smith, president of M.E.S.A., once said of this system:

> This vicious system has resulted in workers being as securely tied to an employer as *the old serfs* were fastened to a specific landowner. Workers do not bother about getting more experience. The tree of knowledge is neglected—the only important thing is to get firmly established in the upper branches of the seniority tree.
>
> An uneducated production worker with ten years' seniority rating is in an infinitely better economic position than the tool designer, who, poor devil, has only worked for the same company a few months.
>
> Today labor unions haven't time to talk of wages, hours, or victimization; all their time is consumed by people claiming unfair seniority treatment.

I will hazard the prophecy that the seniority system in American industry will receive critical consideration by returning veterans, during the next five years.

The aspects of individual existence which we have been discussing thus far have to do largely with the right to live and the right to personal liberty, but I want to consider somewhat in more detail the third great stone in the archway of economic liberalism—the right of the individual to own property, that is, the institution of private property. This is one of the most precious rights any individual can ever possess and probably contributes as much to the pursuit of happiness as any one condition of existence. It has been one of the great motivating impulses that have made America.

I had the privilege of traveling through the Soviet Union some years ago—in fact, I was in Moscow the week the decree authorizing piecework was published. I found everyone living in Moscow in state-owned quarters allocated to their occupants by centralized authority. One of my official companions during my stay in Moscow had a two-room apartment thus assigned to him and his wife. She, however, was absent from the city on government business, and while I was there he was peremptorily ordered to vacate his apartment and move to a one-room habitation because one individual was not entitled under state policy to the occupation of two rooms. I was very much interested to note in the woods in the environs of Moscow many small houses, built very cheaply, and upon inquiry I learned that they were the property of individuals living in Moscow who were granted by the government the special privilege, as a reward of merit, to build these little structures in the woods near to the city for use as recreation places, to get away occasionally from the drabness of their existence in their state-owned habitations. America will never be contented with such a concept of property—state-owned and possessed by the individual as a temporary privilege extended by the state.

By the same token, America is not prepared to accept the thesis that all property used in production and distribution shall be owned by the state or controlled by it to the exclusion of the ownership by individuals and groups of individuals of property so used. The workers of America do not want to work for but one employer, the state, which would fix the rewards for labor in its sole discretion and, in the long run, largely in the interests of the consumer, acting through the mechanism of politics. Americans still want to enjoy the rewards of effort and ability, they still want to achieve, to accumulate, and to put their accumulations to work producing more things that more people want and will pay a price to get. They still want to own property.

I have indicated, however, that there are other types of property now used in carrying on the economic life of the country, that these other types of property will continue to exist and to be so used, and that the extent to which the economic property of the country continues to be genuine private property will depend to a substantial degree upon the success with which the private owners of property are able to compete for public acceptance with the advocates of other types of ownership of property, for use in carrying on the economic life of the country.

This, in turn, will depend, in large measure, upon public understanding of the underlying issues involved and of the effect upon these issues of the day-to-day decisions made, frequently, upon apparently unrelated matters. In the long run public understanding will be the measure of our preservation in America of the institution of private property, with all its implications. This always has been, and I have every hope always will continue to be, one of our most vital and valued possessions.

There is a further question with respect to the use of private property that is constantly being advanced, and merits consideration. This has to do with the right of the user of economic property to participate in the control of its use, regardless of its ownership. Concretely, workers through their organizations are continually advancing the principle that the act of being employed in the use of economic property owned by others gives to the worker an inherent right to participate in vital determinations as to how such property shall be used; in other words, in the function of management. This principle is advanced in the name of democracy, of participation by all in the control of their economic activities. Nothing has been suggested in this connection with respect to a corresponding inherent right on the part of the owners or managers of property to participate in the direction of organizations of workers engaged in the use of property so owned. It would appear obvious that this principle, if ever applied, would, in the long run, have to work both ways. It is of interest to note that a so-called reform of this character was recently proposed by the Provisional French Government. This proposal involves a plan for workers' committees that employers would be obliged to consult once a month. These committees would be selected by labor unions and would have full authority over so-called social institutions such as canteens, nurseries, and recreation programs, and consultative powers in determining working conditions, pay rates, working hours, and the general direction of the enterprise. They would have the significant right of appeal over the management to the Ministry of Production and would be encouraged to exercise this right in cases where it was believed that production or efficiency could be increased. There is nothing novel in this concept of worker control of economic property through worker committees. It was the keynote of the industrial soviets under which the Soviet Union undertook to organize its industry after the Red Revolution of 1917. It is of interest to note, however, that its ineffectiveness was so serious that the Soviet Union has progressively moved away from it, restoring more and more authority to management with responsibility solely to the owner, a government corporation, and through it to the Supreme Economic Council.

Entirely aside from the question of effectiveness, the principle involved in worker participation, as a matter of right, in the management of private enterprise is one that deserves the most critical examination. The principle of participation by all of the people in governmental processes has been applied in America on the assumption that each citizen has an equal interest in the affairs of government and an equal right to participate in them. It will be apparent that the application of this principle to the management of business carried on by the use of private property cannot be effected without far-reaching changes in the accepted concepts of private property—that is, of property owned by individuals or groups of individuals, the use of which is controlled by its owners, subject to impartial, external regulation by government. The parties at interest in business may be said to be the owners of the property used (stockholders in corporations), users of property (employees), takers of the product or services rendered (customers), and the general public. The democratic process of participation by all in the reaching of determinations is applied in corporate organizations through stockholders' election of directors and in taking action upon specific matters referred to them at their meetings. It is applied further through directors' action in the election of officers and in the transaction of specific pieces of business. For the users of property to exercise, as a matter of right, any actual control of the property they use, there must be an irrevocable delegation to them of similar powers to make decisions controlling its use, which obviously would remove, to a corresponding degree, the control of the related property from its owners. Any such change would destroy the private character of the ownership of the property so used and controlled and, by the same token, would change the character of the undertaking so managed from free private enterprise, voluntarily undertaken, to some other form of enterprise.

I believe it will be obvious to any thinking person that the only relation that can exist soundly between the private owners of economic property and its users must of necessity be a contractual one arrived at by negotiation and agreement, existing in each instance for a limited period of time and under defined conditions. This may be accomplished by individual transactions between each employee and the managerial representatives of ownership, or it may be through collective bargaining, neither of which processes, however, can be said to be very democratic in character under existing practices in America. The first is largely determined by the employer and the general economic conditions then current in the community, and the second, on account of the present-day denial of minority representation, is largely coercive with respect to such minorities. All too frequently, negotiations between representatives of management and representatives of employees so chosen are highly autocratic, as between two principals functioning in their own right and with no third party interests of any kind being given consideration.

It is equally obvious that the customer has no justification in seeking to control the use of the property from which he obtains his goods. If the institution of private property is to be preserved, this relationship must also be kept upon a contractual basis, which is not and cannot be democratic in character. By the same token the general public has no right to intervene in the use of private property in the economic life of the country beyond seeing that the public interest is not violated and that the rights of others are not transgressed by the conduct of an individual enterprise. The interest of the public must be looked after by government through regulation and policing, but not through participation in the internal control of the use of the private property being regulated.

This analysis will indicate that there is little opportunity in the conduct of private business for the use of the democratic process. Voluntary consultation between the leaders of a business and their subordinates, the asking for, receiving, and giving of advice, and the general conduct of business relations in a democratic manner and spirit do not constitute, in any general sense, an application of the democratic process since they are not undertaken as a matter of right on the part of those dealt with but rather as a matter of choice on the part of the leaders and of privilege to the followers. Such practices are desirable, of course, in business relationships so long as they do not create conditions detrimental to effective accomplishment of the economic objectives, but they should be recognized for what they are, and their inherent limitations should be accepted by all.

American business leaders are keenly aware, however, of the problems involved in business administration with respect to the maintenance of the maximum freedom of action on the part of the individual and the building up of judgment, power of decision, and ability to exercise free will on the part of individuals comprising an organization. The circumstances under which business is carried on, however, tend strongly to the submersion of the individual into the group in spite of everything that can be done to the contrary. The reasons for this tendency are deep-seated.

Business, which might be defined as the organized effort of man to satisfy human wants, is carried on almost universally by the use of organization. An organization, in turn, might be defined as a group of persons working together toward a given end in accordance with a predetermined plan. It must be more than one person; it must work together; it must have an objective; and it must have plans for achieving this objective.

The plans by which any organization undertakes to achieve its objectives are of two essentially different types, one having to do with the creation and carrying on of the relations between the members of the organization, and the other with the actual accomplishment of specific undertakings. As an organization increases in size and in the complexity of its activities, so that the points of contact it has to maintain are increased in number and variety, its administrative procedures must be more and more crystallized into predetermined routines with a corresponding curtailment of freedom of action on the part of each individual concerned. Also, as the mechanical intricacy and qualitative accuracy of manufactured products are increased, the mechanical processes by which such products are produced must be more and more intensively developed in advance and brought under more and more complete control, with corresponding reduction in latitude for freedom of individual judgment and action. As a business grows in size and complexity and as the character of its product becomes more intricate, it is obliged to narrow constantly the range within which discretionary action on the part of the rank and file is practical, if the required objectives are to be attained. The more highly repetitive the process the more fully this condition will have to be realized. The repetitive characteristics of automobile manufacture are much greater than those found in the construction of an experimental device—hence, there is less opportunity for the play of personality on the part of the individual in the actual production of the product.

This condition with respect to routine activities is in sharp contrast with the very great individuality required of the creative personalities who devise and perfect the ways and means used. While it is true that the rank and file of business possess a degree of creative ability that should be fostered and developed wherever found, yet realism requires recognition of the fact that creative thinking in business is done largely by the few, generally with special training.

It will be seen, therefore, that business is a mixture of highly individualistic activities of the creative type, coupled with highly controlled activities of the performing type. Business management is desirous at all times of keeping predetermined procedure, whether administrative routine or productive process, to the minimum consistent with economical and effective accomplishment of the required objectives, thus giving the greatest practicable opportunity for the play of individuality, but these underlying characteristics cannot be changed in their essential elements.

True liberalism in American economic life will not be found in the destruction or impairment of the fundamental characteristics of private property or of its use in free private enterprise through control of such use by government, by workers, or by consumers; nor will it be found in any freezing of the conditions of employment; but rather in the development of conditions that make it possible for the individual always to find gainful employment; to move freely in and out of employment as and when he chooses and to a large extent where he chooses, keeping his employment upon a thoroughly competitive basis, without monopoly on the part of the employer or of the employee, and without undue interference, by seniority or otherwise, with the individual's moving upward in accordance with his own true merit. It will be found, further, in the protection of the individual in his freedom of choice between work and leisure, and in seeking his maximum compensation for work performed in open competition with others without, however, the creation of monopolies in the field of labor; also in the utmost freedom for the individual in the use of the proceeds of his work in the satisfaction of his own wants so long as he does not thereby interfere with the enjoyment by others of like freedom. And, finally, it will be found in the preservation to the individual of the right to acquire and own property, giving to such ownership the broadest connotation possible consistent with the recognition of the rights of others.

Government has a vital role to play in the accomplishment of these objectives by intelligent regulation of private enterprise and by encouragement of it; also by intervening at critical times to contribute directly to economic stabilization in certain areas of industry. There is no place in the American pattern of economic liberalism, however, for the authoritarian type of economic planning or for the continental concept of the universality or the infallibility of the state.

This is the basis upon which the future economic life of America must be built if we are to have true liberalism in our economic life and true democracy. There is no one formula by which these objectives can be accomplished. They must be reached by evolution, proceeding steadfastly from where we now are to where we wish to be, holding fast to that which we have until we prove out what is better. Above all, education must be the keynote of our future progress—education as to the inherent characteristics of our economic life, education as to the true place of the individual in this economic life, education as to the true values to be sought for in our efforts to satisfy our wants.

X

THE ROLE OF ECONOMIC GROUPS

BY

A. J. MUSTE, M.A., B.D.

The Fellowship of Reconciliation

Labor organizations are among the mainstays of democracy in the modern world and are usually to be found on the democratic side in conflicts between or within nations. It is, in this connection, significant that wherever Fascism has come to power its first objective has been to destroy the organizations of labor—trade-union, political, co-operative, cultural. That accomplished, Fascist régimes have then proceeded to destroy other free institutions, including even the political parties of conservative groups. In a theological seminary special note may properly be taken of the fact that in dictatorships, whether of the Right or of the Left, where there are no genuinely free trade unions, independent alike of employers and of the state, there are presently no genuinely free churches either.

It is difficult to see how at the present stage in history workers in a technologically advanced, highly industrialized society can exercise any control at the point of their economic life, over their livelihood and their status in industry, except through organization on the job. And where a man is deprived of freedom in the economic realm he cannot be genuinely free in other respects. This last was recognized by the Founding Fathers of this nation. It would not have occurred to them to think of slaves or serfs as politically or culturally free men. Political democracy in their view was built upon and composed of men who were free and independent in their economic relationships —farmers tilling their own soil, artisans working with their own tools and machines in their own shops, and, if employed, then free to seek the employer of their choice, to make a contract with him and to leave him at will and engage themselves to another employer on what seemed to them more advantageous terms. Primarily, the Founding Fathers relied upon the first two groups, the free farmers and independent artisans, to sustain a democratic society. In view of the anniversary which we observed yesterday (Lincoln's Birthday) it is interesting to note how as late as 1859 in a celebrated address before the Wisconsin State Agricultural Society Lincoln inveighed against what he termed the "mud-sill" theory, *i.e.,* the idea that "all laborers are naturally either hired laborers or slaves," that "whoever is once a hired laborer is fatally fixed in that condition for life."

A century ago, however, the individual "hired laborer" was also free in a sense that the ordinary unorganized worker cannot be today. At that time there were many employers and each employed a small number of workers. If a man employing five workers lost one of them, he lost twenty per cent of his working force; if the worker who left him joined an employer who had previously had four workers, this employer increased his working force by twenty-five per cent. In such instances a worker by quitting or assuming employment might exercise a real influence on the conditions of employment; more especially since in those days a worker who could not obtain what he regarded as a satisfactory contract of employment on the eastern seaboard could move west and on comparatively cheap land work out his destiny as a self-employer. If in our day, under so-called normal conditions, one of the 250,000 employees of the General Motors Company exercises his right as a free American, who is neither a serf bound to the property of General Motors nor a slave of a General Motors executive or stockholder, and quits his job, General Motors has 249,999 employees left on its payroll. And that is a very different story.

The employer today is not an individual in the old sense but a company, a corporation, a collectivity. The worker, if there is to be that approximation to equality of bargaining power without which there can be no free contract, must also be able to act in an organized, cooperative fashion. This is pretty elementary but it is not beside the point to recall this elementary lesson at a time when organized labor is under attack again, an attack which may become very powerful and vicious after the close of the war.

In a real sense the struggle for freedom of association is as crucial in modern industrial society as was the struggle for the freedom of the individual in an earlier day. We cannot go back to the simplicity and individualism of the horse-and-buggy age; there have to be traffic rules, there must of necessity be more social planning and action. But we do not want to land in totalitarianism at the other extreme. What to do then? It seems to me that structurally, or organizationally, our recourse must be to a multiplicity of organizations: organizations of management, labor, farmers, consumers; free political organizations; all sorts of cultural associations of the people; a free press, free schools, free churches. Through organizations the individual can function in a way he cannot as an isolated individual. But when there are many organizations, each with a considerable degree of autonomy, they will limit each other, the individual will have elbowroom, a chance to throw his weight toward one or another, and no one organization becomes absolutist and dominant, crushing out freedom. Where, on the other hand, there is no association intervening between the individual and the absolutist state, the human being is no longer free. And because, if any element is deprived of its freedom to organize, there will shortly be no freedom of association for any, the workers' right to organize and liberty of action for labor organizations remain the concerns of all progressive elements in the community and not least of the churches which have their roots in Judeo-Christian prophetism.

I shall presently have occasion to raise some questions as to whether the labor movement in the United States is qualified to do its part to defend and enrich our democracy, but before dealing with that very important matter, I wish to comment on some phases of the attack on labor.

In the first place, the closed shop is very often attacked as undemocratic and "totalitarian," and the allegation has a superficial plausibility. Of course, those who are in principle opposed to any form of social compulsion are consistent in also opposing the closed shop. As a firm believer in freedom of conscience, I believe also that exemption from joining unions ought to be granted to individuals whose religious convictions, for example, forbid them to do so. There are cases where Mennonites have thus been exempted from joining unions. But the ordinary cases of people who do not want to join unions are not cases of conscience. They are people who hold individualistic views largely because of tradition or ignorance, who are perfectly willing to accept the benefits of unionism but wish to avoid its responsibilities, and who—often—are the willing or the unconscious dupes of reactionary employers or of other reactionary interests. There are certain types of preachers who get very eloquent about the tyranny of unions because they want to keep uninformed and unsophisticated workers under their own sway.

If workers can contribute effectively to the democratic process in industry, can be citizens and not mere subjects in industry, only through participation in organized activity, then the union becomes a necessary and salutary instrument of democracy. Then it seems to me essentially a legitimate thing to say to a worker who is being hired for a job: "Just as it is expected here that you will behave as a responsible person in such matters as care of machinery and tools, observance of safety regulations, doing a fair day's work, etc., so it is expected that you will function as a responsible citizen in policy-making by belonging to your union and by doing your part to make this union a clean, efficient, and dependable instrument of democracy. You will share in the benefits it obtains, you will be given your vote the same as any other man, and you are likewise expected to put your shoulder to the wheel." The General Council of the United Church of Canada recently set a magnificent example in providing not only for the unionization, but for the unionization on a virtually closed-shop basis, of its printing plant, the biggest, I believe, in all Canada.

For the most part the attacks on the closed shop, the various laws and bills requiring registration of union organizers, public accounting of funds, the open shop, the so-called "right-to-work" measure which was on the ballot in California in 1944, are disingenuous. The purpose is not to make unions more honest and responsible but to discredit them, to weaken them in relation to employer groups, and if possible to destroy them. These purposes according to our view of the role of unions in a free society are antisocial. What we need is strong unions, because only upon unions that are strong and secure can responsibility be placed. A union which has no control over its membership, which is constantly harassed and made to fight for its life, cannot perform a constructive role. Objectively considered, efforts to weaken or destroy unions play into the hands of Fascist forces. Progressive elements will oppose all such efforts.

Of the utmost importance is it in this connection to be on guard against prevalent attempts, which will certainly gain in intensity in the unsettled period following the cessation of hostilities, to drive a wedge between the industrial workers and organized labor, on the one hand, and the men in the Armed Forces and returning veterans, on the other hand. To develop such a cleavage is a stock item in Fascist tactics. Presently a contest for jobs develops and then unemployed veterans are utilized to form Fascist strong-arm squads and shock troops to harass and destroy labor organizations.

The virulent and dramatic public attacks on strikes and unions by Eddie Rickenbacker some months ago are a case in point. So are the attempts made during the election campaign and since to paint the C.I.O.–P.A.C. as a Bolshevik attempt to take over control of American industry and government for subversive purposes. I say this, though I am an opponent of communism and deplore the influence of the Communist Party—under whatever name it may be operating at the moment—over some American unions.

At the moment of writing, the unions—the A.F. of L., C.I.O., Railroad Brotherhoods and others—are opposing labor conscription in the form of "work-or-fight" or "work-or-jail" legislation. I do not doubt there are those who regard this legislation as necessary and patriotic and who are quite honest, therefore, in their condemnation of unions and others who oppose it. But it is dangerous, even when not deliberately dishonest, to keep silent about or to play down the tremendous record of production the unions and workers have achieved and their allegation that the real problem is the intelligent organization of the available working force. There is much in history to support the contention that free labor is more productive than conscripted or enslaved labor. It is fantastic to accuse union people and workers generally of lack of patriotism and of disloyalty to the men in the Armed Forces. Who are the latter if not the sons, brothers, husbands, and sweethearts of the former? And if the unions are unpatriotic in opposing labor conscription, let the lack of patriotism of the National Association of Manufacturers, which also opposes these bills, be blazoned forth.

Another situation that will need to be watched arises from the ruling of the Selective Service Administration that ex-service men shall be given jobs and seniority, even if this means, as in some cases it would, displacing workers who have been on a job for twenty years. The unions themselves are concerned to protect the seniority of ex-service men. The United Automobile Workers Union, C.I.O., alone has 300,000 of its members in the service! They have made provision to count, in reckoning seniority, all the time a man has spent in service. But an arbitrary measure such as this Selective Service edict, carried out arbitrarily without consultation with the unions and management, may seriously affect production and, above all, will be a potent source of embittering relations between service men and the unions and thus will play into the hands of reaction.

We have contended that labor organizations are essential to the defense and effective functioning of democracy and have warned against efforts to destroy or weaken the unions as reactionary in effect, and often also in motivation. We have next to consider briefly the question whether these organizations are likely to play their role in the defense and operation of democracy effectively and what internal defects may hinder or defeat them in the discharge of their responsibilities. This is the most important and difficult problem connected with our subject.

From the standpoint of numbers the unions in the United States are, as is well known, better situated than ever before. Labor unions have a claimed membership of about fourteen million. Of these the A.F. of L. lists seven million. This figure is probably somewhat inflated, for it is based upon per-capita tax paid to the Federation by affiliated international unions, and there are powerful affiliates, such as the Carpenters headed by William Hutcheson and the Teamsters headed by Daniel Tobin, which regularly pay more per-capita dues than their actual membership in order to obtain greater representation—also based on per-capita tax payment—at annual conventions.

The C.I.O. claims from five to six million, and these figures are also somewhat inflated. The remaining members are in the United Mine Workers headed by John L. Lewis, in Railroad Labor Unions independent of the rival national federations, and in other less important independent bodies. In the process of reconversion from a war footing, and with possible large-scale unemployment, the sprawling and comparatively new unions of the C.I.O. are likely to suffer more than the older, more closely knit and better financed A.F. of L. unions. It must be borne in mind also that there are still considerable sections of industry on an anti-union, open-shop footing. This is true of the textile industry in the south and largely so of agricultural workers and the poorer farmers throughout the country. To cite another instance, which is brought out in the current (February, 1945) issue of *Fortune,* whereas labor in Seattle is now about 90 per cent organized and in San Francisco 75 per cent, the figure for Los Angeles is down to 30 per cent.

Furthermore, the history of labor and of revolutionary movements throughout Europe reminds us that, even if they are powerful not only numerically but in other respects, this does not guarantee that they will be effective and victorious in the effort to stem the tide of reaction and totalitarianism. It is clear from this European experience that one of the serious sources of weakness was that labor could not achieve unity within its own ranks, not to mention effective working relationships with other progressive elements. In Germany, on the advent of Hitler to power, the imposing German labor and radical movement did not offer a gesture of resistance, either violent or nonviolent. Obviously, something must have happened within the movement itself to bring things to such a pass. The long and bitter controversy between Socialists and Communists for control of the unions and other workers' organizations had played an important part. The role of the Social Democrats is certainly subject to grave criticism and in the early 1930's there were trade unions—as there were unfortunately also church leaders, including some who subsequently and at great cost to themselves changed their course—who were not so much concerned about resisting Nazism as in coming to an understanding with Hitler which would enable them to maintain their vested interests in trade-union leadership and to get even with the Communists. On the other hand, the Communists had stopped short of nothing in their factional struggles against the social Democrats and the officialdom of the unions; had confused German political life by their slavish pursuit of the course dictated by the Soviet foreign office policy, which often performed the most amazing zigzags and had even joined with the Nazis in strikes in order to embarrass the Social Democratic régime in Prussia. As some one has put it, each side habitually denounced the other as liars and betrayers of labor—and the workers presently believed them both! No one trusted anyone else any longer.

It is not necessary to dwell upon the fact that this evil of division and factionalism already afflicts the American labor movement. It is patent in the breach between the A.F. of L. and the C.I.O.; in the absence of the powerful United Mine Workers from either Federation. At the moment a rapprochement between the U.M.W. and the A.F. of L. seems to be in the making, but it is doubtful whether if it is consummated it will be a contribution to true labor unity. It seems much more likely to be a move to sharpen the fight between the A.F. of L. and the C.I.O. The phenomenon of which we are speaking is manifest also in the controversy centering around communist influence or domination in certain unions and in the political field between the Liberal Party and the American Labor Party in New York. At the moment of writing the situation is reflected in the absence of the A.F. of L. from the international labor-union conference in London and the presence there of a weighty delegation from the C.I.O., the presence of the Soviet unions which the A.F. of L. refuses to recognize as genuine free unions, because of their relationship to the state and to the Communist Party, being the reason for the absence of the A.F. of L. The A.F. of L. is in the meanwhile engaged in exploring the possibility of rescuing and revitalizing the old International Federation of Trade Unions or forming a new International. The indications are that in the postwar period these controversies, particularly as they affect the situation in the United States, will be sharpened rather than resolved.

Another factor which hampers the unions in helping to save and advance democracy is their own lack of internal democracy. The railroad labor unions are perhaps least subject to criticism at this point and probably the International Ladies Garment Workers Union belongs in the same category. Otherwise, undemocratic conditions are all too frequent both in the more conservative unions and in those generally regarded as more radical. In the former, officials are often firmly entrenched, virtually self-perpetuating, and the members are expected to pay dues and keep still, accepting the benefits obtained for them by officialdom, benefits which, so far as wages, hours, and certain working conditions are concerned, are at times real and substantial enough for those who are willing to obey orders. In other unions the chief problem is created by communist manipulation, sometimes subtle and concealed, sometimes open and crude, but in any event precluding genuine discussion of issues on their merits and a real challenge to the control of the dominant group. Attacks from without calculated to weaken or destroy the unions will not remove this evil but confirm it or replace it with something which is at least as bad. But labor organizations which are not themselves democratic in spirit and action will not in the long run or at crucial moments serve the general cause of democracy, and those who are concerned about the future of democracy must take this into account.

Another undemocratic attitude encountered in certain sections of the labor movement must be recorded in passing, though there is no time to discuss it. I refer to the discrimination against Negroes and other members of minority groups. It is practiced openly and deliberately still in a good many A.F. of L. unions. The C.I.O. has on the whole a clean and enviable record and in the south has done more than any other single agency—far more than the churches, be it said to their shame—to overcome discrimination and Jim Crow practices. Among the membership of all the unions, however, the prejudices characteristic of American culture in this realm are to be found in large measure. It may be questioned whether even in the most progressive unions as much as might have been done has been done to remedy the situation and to prepare for the almost inevitable increase of tension that will occur in the disturbed period following the war, and more especially in the major economic crisis which the country seems certain to experience, if not soon after the war, then at a somewhat later date when our accumulation of surplus goods is exhausted.

The brief concluding section of this paper will be devoted to an attempt to state some of the dilemmas with which the labor movement in this country is confronted as it tries to work out its answer to the economic and political problems of the postwar period. One of these dilemmas may be stated thus. For the most part, unions have abandoned the "class-struggle" philosophy that employers and employees have little if anything in common and that unions must be, above all, instruments for carrying on the struggle against encroachments of business and finance on the rights and income of the workers. The prevailing idea is that workers are interested in the prosperity of industry as much as employers and that their unions must, therefore, in order to serve the workers' interests, look out also for the employers' interests. The instrument by which this is to be accomplished is union-management co-operation. It is unquestionably true that the prevailing philosophy of collaboration, "no-strike" agreements, etc., has been in part accepted in the supposed interest of the workers and the nation under war conditions. It represented, however, the dominant trend before the war and is widely advocated as a postwar policy, though not always in the extreme form propounded by Harry Bridges and his Longshoremen's Union on the Pacific Coast. But if the earlier attitude of belligerency was an oversimplified one and against the true interests of society, it may be that this is true to some extent also of the prevailing philosophy of collaboration. At certain points this is tacitly admitted and as a result the unions find themselves in politics on opposite sides of the fence from employers with whom in the shop they work hand in glove.

Employers continue to espouse the theory of what they call "free enterprise," which in some cases means a desire to return to competitive conditions that would presumably give the "little fellow" a chance but in the case of the more powerful employer groups expresses a desire to maintain corporate monopoly as free as possible from government control and "interference." The unions pay at least lip service to the same concept, both the A.F. of L. and the C.I.O. coupling advocacy or support of "free enterprise" with labor-management co-operation in the statements of their recent conventions. This is, it may be worth noting, in rather glaring contrast with the positions taken by labor after World War I, when railroad labor was vigorously agitating for nationalization of the railroads and the 1920 Denver convention of the A.F. of L. called for the socialization of the key monopolies. But on certain concrete issues now coming to the fore, the disposition of which will largely determine the fate of labor and of democracy, there is a sharp divergence of view between dominant employing interests and at least some sections of labor.

A case in point—perhaps the most crucial—is the question of what is to be done about the war plants built and equipped with Federal funds. Plants built and owned by the government represent one fifth to one fourth of the nation's manufacturing facilities, including 50 per cent of capacity to build machine tools, 70 per cent of aluminum, 90 per cent of synthetic rubber, aircraft production, and shipbuilding and repairs, 96 per cent of magnesium, and an investment of five billion dollars in plants for the manufacture of explosives, ammunition, combat vehicles, and guns. Government investment of public money in new plants is greater than the total investment of private enterprise in the ten years 1930–39. Business interests in general want these plants sold cheap to private purchasers under conditions that would put corporate monopolies in an advantageous position. This might very well mean the scrapping of these plants or of others now owned by these interests, thus serving to maintain the old scarcity economy, rather than their utilization to maintain full employment and full production. The current controversy about the appointment of Henry A. Wallace as Secretary of Commerce arises largely because this problem of how these publicly financed properties are to be disposed of is involved. So far, the unions and others interested in having the social interest put foremost in this situation are fighting a losing battle. There is no evidence that labor organizations have thought through the question as to how far their own and society's interests are identical in such matters with those of the present owners and managers of industry and what this means for the policy of labor-management co-operation.

In another area the policy of the unions coincides with that of employing interests, and they believe this to be in the interest of their members, but they have not faced the problem of whether this is truly in the public interest, especially when international factors are taken into account. Both the A.F. of L. and the C.I.O. unions in the shipbuilding industry are for a large, government-subsidized merchant marine. Their arguments parallel those of the shipping lobby. The reason is plain if not cogent. The prewar low in employment in this industry was two hundred thousand. The present figure is seventeen hundred and fifty thousand. It is feared that the bottom will be reached again unless some such program as that just mentioned is adopted, which would practically wreck these unions. But under the program proposed the policy of labor is actually an endorsement of imperialist expansion without regard to the economies of other nations, such as Great Britain, and to the needs of world trade.

Another point at which the unions face a dilemma is that of their relationship to the state and the agencies of government. The old trade-union philosophy, so tenaciously held by Samuel Gompers throughout his career, wanted government to keep its hands off the relations between employers and unions. What the government or politicians gave they could also take away and probably would. What labor won from the employer by its bargaining strength it could, by the same token, keep. But the depression gave that philosophy a jar even in the A.F. of L., and the C.I.O. has from the beginning largely depended on government support through the Wagner Act and other measures. There is no question that the Labor Relations Act gave a great impetus to union organization. But when government boards virtually have the power to fix wages, hours, and conditions of work, the bargaining with employers in which union leaders engaged on behalf of their members is superseded. When government goes on to provide social insurance, workers are likely to look increasingly to the government rather than to their organizations, and union leaders may become more concerned about how they stand with government bureaucrats than with their own membership. One illustration of the perplexities which ensue is furnished by what has happened with "labor representation" on government agencies. At the beginning of the war the unions, particularly the

C.I.O., clamored for such representation. But experience has dampened the enthusiasm, for in practice "labor representation" has tended to tie labor's hands and to make it an agency of the state in enforcing government decisions.

The same problem of what government intervention implies faces labor in connection with the foremost item in its postwar program, *viz.,* "full employment." Traditionally, unions existed to protect jobs when jobs were scarce. When economic conditions created a demand for labor, unions got the credit and earned the gratitude and support of the workers. But "full employment" in the present context implies state action to underwrite jobs when a slack appears. When the state underwrites the job, the traditional role of the union leader has been undercut. There is a danger that under such circumstances unions, having seemingly become superfluous, may be eliminated or may become agencies of the state. Neither development would appear to be desirable from the standpoint of democracy.

Another problem with respect to which labor's thinking has not been clarified and a viable program developed, is that of war and the war system. Organized labor in the United States, and especially the C.I.O., felt itself so deeply beholden to the Roosevelt administration because of its domestic policies that it was disposed to "go along" almost automatically with the Rooseveltian foreign policy. Its support of the war has been thoroughgoing. The leaders have been willing to incur deep-seated dissatisfaction on the part of their membership, as over the maintenance of the Little Steel Wage Formula in face of rising prices and high war profits, rather than to risk a break with the President.

Labor pronouncements about the peace and the postwar world are mildly liberal. But there is no evidence that labor will work out an independent and imaginative policy—and back it vigorously— which would give substantial promise of radically altering American policy and international relationships and thus give promise also of a just and durable peace. Labor, for example, is not likely to demand any substantial change in American immigration and tariff policies. We have pointed out that the shipbuilding unions are, in the supposed interest of keeping employment up to war figures, supporting economic expansionism and imperialism. Though by no means always clearly aware of all the implications, the unions generally act on the assumption that they have a vested interest in American imperialism as a guarantor of high American wages. They believe that for purposes of "defense" the United States ought to keep a big military establishment and naval and air bases in various parts of the world. But such policies and attitudes as this brought this country into World War II and assured the government of labor support in that war. These policies and attitudes will mean, on the one hand, keeping the rest of the world out of the United States market and, on the other, an attempt to maintain and extend United States economic hegemony in Latin America and to make the Pacific an American lake. This in turn means World War III and labor participation in it. And all this is suicidal for the masses of workers and for the labor movement itself.

This brings us naturally to our final observation. Labor, like most of the rest of us, is still obsessed with the essentially materialistic, mechanistic notion that the solution of our ills is something called "maximum production" as a result of "the liberation of the productive powers." But, as John Middleton Murry pointed out in an essay in *The Adelphi* magazine in the fall of 1943, (London, British Periodicals Co.) "maximum productivity is achieved only in time of war. Compared with a war-boom a peace-boom is nothing; and it is always followed by a peace-slump." The idea that under present conditions we can maximize production for peace "is an illusion. Maximum production of goods for peace must always be potentially production for war. Industrial peace-potential is war-potential." A writer in *Harper's Magazine* for January, 1945, contended that the United States could almost get along without a military establishment in the usual sense of the term, since the industrial potential of a nation is indeed its sole, certainly its decisive, means of preparation for the supermodern war of the future. "Unless therefore war is made impossible, maximum production for peace is self-deception: a device for not letting the nation's right hand know what its left is doing."

If we were not constantly proceeding, though unconsciously for the most part, on the assumption that we live in a war economy and that war cannot really be eliminated, we would probably long since have recognized the abstract, essentially dehumanizing and degrading nature of the concept of "maximum production." It makes the worker himself a piece of mechanism to turn out goods, a slave of the "productive forces" rather than their master. It makes the means to living the end of life. If we lived in another atmosphere, we could get the fog out of our eyes and see realities instead of fantastic shapes through the mist, we would realize that the problem is not the liberation of the productive powers but their control for the common good. We would see that there is no sense in being slaves in order to increase by geometric progression the so-called standard of living and that it is more important for moral and spiritual beings that they should work for ends which are rational and under conditions which are psychologically and spiritually satisfying, than that the output of machines they operate should be big in monetary terms or even in terms of gadgets produced. Only as we begin to think in such terms shall we give peace other than a negative content and only thus shall we be able to save or achieve democracy, which can apply only to a society of rational beings who are free not only in relation to each other but free also from any impersonal tyranny such as that of the machine. As yet there is little awareness of this problem in labor ranks.

The churches and religious leaders, then, should defend organized labor from attack at the hands of reactionary forces; but they should not place uncritical confidence in it as the savior of democracy nor regard it as any service to labor or democracy simply to endorse labor's program and activities. They have a responsibility to apply to labor as to other groups the standards of judgment given us by God through the prophets of our faith. Above all, they must help labor and all progressive forces in modern society to clarify their objectives in the light of that faith, to cultivate the grace of humility and repentance, and to generate the moral passion without which we shall not achieve a democratic society, which is nothing but a fellowship of free men who are akin to one another because they are children of God.

XI

DEMOCRACY IN A COLLECTIVIST AGE

BY

GOODWIN B. WATSON, Ph.D.

Professor of Education, Teachers College, Columbia University

Voltaire in his *Philosophical Dictionary* observed that "Democracy seems suitable only to a very little country." The models of democracy which we usually have in mind when we frame its definitions are face-to-face groups like town meetings, debating societies, fraternities, progressive schools, and legislative assemblies. Thomas Jefferson grew up in a community so small and isolated that until he was eighteen years of age he never saw a town with more than twenty houses. He thought with rural premises. In his comments on the proposed Federal Constitution written to James Madison (December 20, 1787) his one reservation was that cheerful reliance on the will of the majority could be expected only "so long as agriculture is our principal object." "When we get piled upon one another in large cities, as in Europe," he predicted, "we shall become corrupt." In another famous passage he was even more vehement. "The mobs of great cities add just so much to the support of pure government as sores do to the strength of the human body." When we admire the extent to which economic progress has been made with substantial retention of democratic traditions in countries like Sweden, Denmark, Switzerland, Australia, and New Zealand, we are bound to remember also that not one of these countries has in its entire area as many persons as are presided over by Mayor La Guardia in New York City.

Our problem concerns the fate that may overtake democracy if our lives continue to be increasingly influenced by huge collectives. The little neighborhoods of Jefferson's day became industrial cities clustered about water-power sites and steam-driven factories. The economy within which our democracy was born was one of farmers and small businessmen, but both of these groups are dwindling. In 1820 75 per cent of the American people were engaged in agriculture, forestry, or fishing. Already that proportion has dropped to 15 per cent, and social scientists tell us we shall come out of this war with 2,000,000 more families on farms than we really need. This last summer a crop of cotton was planted by machinery, weeded by mechanical flame throwers, picked and ginned by more machinery, completing another successful demonstration of mechanized agriculture, adaptable to large-scale operations. The postwar epoch is likely to see farming revolutionized as automobile production was after World War I.

The little businesses of frontier days have now grown into huge factories and department stores. That extraordinary social invention, the modern corporation, has further transformed the business scene. A decade ago more than half the business of the country was done by 200 nonfinancial corporations; today these same 200 probably do nearly two thirds of the nation's business. Small retail establishments are bound together in huge chains. Every week brings to the financial pages announcements of new mergers. Wartime contracts have overwhelmingly favored big business, despite Maury Maverick's intelligent fight on behalf of the little fellows.

We have reason to be particularly concerned over the advance of collectivism in the agencies which make up public opinion. A generation ago there were more than 3,000 daily newspapers in this country. Today there are about 1,800. There is more concentration, however, than this figure suggests. Many of these are owned by newspaper chains. Only one city in six has any choice of local daily newspapers. There are 111 cities in the United States where there is only one newspaper and where the publisher of that newspaper owns also the only radio station. Even when newspapers are under different ownership, they are dependent mainly upon three great news services—Associated Press, United Press, or Hearst's International News Service. The men who sit at the controls in those news services determine what millions of people shall know and what they shall not be told.

In radio the concentration is equally great. It is true that there are some 900 radio stations, but they are tied up in four big networks which give us 95 per cent of our evening programs. We get programs, in three cases out of four, through the food industry, the drug industry, the soap industry, or the tobacco industry. A handful of advertising agencies are the bottlenecks through which finances flow to magazines and radio stations.

The concentration in industry and in the control of communication is necessarily paralleled by growing centralization in government. Only the Federal government seems powerful enough to cope with the modern economic giants.

The Committee on Economic Development has made laudable efforts to get local groups of businessmen to lay out plans for increasing employment after the war, but most citizens today believe that there is no hope for sixty million jobs in this country in 1950 except through drastic action by the Federal government. There are still millions who carry insurance with private companies or through fraternal lodges, but the bulk of voters in all political parties now accept the idea that extending social security is a national obligation. To fight the war we introduced planning and collectivist control on what is for America an unprecedented scale. We rationed raw materials, fixed prices, froze men in jobs, clamped ceilings on incomes, and compelled saving. We recognize that it may be necessary to keep many of these controls for some time to prevent inflation and to provide postwar employment.

Modern transportation and communication are making new collectives international in scope. In business we damn cartels or perhaps explain them as necessary and not so bad. American interests patently have extended to include Middle Eastern oil and African and Pacific air bases. The main tenor in liberal criticism of the United Nations is that it does not go far enough toward setting up collective controls. The Great Powers and zones of influence seem still too decentralized to deal with the kind of problems presented by an integrated world. A neat trick of name-calling has led to avoidance of the term "global," but more than ever before we are involved in international operations which can be intelligent only if they are planned on a global scale.

It seems clear that the issue between collectivism and democracy is one which is developing within all modern industrial cultures. It is not, as some have supposed, focused in the unfortunate antagonism between the Anglo-Saxon democracies and the collectivist Union of Socialist Soviet Republics. Vice and virtue are seldom neatly divided by national boundaries. There are democratic aspects and dictatorial aspects of the life of the Soviet Union and both can be found also at different points and in different forms within the United States. England remains democratic but sees collectivist patterns as essential for her international trade, while the Labor Party follows Sir William Beveridge (Liberal) toward a program for full employment which uses collective planning for the ends of freedom and democracy. America and England, no less than any other country in the world, have still to solve the problem of reconciling necessary large-scale planning with absolutely essential democratic liberties. The clash between the Russians and the Anglo-Saxons is in part a clash between certain freedoms and others. There are freedoms that seem incompatible, and we do not solve that problem by shouting "Hurrah for freedom!"

The real conflict between collectivist trends and democratic aspirations can best be defined by a look at the proposed solutions.

1. One answer is that of *economic monopoly*. This is the program of bigger business. It rests upon the claim that American prosperity is the product of "free enterprise," and that "free enterprise" is inseparably bound up with democracy. Our safeguards, from this point of view, are billion-dollar corporations and the National Association of Manufacturers. The collectivist danger which monopolists fight is that of "government interference." When they say "freedom of the press" they mean only freedom from laws by which the state might hamper whatever profitable policies the news monopolies would otherwise follow. They muster all possible evidence in favor of the efficiency of private enterprise and the deadly sins of bureaucracy. They recall with affection Thomas Jefferson's remark that the best government is that which governs least. This is not what they really mean. They are not opposed to government action to emasculate labor unions, to tax co-operatives, to prevent price cutting, to subsidize exports, to exclude competitive imports, to persecute radicals, or even to buy off with the most inexpensive possible concessions any poten-

tial revolution in time of distress. They are opposed to the power of the state only when it conflicts with their own power—they welcome it as a subservient aid. They are ignorantly or wilfully blind to the dangers of the economic collectivism on whose behalf they battle against our growing political collectivism.

2. The *totalitarians* have the converse concern. Theirs is the positive program of the all-powerful state. They cannot say too much about the evils of concentration of capitalist economy power. Their answer to all problems is to have the government step in. They argue that, since our American government is ultimately responsible to the people, democracy will be extended rather than injured if the government takes over the basic industries and plans the economic system as a whole. They find the trend toward centralization of industry to be irreversible, and they follow it to its logical conclusion: a single central body ultimately responsible for co-ordinating all aspects of our economic and political life. We have found it efficient to bring all the diverse activities of a great industry under the central control of a parent corporation. Merely extend what is now the rule within corporations to the relationships among them, they say, and there will result an efficiently planned and co-ordinated social order. The correlative blind spot is the inability of these totalitarian socialists to appreciate the limitations and dangers of concentrated power. They may repeat, as Laski does, after Lord Acton, "Power always corrupts, and absolute power corrupts absolutely!" but they expect that in a country used to democratic procedures, these will survive to curb and to guide the all-powerful state. Or perhaps they argue, in defiance of some pretty sad experience with boss-ridden labor unions, that representatives of the proletariat can be trusted not to abuse power. Does anyone still look for the state to "wither away" in Russia? Sensitive as these social planners are to the irresponsible and ruthless rigidity of such collectives as armies, state churches, mass-production industries, and huge financial combines, they do not see that centralized state power is likely to be an even greater menace.

Each of the other agencies of society operates against checks and under some superior controls. A centralized and autocratic business like that of the X family in Middletown is bad, but its interests clash with other enterprises, and there are areas of life it does not pretend to occupy. Monopolies must deal with other monopolies, and none is the whole show. Theoretically, the power of the state, with some measure of independence and some constitutional safeguards, operates over and above any economic collectives, military collectives, or religious collectives. If and when the state, in the sense of our supreme coercive power, takes direct responsibility for managing all areas of life there will be no appeal short of Providence. If the rulers of such a state tended to become self-perpetuating—and what concentration of power does not?—relief could be sought only in revolution or in conquest by some stronger state. Hitler's speeches often remind the German people that the Nazis came into power by "legal means," through the channels of representative government and under constitutional provisions. Totalitarians may come in that way, but they make sure they are the last to do so by pulling up the political ladders and drawbridges behind them.

3. A third type of answer is provided by a variety of powerless but interesting groups of *decentralists*. A few individuals follow Thoreau to Walden Pond, rejecting at every possible point the pressures of every kind of collectivism. Most of us share this impulse at times, but find the realities too grim for action. Millions in India follow Gandhi's thought away from modern industrialism back to home-grown food, home spinning wheels and looms. Ralph Borsodi's theories are a little more acceptable in this country because they allow for something like a quarter of our needs to be met by mass production, while inviting us to learn the multiple skills essential to doing the other three quarters ourselves. Small idealistic communities have often been founded, but the only ones to survive seem to have been those that were somehow incorporated within a vast centralized collective like the Catholic Church. We shall doubtless see many new attempts to form islands of order in the chaos of Europe and Asia after this war. If the experience of history is repeated, they will not survive as little independent social units beyond two generations.

The first two answers—monopoly and totalitarianism—would be feasible enough, but they threaten to crush democratic values that generations of Americans have fought to defend. The decentralist answer in some of its forms is attractive and soul-saving, but it seems most unlikely that the hands of the cosmic clock will move backward. It is too hard to unlearn airplanes, kindergartens, automobiles, symphonies, typewriters, highways, theaters, apartments, all-year orange juice, exotic foods, books, laboratories, magazines, social security, and the countless other luxuries of our collective order. Is there a possibility that the spirit of democracy can find new implementation within the technology of collectivism?

4. *Democratic collectivism* is the only answer that combines both feasibility and desirability. Few students of social trends doubt that government participation in our economy will continue to increase. Even though socialism lags in the United States behind its rate of advance in every other industrial nation of the world, the realities of America today often go beyond the socialist platforms of a generation ago. The writer spoke recently to a group of able college students —pioneer thinkers of a sort which in the mid-1930's would have included mostly Communists or fellow travelers. In the mid-1940's they showed little excitement over economic radicalism. "Those problems are solved!" they announced. "The fight drags on but the issue is no longer in doubt. Government control and, where necessary, government operation may be taken for granted. Our interest," they said, "is in the use of our new resources and our new freedoms to create the good life!"

What could they have meant by new freedoms, springing up within the matrix of expanding collectivism?

Perhaps they had in mind the reduced man-hours required for production. This makes possible increased leisure, with corresponding increase in each individual's time to live in accord with his own tastes and values. Score one for greater democracy.

The students might also have had in mind the important demonstration of the T.V.A.—where collective planning has emancipated millions of valley dwellers from slavery to ignorance, disease, poor soil, and lack of mechanical power. Score some more for democracy! David Lilienthal has probably done more than any other man now living to demonstrate that giant social organizations can be harnessed under continuous control of the democratic will.

Within collectivism itself are being forged new social instruments that can be used not only to preserve democracy but even to extend it. Our American public-school system is one of the most familiar of these instruments. It is itself a powerful collective, providing for the many an enlightenment which might otherwise be confined to the few. Its greatest limitation is probably that it is not yet sufficiently collective. Only through a program of federal financing will it be possible to provide decent schools for children in some impoverished sections of the land. The ever-expanding schools are a clear demonstration that federal aid does not necessarily involve the imposition of a uniform system devised in Washington. Social inventions commonly permit the national machinery to serve under local, grass-roots control. Many a school today works out its actual plans and policies in groups no larger than the classroom or neighborhood, while much larger social units raise the bulk of the funds and offer to the local authorities a stimulating variety of possible books, methods, ideas, and services.

The agencies of mass communication are giant collectives which, even under the lingering limitations of private control, reveal their potential contribution to democracy. It is a first principle of democracy that the people must know what is going on. We may justly deplore the profit-seeking censorship exercised by the radio, the movies, and by emerging television, but it is clear that these instruments are peculiarly well adapted to reaching millions who could never be given by the traditional methods of print any effective grasp of current issues. One reason why Franklin D. Roosevelt could be reelected in 1936 and in 1940 and again in 1944, against the united opposition of business interests and most newspapers, was that his cultured friendly voice could reach the family about the stove or fireside in almost every home.

Bode has defined democracy with emphasis upon increasing the area of *shared concern*. Modern collectivism enables us to share on an unprecedented scale. By television we shall have ringside seats at major events anywhere in our country or around the world. Air travel will take us to the Philippines faster than the stage coach took our first congressmen to Philadelphia.

We can know better what is going on, and, thanks to modern technology, our views can more easily be heard. A penny postal will reach our representatives in Congress and we can telegraph or telephone them for less than the price of a theater seat. There are other possibilities still undeveloped. Technically, it would be quite feasible to equip each radio with push buttons through which citizens could register approval or disapproval of any ideas being expressed at any time.

Collectivism does not even wait for our initiative. Opinion polls now seek out our reactions to proposed new products and proposed new policies. Likert's work with the Department of Agriculture in developing, sampling, and interview methods by which government administrators may know at all times what the average citizen likes or dislikes about specific measures, is a notable advance on the pathway toward democratic collectivism.

Another contribution of collectivism to democratic participation is in the development of new social units through which the individual can influence big economic and political agencies. It takes a collective to fight the collectives. So we have labor unions and an emerging Labor Movement. Labor unions are the necessary collective adaptation of the American dream. When the individual can no longer advance by moving to free land in the west, or simply through his own ambition and energy, he joins with others in a similar predicament; and, in co-operative, united fashion, they are able to make progress which they could not make as individuals. Consumer organizations are relatively weak as compared with labor unions, but they too represent a form of collectivism in which the concerns of the individual can find channels reaching to the effective controls in our economic system. The political activities of the C.I.O. and its Political Action Committee during the recent election, represent another achievement in building collectives through which the common man can increase his influence in public affairs. We have not yet solved all the internal problems of these new collectives. Some of them are controlled by a small clique of insiders who manipulate the organization that is supposed to provide mass expression. One of the major tasks of teachers of social science in secondary schools of this country ought to be to equip every citizen to work in a union or a co-operative or a party in such a way as to thwart efforts of a few to retain domination.

To participate in groups or organizations does not necessarily imply becoming a rubber stamp, a robot, or a carbon copy of the mind of the group. George Albert Coe, more than twenty years ago, gave us the very important distinction between a crowd and a democratic group. In a crowd the individual personality is *submerged;* in a democratic group individual personalities *emerge*. This distinction is supported by contemporary experiments in social psychology. Kurt Lewin has demonstrated how democracy can release individual potentialities in club groups and on playgrounds. Roethlisberger and Dixon describe experiments in industry where greater democracy and self-realization for individuals were a major factor in higher levels of production. The Massachusetts Institute of Technology has inaugurated its new Institute for the Study of Group Dynamics. We are only at the beginning of a development which may carry us far toward new social techniques, permitting and encouraging individual spontaneity within our many collectives.

Let no one assume that because collective instruments *may* facilitate popular enlightenment and individual participation they necessarily *will* be used in this way. That is what the struggle is about. Social inventions are as two-edged as are new advances in physical science and machine design. They may release or enslave. Regional development may be as democratic as the T.V.A., or it may be dictated by a Washington official with military concepts of administration. Our schools are under public control, but that has not prevented rigid anachronisms or such abuses as the hysterical tossing out of the Rugg textbooks at the instigation of a few manipulators. FM stations open the possibility of local control in the public interest, but there is still a danger that they may be linked up in a few huge chains devoted to profits from advertising. Public-opinion polls, labor movements, co-operatives, even the techniques of enlisting group loyalty through giving each member a sense of participation, are subject to misappropriation. It would be fatuous to suppose that collectivism inevitably fosters democracy.

Our contention is more modest and more challenging. Collectivism does not necessarily bring totalitarianism. A collectivist age *may be made* an age of increasing democracy. Collectivism builds up social giants that are difficult to control, but it also brings forth new agencies of control appropriate to the new giants that must be harnessed. It is as naïve to contrast planning and democracy as it is to equate them. The decisive factor remains in the attitudes and efforts of the people. We are not doomed by the machines with which we have harnessed the energies of the universe, nor can we rely on them to defend us. The defense of democracy lies in our dedication to democracy. We can have, in a collectivist age, only—and fully—as much as we are determined to have. New inventions, mechanical and social, confute many ancient maxims, but one abides: "Out of the heart are the issues of life!"

XII

EDUCATION FOR FREEDOM

BY

SCOTT BUCHANAN, Ph.D.

Dean, St. John's College

In connection with the controversial connotation, at least of the title of the lecture, perhaps I ought to say just a few words. They are not important, but some of you may have expected something different from what I am going to do. I believe that this phrase got its currency from Mr. Hutchins' book of that title. I am sure all he meant by the title was to translate "liberal education"—the word "liberal" connoting "freedom," and "education for freedom" being a possible translation. I am sure there was no political, ulterior purpose in that title.

Some of you may know of the controversy that has been going on concerning an organization called "Education for Freedom, Incorporated." That was a curious kind of organization, which never stated its views very clearly. It was a kind of place of meeting for people who were concerned about American education at the present time. Because some of us at St. John's and Chicago are more vocal about it than others, it came to look as if the organization was an agent of St. John's and Chicago. You may be interested to know that it is probably dissolving at the moment, because of internal disagreements. I think it almost inevitable that it would. It has been rather amusing but a little bit disturbing.

I am not going to talk about St. John's and Chicago, or Education for Freedom, Incorporated. I have taken this opportunity to do a thing which, I realized when I started, I have never done before: I have never talked for an hour about freedom. I would like to talk about freedom for this hour, not because it is an easy topic to discuss;

I have discovered in thinking about it that it is not. I do not suppose human beings know less about anything than they know about freedom, in spite of the fact that it is their most common experience. It is almost like the scandal about sleep in medicine. You know, the doctors have no explanation for sleep, and yet it is a common human experience—or lack of experience.

Well, it is like that with freedom, I think. It is, of course, very difficult to discuss the subject at this particular time, during a war, when opinions about it are pretty heated—and a war which came on us, in some sense, because we were short on freedom. We had forgotten it. I do not think there is any question about our recognizing and loving freedom, but it is a very serious question whether we understand it at all these days. Therefore, "education for freedom" is a phrase that requires clarifying. I am going to see if I can make the idea of freedom a little clearer. I could not possibly do an adequate job, but perhaps I can furnish an emphasis that will start you, as it has started me already, on a kind of speculation and analysis of what we mean by freedom.

Discussions over the past two or three hundred years are notable because of their specific nature, revealing the antithesis of freedom in the minds of the people who discuss it. Take a writer like Spinoza. I think his statement of determinism in the relation of cause and effect—that is, that everything that happens happens of necessity—is one of the clearest statements in the history of thought. Freedom, then, becomes a very serious problem; and you may remember that he denies that man's will is free. We have a strong opinion that our will is free, but that is merely an opinion, and an illusion. On the other hand, he ends with a doctrine of freedom—not freedom of the will, but of human freedom, which I suppose has never been bettered in its clarity and its lyricism: that is, in the real joy that is expressed in it.

Kant did almost the same thing, but with quite a different notion of determinism, and a different basis for it, although with some connection. He stated the doctrine of determinism in such a form that a good many people think he just fooled himself when he afterward talked about freedom. Freedom, he believed, came into human experience because of our living in two worlds: the world of nature and the world of the "kingdom of ends," as he calls it. I think Kant has a real solution for his particular statement of the problem. I will not attempt to state it, because it is difficult and would take too long for this particular occasion. However, there is here a notion of freedom which has a great deal to do with politics—I think, more than Spinoza's notion of freedom; that is, the notion of political freedom can be derived from Kant with the help of Rousseau and some other writers, in a very interesting way.

Our own Founding Fathers, who were very much aware of the problem, were stating their notion of freedom, in so far as they ever defined it, against a doctrine of tyranny. It is in the political field that you find their statement of the issue. I think our institutions are dominated now by a kind of fear of tyranny—a quite justifiable one, but still restricted to that notion rather than extending to any broader conception of human freedom which would go beyond the political realm.

The reason I am saying this is not merely to review the subject for you, but because I think we have a different problem now, and our thinking about freedom will have to go through a complete revision, a ransacking, with perhaps some very shocking turns on the way.

The present threat to freedom has been set up in the very name of freedom. Now, perhaps that has always been so, but I think it is pretty obvious that it is so now. Read the Fascist and Nazi literature, and you find that what they are talking about is freedom. We tend to think that that is all hokum and off the point, but if you notice what is being said—whether they are sincere about it or not—you will see it is the same thing that we are saying about many of our institutions at present.

I have just been reading Lilienthal's account of TVA. I am a little late in reading that. I recommend it to all of you. There is a kind of freedom implicit in what Mr. Lilienthal is talking about in TVA which comes pretty close to what even our enemies are wanting: that is, freedom for groups of people.

We have freedom of assembly in our Constitution, but I think we are a little afraid of groups of people having freedom; in fact, we call that "factionalism" when it happens within our state. When it happens to a nation, and the nation comes under dictatorship, it is a very dangerous thing. And yet, the thing that is being sought there is a thing we are all very much concerned about.

To put it in other terms, our problem of freedom has to be stated against the background of a sense of frustration. I think we all feel as persons, whether we recognize it clearly or not, a degree of frustration. The term I have chosen to use here is taken from psychology, of course; it denotes the Freudian theory of frustration; but I think we find it in our economic and political life. We find it now in our technical organization. The whole problem of monopolies and cartels, of course, arises from frustration of the purpose of technology. I think we experience this perhaps most deeply in our personal and religious life.

I use the word frustration here perhaps not exactly in the Freudian sense; in fact, I am always interested in the word whenever I run across it. It presents an image which you have to look at twice. Frustration, I believe, means making a frustum out of a cone: that is, cutting off its apex. Now, in human activities, I take it the figure of speech means that you have lost the end, you do not know what the end of your activity is; and your frustration, in the sense of the hindrance to action, comes not from lacking the means but from not knowing what the end is.

This is a peculiar way for the problem of freedom to arise. You ordinarily think you are free if you can get the means you require and if you are not hindered from doing what you want to do; but I think this puts the matter in reverse. We do not know what we want to do and therefore we are not free. This is not an original formulation of mine. I have seen it in the literature of the past five or six years. It is pretty common. I wonder if that is not what ought to be talked of now.

I have a thesis which I want to propose to you. You may not accept what I am saying about frustration; but if you will agree on this, we will get closer to our solution of the problem. First, a statement of it, and then, the solution. We will get closer to the solution if we look at the problem as an educational one.

Education has something to do with the discovery of the proper ends of human action. I do not know any other activity that has, unless it is religion. Religion has to do with discovering and preserving such ends, I suppose; but even then, education has to play a large part. This is true in politics, certainly; and I think it is true in individual living. People do not know what they want; and, as long as they do not, they need education of a very special kind—probably liberal education. Liberal education will acquire a new meaning if this is the case. Putting it in other terms that may be less high-sounding, we have got to learn a good deal in order to solve our problem. We must learn, in order to solve this problem, definitely what our ends are.

My hypothesis—very distant in realization but, I think, all-controlling—is the famous quotation from the New Testament, given widest currency in this country, I believe, by Thomas Jefferson: "Ye shall know the truth, and the truth shall make you free." The tenses in that statement are interesting. It does not say that you know the truth and therefore you are free; it says you shall know, and it will make you free. Thus we have it in educational terms.

If I may be allowed, I want very briefly—and I assure you this will be very inadequate—to state what I think the problem of freedom is in religion, in politics, and in personal life.

Some years ago I went to the University of Virginia to teach, and one of my great interests in going there was to learn more about Thomas Jefferson. One does learn a great deal about Thomas Jefferson in Charlottesville; one learns a great deal about the people who have forgotten him; one learns a great deal about the University that was founded by him, and so on. On his gravestone, up in Monticello, he asks to be remembered for three things: the writing of the Declaration of Independence; the bringing of some seeds from France to this country; and the writing of the first article on religious freedom into the University Charter.

He was very proud of this last. It is a great article that he wrote; it has to do, of course, with the freedom of the University from sectarian domination. But it interested me to learn what he really thought about this. There is a very interesting drawing of the campus made by him. He made a great many, as you probably know. Only one was finally used, and I believe the choice was the result of a great deal of discussion and fighting over the different plans. The plan that was chosen was a picture of the "academic village," as he called the central part of the campus. Around the edge of this were religious houses—a dozen of them, I think. They were not on the campus; they were just off it. In fact, they were right on the boundary line. These were to be set up by separate sectarian institutions, and students who were interested in these sects or connected with them were to be allowed to go there. Of course, there were not merely Christian sects; Judaism was represented, and I imagine he would have wanted Mohammedanism and Buddhism, and so on, there. That was the pattern of his thought.

It is an interesting proposal as a solution of our problem of church and state, religion and politics, in this country; it is about the only solution, it seems to me. But what has come of it now? I noted that at the University of Virginia there was perhaps more intense conviction than you will find at other places, but the same conviction found elsewhere, that a university should have nothing to do with religion. Religious freedom had come to mean freedom from religion: no domination by it and no responsibility for it. Now, I do not believe that is what Thomas Jefferson meant. He saw a real problem and he meant that religion should somehow be free; that the university should create freedom for religion.

I have presented this as a problem because I think concern about the relation between educational institutions and religion is very widespread in this country. Our public schools are involved in this issue.

Let me jump to the center of this question, although there is a lot to be said besides. I would like to tell you about the problem at St. John's but there is not time. I think at the center of the problem of freedom for religion is the problem of love—human love. Again, Spinoza seems to me one of the best formulators of this problem. You remember, he begins *The Improvement of Understanding* by speaking about the ends of human life, the *goods*. He talks about pleasures, riches, fame, friends, and the like. These are in some sense unsatisfactory objects of love. They do not last. They are subject to disillusionment and change. Terrible things happen to people who set these things up as their ends. He says that the great problem is to find the proper object of love. Of course, he finds, in the end, what many philosophers before him had found to be true; that is, that the only adequate and proper object of human love is something eternal and unchanging, and therefore dependable. This is not a new discovery but he stated it rather well. I was interested in finding out and reflecting on the other objects besides God that he brings up to satisfy that criterion. As nearly as I can make out, there are three such objects: God, reason, and—what Plato so strongly emphasized—the laws.

I think the most common one of all these adequate objects of human love, the one that has been most widespread and characterizes more schools of thought than anything else, is the laws. This does not mean merely patriotism; it means human reason operating in society, where it can be known and loved.

One of the things said about this object of love is this: "in whose service is perfect freedom." It is a very strange notion: if you give yourself completely to the adequate object of love you find freedom. Now, that is very far from the idea of doing what you want to do, in the ordinary, whimsical sense. It means trying to find something to which you can sacrifice your freedom, and, in so sacrificing, find the thing you are sacrificing. Perfect freedom would be the return for the imperfect freedom you are giving up.

Here is a statement from Cicero about it: "We are all servants of the laws, in order that we may be able to be free." This is nonreligious in form, but I think it contains a religious thought. The highest statement of it, it seems to me, is in the doctrine of the angelic knowledge and in the beatific vision. Angels know God and love him; but there was only an instant in which they had a choice. That was the instant of their creation. They could either choose to know and love God or they could choose not to, but to become demons. As you know, some of them fell, and some of them chose to love God. Their love of God is unchangeable. They have no freedom of choice any longer, but they are free, still, because they have found an adequate object of love. (Now, you may not believe in angels; it is not necessary; you may take this as myth, or as an interesting formulation.) That is one type of freedom. The beatific vision is concerned with the Last Judgment. When human beings are saved, their salvation consists in knowing God and therefore loving Him in a direct and intuitive way, eternally, because they could not possibly wish anything else after they once found the object of all human desire.

This is the positive notion of freedom, it seems to me, and a very puzzling one when you realize how complicated are our problems of freedom in politics and in personal relations. I think we can perhaps get the clearest sense of it when we are in love with someone. The question is: "Is the object of our love worthy of all we are giving?" And of course, if you once get in that mood, you pass into the opposite mood and wonder if you are worthy of the object of your love. I think that puts the problem of freedom in its positive, religious form more clearly than anything else. I am not trying to solve it. I would like to say something later that may have a bearing on how freedom is actualized in the sense of choice, but I will only suggest it now.

I think in this kind of love—of God, or of persons, or of laws—there is always a doubt which puts faith in the place of knowledge. In other words, this kind of freedom is a freedom that comes from believing; it has a tension in it; there is always some doubt about it. Raised to the highest point, of course, as in the case of the angels with beatific vision (mythical, if you like), that doubt disappears. But even then, at one moment there was the possibility of choosing, in the cases both of angels and of men.

In most religions that I know about, God is never in a position of coercing human beings to love Him. He is demanding the freedom that comes from the love of Him. I believe that is deep in religious doctrine.

Let me pass quickly now to political liberty. I want to read you a quotation here from Montesquieu. I found this quotation very disturbing when I first read it, and I have been trying to understand it ever since. I think I understand some of it, and I think it has an important bearing on our contemporary problem of frustration and freedom. "In governments—that is, in societies directed by laws—liberty can consist only in the power of doing what we ought to will." You probably think you mis-heard that. Let me read it again. "In governments—that is, in societies directed by laws—liberty can consist only in the power of doing what we ought to will, and in not being constrained to do what we ought not to will."

Aside from the question whether the word "only" is proper there—that is, whether it consists only in this—let me ask you if it does not remind you of, and describe the feeling you have about, Europe at present. What has been violated in Europe, it seems to me, is people's sense of what they ought to do. What the violence has been doing is making people do things they ought not to will, and also taking away their power of doing what they ought to will. There is a moral sense of freedom, which I think is terribly important and which Montesquieu is stating here for a very specific purpose. This is in the context of his whole discussion of the division of powers in government. If you think of it that way, you will see what he is talking about. If you think of his officers in the government, you will get the idea. Of course, Montesquieu is thinking of citizens as officers, too, and therefore political freedom consists in this nonfrustration of function.

There is a paraphrase of this. I do not know whether it came from Montesquieu or not, but it is a nice rendering of it. "Political liberty is the practicality of social purpose." It is quite characteristic of Dr. Whitehead to use words that way. I take it he means the practicality of doing what you ought to do, socially.

This raises a tremendous problem, of which I can only remind you. I would like to talk about Rousseau in connection with it; that is, Rousseau's doctrine of freedom, which consists in saying that human beings get freedom only when they give up all their freedom to a sovereign, who in turn governs them, and who in turn is their agent. There is in Rousseau a complete political re-forming of personal liberty, the most radical and drastic that I know. It ends in something very close to pure Athenian democracy, with the idea of representation added; that is, the representative agents of the people are the governors.

I think we have to face this problem as one of the most serious. Perhaps some of you know Mr. Meiklejohn's book, *Education Between Two Worlds*. It is chiefly about this problem. If you want a new exposition of Rousseau, a new understanding of him, you may be interested in that book.

Our present problem in this connection, which you are probably thinking of as much as I am, is: "What is happening in Washington at present?" or "What is happening in Albany at present?" Personally, I feel what I might call "the frustration of assent" in relation to what is happening in those places. I am not really disagreeing with what they are doing. I have great sympathy with them in their tasks. I do not know, as a matter of fact, how to agree or disagree.

I know that there are pressure groups in Washington and in Albany, and in various other places. I know that the representatives of the people are thinking of themselves as agents of pressure groups—agents of localities, of interests of one kind or another. Very few of them—there are some, thank God!—are thinking of themselves as representatives of the people in quite another sense. These are the people who realize that they are sent to these places to deliberate about the common good, with all the knowledge that their local experience may give them. They are thinking about the common good; they are in that sense representative intelligences. They are not representative agents, but intelligences. They are our better intelligence working for us about matters that concern everybody.

The term "representative" is very interesting: how one represents, what one should represent, and what the office means, are terribly important questions. I think what is chiefly missing is the idea of the common good. Most people think of the common good as the greatest good for the greatest number. Of course, as I understand it, that is not at all the notion of the common good. Common good is justice. It does, of course, insure the greatest good of the greatest number, but it is in itself a very abstract principle, to be applied to very complicated situations. What is required, both in our representatives and in ourselves—in order to give assent or withdraw it properly—is a certain capacity for abstract thought. I will return to this at the very end of my address. It is involved in the problem of religious freedom, too.

Let me pass on now to personal freedom. I am going right to what I consider the center of it without any discussion of the peripheral problems. Personal, individual, human freedom consists in the power of choosing between alternatives. Now, the conditions are not often seen clearly, but it is obvious that you cannot choose unless you have at least one alternative. Even the situation presented in "Do this, or else—" contains an alternative. But we do not demand that the alternative be clear when we are choosing between goods or courses of action that are widely different in quality.

No, it takes a good deal of imagination, of abstract thinking, to be able to supply ourselves with alternatives on all occasions when we want to be free. I say imagination, because the situation is so stuffy and depressing at times. Most of us in this country are "middle class," as they would call us in Europe. One characteristic of the middle class is that at the age of thirty or thereabouts—at the beginning of middle age—we all think of ourselves as settled. One of the consequences of being settled is that we do not think of alternatives; we think we are doing the only possible thing we can do. Our jobs are like that, and our homes, our social life, our institutions, our religious life—everything. We are not aware that there are always alternatives.

One of the most disturbing things that I have run across in this country is that very few people are aware of the alternatives to anything that a dictator might demand. Some of you probably have read Epictetus, and know the conversation he had with the tyrant.

The tyrant said, "Do as I say, or I will flog you," and Epictetus said, "Go ahead and flog me. I will do what I want to do; I won't do what you want me to do."

The tyrant said, "Do as I say, or I will behead you." Epictetus said, "You can have my head; you can't touch me."

There is always the possibility of a choice. But I think very few people in this country really believe that there is always an alternative to anything they are told to do. Of course, Epictetus's freedom is a very abstract and empty one in the end, as far as this world is concerned. On the other hand, it is, I should say, an essential, abstract principle to grasp if we want to understand human freedom at all.

Some very strange things are encountered in thinking about freedom. In passing from religious freedom to personal freedom, one moves from what might be called "the eternal 'yea,'" in acceptance of the adequate object of love, to an eternal "nay." These are the two marks of human freedom. This is not hard to understand when you realize that in any choice you are choosing something and denying something at the same time. Those are the two acts which have to do with human freedom. In choosing the eternal good, Spinoza was very definitely turning down riches, fame, and pleasures—not necessarily to lose them, but to place them in another relationship.

To sum up, then, it seems to me that religious freedom is concerned with our ends, our ultimate ends, and freedom in respect to them is our ability to find them. They are hard to find, and to keep them in mind after one has found them is even harder. Ends get reduced to means so quickly that we sometimes lose them more easily than we find them.

Political freedom, it seems to me, is chiefly concerned with means, and that is the reason why Montesquieu could make his statement. It means the ability to do what we ought to do. It is expressed in terms of power, of means, of understanding; for political freedom includes economic, technical, and even scientific knowledge. We have to know what the material arrangements are in society which make it possible for us to act together and do what ought to be done; we must have knowledge about nature too, in order to do that.

I have spoken of Mr. Lilienthal's book on TVA. The great defect in that book seems to be that he has no notion of what the end of human society is. In other words, he is short on religious freedom; perhaps not personally, but the book does not deal at all with the purpose of society as a whole. He is very strong on organization of means, and the book is very exciting for that reason. It deals with the agreements which preserve freedom rather than destroy it, even under government control. It is a terribly exciting picture that is presented. The most extraordinary thing I know of at present is the dam on the Dnieper River in Russia, because of its possibilities. But it seems now that the Tennessee Valley has come closer to revealing such possibilities than anything else.

Individual freedom seems to me to reside inescapably in the human intellect. I would like to say something about that. Forgive me if it seems too brief and abstract. Without this the rest of what I have said will not be completely intelligible. The intellect knows what it knows—and that is a good deal—by the use of abstractions. The intellect is part of us, our reason, our power to grasp abstract objects. Here we have "the one and the many"; the common character possessed by a lot of complicated things. This is why it is terribly important in political matters for our representatives to be able to do abstract thinking, and for us to be able to do it: because if we do not, we will never get any clear statement of alternatives in assents and dissents.

But this power of abstraction never realizes itself, never comes into action, without the help of the imagination and of our passions, our appetites, our desires; and, *vice versa,* in human beings, our imaginations and our desires never act in any human way—they may act on a low, automatic level, but they never act in a human way—without the intellect being involved. For that reason, everything in a man is touched by this freedom which is involved in the intellect. The intellect is not a separate power in a man; it is something immanent and permeative throughout all his life and activity. Even our digestions, as some people have said, are different because we have reason within us.

The reason the intellect is the seat of freedom is that it can do something that apparently no other power in nature can do, entertain opposites, contraries, contradictions. In other words, we can put before ourselves alternatives. When you watch animals behave, you imagine they are doing something like that, but it only seems so. Now, a cat, I think, is the most eloquent animal in this respect. A cat sees only one thing at a time. He will watch something for a time and be very much interested, and suddenly his attention is away off to something else. To be sure, people behave like that sometimes, but cats characteristically do it, while human beings, on the contrary, are always seeing one thing in relation to another, as opposites. When they are bereft of all alternatives—as some people in the occupied countries seem to have been, and as we are, at times, here—they then can do what Epictetus did.

You can, it is true, say "No," without its having any particular content that you are aware of at the time. "No" to any order that is given us means, "I can't think now, but I will think of an opposite to this thing." And you can think of it only in terms of the negation that is involved.

Since the intellect alone is capable of this and since it is deeply involved with our imaginations, our appetites, and our desires, in order for it to operate well, there must be training and building up and underpinning for this exercise of choice. It is not easy to find alternatives and to state them in such a form that they are really clear, not false double questions, false imaginings of various kinds. One has to get to a level of abstraction in order to do it; and one cannot do this without training.

Therefore the life of freedom will be a life of learning. Learning is the typical activity of the free mind. To put it the other way, you may say that the intellect is not alive unless it is learning. If this is the case, then education is not just something that would be a good thing to have in the interest of freedom; it is an absolute necessity for freedom. Human freedom cannot be preserved in any effectual way without the continuous processes of education, not merely for children, but for adults. The learning process is, indeed, always going on. I do not mean necessarily formal education. Any institution must have within it the conditions for continuing learning. It must be organized in such a way that people can use their curiosity and think of alternatives, with the power of criticism and dissent that is involved. That is what we mean by democracy.

The kind of learning, however, that is the deepest and the most important is a very painful kind. It is the kind which has often been called "tragic." If people think abstractly, they will go in the direction of an overt intellectualism; they will overintellectualize their lives. They cannot help it. This is not a perversity of academic people; it is a perversity of the ordinary man on the street. As a matter of fact, children and men on the street are much better at abstraction than academic people are. They go off on an abstraction very easily, and find they are wrong. The coming back to reality which is involved in finding oneself wrong is the most fundamental kind of human learning, and is always painful. Disillusionment is one of the perennial fates of human beings.

Well, then, very briefly to summarize all I have been saying: liberal education is necessary for freedom. It consists, not wholly, but mainly, in learning to deal with abstractions—and I mean, not merely to think abstractly, but to deal with the problems with which abstractions confront us, the tragic craziness that is in them that we have to correct. We cannot avoid using them, but we must continually correct them.

The process never ends, because, as a matter of fact, human experience is essentially this; the intellect is always involved in it. Thus human experience takes the form of learning. The time sequence of life is marked by moments of tragic learning, of supposition, action on hypothesis, failure, recognition, correction. It is by reference to these that we can measure human history.

Liberal education, then, continues throughout the life of every individual. To go on to school a while and then, as some ten per cent do, to college, and then have further study and inquiry prevented, as often happens to college graduates, is a terrible, a menacing thing. We will lose our freedom if this continues, it seems to me. We must have, then, not only liberal colleges for everybody; we must have adult education for everybody, of a liberal kind.

In the end, a democracy demands that its government shall be educational. It demands that its government shall be run in such a fashion that everybody in it can learn. That, of course, would be the ideal thing; but, until we accomplish that, I think government must be supplemented by very special institutions to carry on the educative process. It would be grand if we had liberal colleges for everybody, and people's universities for all who are graduated from the liberal colleges, thus carrying on learning throughout life!

XIII

DEMOCRACY IN EDUCATIONAL PRACTICE

BY

HARRISON S. ELLIOTT, Ph.D.

Skinner and McAlpin Professor of Practical Theology and Head of Department of Religious Education and Psychology, Union Theological Seminary

Education in the wider sense of this term involves all of life because there is no aspect of the experience of children, youth, and adults but has its influence. There is truth, therefore, in the statement that the educational process is the experience process. But our topic refers to education in a more restricted sense as applied to the agencies in the community organized for this purpose. Among these the school would probably be considered the primary institution for education, but the family, the church or synagogue, and various community agencies should be included. These agencies differ in that some of them are public and others private. So far as the issues of democracy are concerned, they can be considered together because they are alike in that they have definite educational functions and because they are compassable and can be managed in ways that may be determined.

The educational influence of all of life's experiences can be altered only as changes are effected in our cultural patterns; but homes, schools, churches or synagogues, and community agencies, while they are inevitably influenced by the cultural patterns, are units within which may be developed a distinctive life. They may become experiment centers for ways of living together which are divergent from the commonly accepted standards and practices. This is notably true with reference to democracy. Under the controlled conditions of an educational institution it ought to be possible to attain a greater degree of democracy than has as yet been achieved in our common life. Whether or not this is possible is a crucial issue for the realization of a democratic way of life. If democracy cannot be achieved under the controlled conditions of an educational institution, there seems little hope for developing it in the wider social order.

In considering democracy in educational practice there must be some measure of agreement as to the meaning of the term democracy. It seems to me to be that arrangement of life by which the members of a group, small or large, have the opportunity to participate responsibly and co-operatively, in proportion to their maturity and ability, in deciding, planning, executing, and evaluating all matters in which the group is involved, matters both within the life of the group and in the group's relationship to other groups and to the common life of which the group is a part. Deciding and planning what to do, carrying out these decisions, and appraising the results are the steps in any democratic procedure.

This definition of democracy includes both rights and obligations. In it there are assumptions, first, that any one who is affected by or must carry out a decision or a plan has the *right* to have a voice in making the decision or determining the plan and, secondly, that those who are affected by a decision or a plan have an *obligation* to do their part in putting it into effect.

On this definition of democratic practice it must be admitted that organized education is far from being democratic. Those who are being educated and who carry out what happens in the school, church or synagogue, or community agency, usually have little or nothing to say about what is to be done. They are supposed to participate in carrying out plans and regulations made and evaluated by others. This lack of opportunity to participate responsibly, characterizes both the planning of the program and the determination of the provisions and regulations for the management of the life together in the institution.

Public education is supposed to be the great bulwark of democracy, and yet those engaged in or affected by this enterprise often have little responsible part in determining policy and program. Usually the teachers have an outlined curriculum provided for them and their opportunity for responsible participation is limited to working out methods by which they can teach the assigned subjects. They can vary procedure within a prescribed framework but the course of study, regulations for the general administration of the school, and even the rules of conduct, are often out of their hands. At times the principal and the local board of education are under a required curriculum outlined by a state board of education. The parents of children and the citizens of a community have a stake in education, but, aside from electing a board of education to represent them, they usually have no opportunity for responsibly influencing policies and practices affecting the children of the community. Parent-teacher associations are in most cases used to secure support of what is going on, but very little is being done to relate parents responsibly to the enterprise in which they have a stake because of their children. Sometimes pressure groups are formed of parents or of citizens to try to influence the policies or practices in the schools, but these are very inadequate methods of democratic participation. Certainly in the great majority of schools the pupils, who are the ones most affected by what is happening, have no opportunity for responsible participation in determining program or regulations. They can show their disapproval only by passive resistance, active disorder, or by various methods of "getting by."

The situation is somewhat similar in churches or synagogues and in community agencies. The policy and program in these institutions are usually determined by the administrative officer or officers or by an elected board. At times teachers and leaders participate in determining what shall be done. Often, however, the curriculum is outlined by a national agency and printed curriculum materials are furnished which a local institution is supposed to follow. Parents are usually not related responsibly to the religious education of their children in the church or synagogue, and the only thing they can do is to protest if they do not like what is going on or withdraw their children. The general congregation usually is uninformed about the program provided for children and youth and as a result does not give it adequate support. Children and youth usually have no more part in determining the policy and program than they have in the public school. The adult program is much the same. The minister determines the sermon he will preach without consultation with others. He decides the content of the public worship, or an established ritual is followed. In adult classes or clubs the program is usually developed by some individual or small group and an appeal is made to adults to enroll in the enterprise.

What has been said is also to a great extent true of homes. Children have little or nothing to say about the life in the family. Usually their only participation is in carrying out the arrangements and regulations made by their parents.

No one assumes that democratic procedures can be set up on a dead level so that everybody decides about everything. Participation must be "in proportion to maturity and ability." But even for children there are unutilized areas in which they are competent to participate, and certainly on the high-school, college, and adult-age levels, there is far more capacity for deciding, planning, and evaluating than is now being utilized.

Democratic procedures are important not only in planning program but also in the management of the life of an educational institution. While a school, a church, or a synagogue, or a community agency, is from the viewpoint of the program an alternation from ordinary life activity in order to give the individuals enrolled the help that will enable them to re-enter life experience and carry it on more significantly, it is from another point of view just a continuation of life. Principals, teachers, and pupils are spending time together each school day. While the school is organized to prepare individuals for life outside the school, it is for those in the school during the hours they are there life itself. It is a small and compassable grouping within the larger community in which individuals have to live with each other and in which they face all the problems of living. It is interesting, if not indeed tragic, to note how little advantage is taken of this opportunity for training in democracy. The importance of this opportunity is emphasized by Hollis L. Caswell, who says that "direct provision should be made for democratic organization and direction of the school community. If the school is to be a constructive social force, the beginning in democratic procedure must be made in its own organization." ("Developing the Design of the Curriculum" in *Democracy and the Curriculum,* Harold Rugg, Editor, p. 418,

Ginn & Co.) Dr. Caswell indicates three requirements if the students are to participate democratically in the management of their life together: the operation of the school community must be given a significant part of school time; students must actually be given a determinant part in carrying forward the activities; the areas of democratic control must be extended far beyond disciplinary and similar problems. (P. 419.) There are interesting illustrations of schools in which provision exists for significant participation by the students in the management of the life of the school. (See Koopman, S. Robert, Miel, Alice, and Misner, Paul J., *Democracy in School Administration*, Chapter 7, and *Educational Policies Commission, Learning the Ways of Democracy,* Chapter IV.)

In the efficient practice of democracy a distinction must be made between the formulation of basic purposes and policies and the detailed plans for attaining the purposes and carrying out the policies. Everybody affected should have the opportunity to participate in determining controlling purposes and basic policies; the responsibility for working out the detailed plans in accordance with purposes and policies frequently should be assigned to individuals or smaller groups who have competency in a particular area. For example, if there is to be a social event or a recreational program, all involved in it should determine what kind of social event or recreational program is desired; but the working out of detailed plans should be assigned to committees responsible for making the arrangements. In the same way, what should be the controlling purposes in the curriculum and what kind of program should be developed to attain these purposes are the concern of all involved in the program, and they should have opportunity to participate in making these decisions. Working out the details of the curriculum, selecting curriculum materials, and the like, may be assigned to the teachers and others who are especially competent in this area and who are charged with carrying out the program. They must keep in touch with and report to the larger group to ensure that their detailed plans are in line with the basic purposes and policies.

Democratic planning does not involve ignoring the expert in any field, but it does mean that the function of the expert is different in a democratic institution from what it is under autocratic control. Instead of determining what shall be done, he brings to the planning his wider experience and greater competency in helping those involved to understand the situation and to formulate plans. After policies are determined, his skill is utilized in working out the detailed plans in line with the basic policies. This can be illustrated from a community survey. An expert who is asked to help a community work out its problems, for instance, in an area like delinquency, follows one of two procedures: one autocratic and the other democratic. Under the autocratic procedure he studies the situation, gets at the causes of delinquency, and works out a plan for meeting the problem that the community is supposed to adopt and follow. Under the democratic procedure he works with the community in helping it to study the situation, define the problems, and work out a plan. He also co-operates with reference to ways and means of carrying out the plan. The first method usually fails, since the community neither understands nor believes in the plan proposed because they have had no chance to develop understanding and conviction by participation. Under the second procedure all the experience of the expert is made available, but the plan arrived at has chances of success because the community has helped form it and has some understanding of, and confidence in it.

The difficulty with the present lack of democratic practice is that those related to educational institutions are robbed of participation at the points which are most significant for the development of their competency in democratic responsibilities. A democratic arrangement of life depends upon individuals who have the ability to face situations, understand the problems, determine purposes and goals, and make decisions and plans which will meet the situations and attain the goals. Evaluating the results of these decisions, when they are put into effect, is also essential if progress is to be made. To carry out plans and to follow regulations made and evaluated by others, is to be robbed of experience and training in the most crucial and significant aspects of democratic practice. Indeed it gives training in an autocratic rather than in a democratic way of life. Small wonder that as a result we have so many individuals who are at the mercy of demagogues of various types and are so easily swayed by propaganda. Most serious is the loss, to a great extent, of a golden opportunity for training in democracy. It is not enough that there should be teaching about democracy. Children, young people, and adults "learn the ways of democracy" best by responsible participation in life that is democratically organized.

The present practice is not only undemocratic but inefficient. More is involved than the rights of individuals to have a part in making decisions by which they are affected. Only those who have had a part in making a decision or determining a plan can carry it out intelligently and effectively. Execution of policies cannot be a distinct operation, separated from their formation, if they are to be carried out effectively. L. Thomas Hopkins illustrates this from school systems "where courses of study are made by a small group of individuals, but are put into operation by all teachers of that subject. The intelligence which the committee members developed in the process of formulating the course of study is not transferred to those who will use it by the instrument itself. The result is an unintelligent use of what may have been a highly desirable experience for those who made the course of study" (*Interaction: The Democratic Process*, p. 412, D. C. Heath & Co.). Hopkins says that not even the janitor can do his part effectively in the heating and ventilating of the building unless he has had opportunity to have some understanding of the policies and the program of the school.

This relationship between the formation and the execution of policies has particular importance with reference to regulations of life in an educational institution. Student self-government, when it exists, usually is confined to dealing with minor details or with problems of discipline which emerge within the prescribed regulations. When the regulations are not those which the students believe in because they have helped form them, various methods have to be used to enforce them. Only those regulations will be followed wholeheartedly which the individuals affected by them have helped to form and, therefore, believe in. A law on the statute books which does not represent the will of the people becomes a dead letter, and it is not possible to enforce it. It is not a case of asking children to work out the regulations for their life together without any advantage of the insight and experience of adults. Both teachers and pupils are a part of the school community. It is student-teacher government and not student government which should be developed. But the teachers and the administration must not use the form of democracy as a way of getting assent to their desires. Provision for responsible participation on the part of the pupils is important if the life of the school is to be democratic.

Democratic participation is requisite for the best motivation. When someone else makes the plans, what is in the program often lacks meaning and significance in relation to the "whole of which it is a part" and in relation to life outside of the institution. The best motivation results from seeing the meaning of what is being done in relation to a situation in which one is involved and in relation to a purpose to which one is committed. Without such motivation extrinsic methods have to be used to get individuals to participate in the activity, such methods as competition, awards, grades, or even coercion and punishment.

While teaching about democracy in an undemocratic institution is ineffective, it is also true that democratic practices without opportunity to understand democracy are inadequate. There must be opportunity for consideration of the meaning of democratic experience. It is sobering to note that in life as it is now organized many individuals seemingly would prefer to have somebody else do the deciding for them and are quite willing to carry out the routine assignments made by others. Unless there is an opportunity to consider democracy itself and to make an intelligent decision to engage in democratic procedures, an educational institution may be giving practice in democracy without securing understanding of it or securing commitment to it as a way of living. Consequently, there must be full opportunity to consider what is involved in democracy and to come to personal judgments in regard to a democratic way of life. This may be provided incidentally in connection with the program and the management of the school, or there may be related groups or classes in which democracy is considered. In these ways those who engage in a democratic enterprise will have opportunity to develop a democratic philosophy.

Democracy as interpreted in this address goes beyond a "representative" form of life. Our government was developed on a representative basis. At the time our Founding Fathers initiated the enterprise of free government, they did not have faith that the rank and file of the people had competence democratically to determine what should be done. They did feel that they might be competent to select individuals who would make the decisions for them. Even the election of the President was not left to popular vote, but the people were given the right to select a Board of Electors to decide who should be the President. This representative form of government is about as far as democracy usually is developed. Boards of education are elected to determine educational policy for the school. Boards and committees are selected by congregations to determine what shall be done in the church or synagogue. Student self-government usually means the election of students to form a council which will decide what should be done. If the full significance of democracy is to be realized, provision must be made to go beyond a representative form of government to one in which the rank and file of the people have a significant part. This is not impossible in any educational institution. It need not be done just by mass meetings; any issues of basic policy can be considered in various groups or classes in the institution. After this small-group consideration there can either be a general meeting or individuals can be selected who have participated in the smaller group discussions and who can truly represent the points of view of their constituency.

The significance of full democratic participation in the school and in the church or synagogue is evident. At present the rank and file of the members are not really responsible either for policy and program or for the management of the institution. As a result they do not feel themselves vitally a part of it. This is notably true of children who are being brought in to be educated so that later they may take their place as members. Unless they can participate significantly as children in relation to the institution as a whole and feel themselves a part of it, they are not receiving the best training for adult responsibility. The comment of Paul R. Hanna is pertinent: "With no sense of belonging to a great enterprise which demands their loyalty and their labors, with no responsibility for making a contribution to the larger group, the young develop few of those character traits which are so essential and basic in a highly interdependent modern society" (*Youth Serves the Community,* p. 33).

What has been discussed has religious implications. Democracy is not to be identified with that "Kingdom of God" which is the hope of Jews and Christians alike. It does, however, represent the arrangement of life most nearly embodying the values which the followers of these faiths cherish and the conditions under which the religion in which they believe has the best chance of being developed. Democracy, along with the Hebrew-Christian tradition, places its emphasis upon the worth of the individual and respect for him. It seeks to ensure the rights of individuals, but it goes beyond individual rights and provides for ways of living together in mutual respect and co-operative endeavor toward common goals in which these values of life are embodied. Democratic functioning provides a means for human beings to use their freedom for individual growth and for human welfare.

XIV

DEMOCRATIC CONCEPTIONS OF AUTHORITY, REVELATION, AND PROPHECY

BY

F. ERNEST JOHNSON, D.D.

The ideas that furnish the content of this lecture will be considered in a religious context and with reference to the basic problem of democracy: how to reconcile freedom with order and law. Authority is the key concept; revelation and prophecy must be considered in terms of their bearing upon authority within a framework of democratic assumptions.

At the outset we are confronted by the question whether authority, as expressed in religious systems, is compatible with any genuine conception of democracy. Merely to raise the question is to distinguish between authority and authoritarianism, for the latter by definition is in contrast to the democratic principle. The tendency to identify the two is responsible for no end of confusion, in secular as well as in religious thinking. Authority is a prerequisite of order and is as relevant to a democratic society as it is to any other. Authoritarianism connotes a particular way of meeting the requirement of authority in which the bearer of it tends to be singular and isolated and the method of its administration tends to be prescriptive and arbitrary. A democratic conception of authority places primary emphasis not upon the bearer but upon the people in whose interest it is exercised. Authority is conceived not as wielded by persons who hold it as a prerogative, but as appropriated by persons who utilize it for the ordering of their lives. "Authority," says Chester I. Barnard, "is another name for the willingness and capacity of individuals to submit to the necessities of co-operative systems" (*The Function of the Executive*, p. 184, Harvard University Press).

It should go without saying that religious systems, both historical and contemporary, present many examples of these opposing views of authority and of attempts to mediate between them. There are types of religious doctrine and organization that can be reconciled with democracy only by tortuous rationalization. On the other hand, there are democratic implications in some of those religious formulations and practices that are commonly dismissed as undemocratic. The ancient Hebrew theocracy is a case in point. It merits study today because it is in the line of both Christian and Jewish inheritance and because there is in modern political theory and practice a counterpart, often unrecognized, of the ancient theocratic principle. The subordination of human purposes, as expressed in society, to divine sanctions, served to place all political action in a perspective transcending the immediate present and thus to give a quality of permanence to the value judgments expressed in political action. When former Chief Justice Hughes in his famous dissent from the ruling opinion in the McIntosh case, declared that men have always recognized a loyalty higher than that directed toward the state, he was making recognition of this principle of transcendence.

A glance at Hebrew history is instructive at this point. In the eighth chapter of the First Book of Samuel occurs an account of the institution of the monarchy. It undoubtedly belongs to a late period and reflects a judgment which matured long after the event. But it illuminates the theocratic conception. In dramatic fashion the struggle of Samuel with the people is portrayed. They wanted a king and his protests against such apostasy were of no avail. Then he cried unto Jehovah, only to be instructed to do what the people said. " 'Hearken unto the voice of the people in all that they say unto thee: for they have not rejected thee, but they have rejected me, that I should not reign over them' " (I. Samuel, 8.7). Warn them first, was the divine command, but do what the people say. And how Samuel warned them! No modern revolutionary protest against tyranny is more eloquent in its indictment. " 'This will be the manner of the king that shall reign over you: he will take your sons, and appoint them for himself, for his chariots, and to be his horsemen; and some shall run before his chariots. And he will appoint his captains over thousands, and captains over fifties; and will set them to plow his ground, and to reap his harvest, and to make his instruments of war, and instruments of his chariots'" (I. Samuel 8.11, 12). All this and more, the prophet declared, the monarch would do, yet the people were unmoved from their purpose. And so Jehovah sadly instructed Samuel, "'Hearken unto their voice, and make them a king.'"

It has seemed strange to me that this, no doubt highly idealized, account should not have been regarded as an explicit sanction of what we would today regard as a democratic principle. Samuel was not instructed to wash his hands of the stiff-necked people and leave them to their own devices. Not at all. The king they chose in their rebellious act was nevertheless the "Lord's annointed." The people must have their way.

The monarchic principle, as developed under religious sanction, has probably never been free from democratic elements. The development of the doctrine of the divine right of kings was in some sense a historical accident, serving as a means to securing the sovereign independence of the nation states that arose upon the dissolution of the Roman Empire. Progressive limitation of kingly prerogatives has been demanded in the name of God and the people. Magna Charta, forced from King John in 1215, was addressed to the archbishops, bishops, and abbots of the Church as well to the earls and barons and other secular personages. It declared that the rights prescribed within it were granted "by divine impulse, and for the salvation of our soul" and "for the honor of God, and the exaltation of Holy Church." The Catholic doctrine of monarchical sovereignty maintains the line of authority not directly from God to the king, but from God to the people and thence to the king. Modern constitutional monarchies recognize the ultimate sovereignty of the people, under God. The founding of our Federal Union was the outstanding illustration in modern times of the theocratic principle in a democratic structure. It is difficult to locate and define any typically Protestant conception of political authority, as it is to fix upon any typically Protestant conception of spiritual authority. It seems safe to say, however, that the Protestant churches have, like the Catholic Church, regarded governments when duly constituted as having divine sanction. "The powers that be," said Saint Paul, "are ordained of God."

But, except for the aberration that for a time sustained the spurious doctrine of the divine right of kings, Protestant thought has fitted into the mold of constitutional government, affirming, in effect, that the reasoned judgment of men living in community is the only instrumentality for validating political mandates. It is a pity that what is implicit in the acceptance by religious men of constitutional government is not often made explicit; namely, the divine right of the people. No doubt, the dictum, "The voice of the people is the voice of God," is less than true in an absolute sense. But the voice of the people is the only voice through which the sovereignty of God can be actualized in political affairs, once the constitutional principle is accepted. For one who stands in the Judeo-Christian tradition, democracy becomes a faith in the people as the authentic bearers of authority, a conception given classic expression in Lincoln's phrase, "This nation under God."

It is necessary, however, to push our exploration further, for the question insistently arises whether the concept of democracy is relevant to religious institutions. Here no generalization is possible, for the answer given is sometimes No, sometimes Yes, and sometimes it is evasive. To the extent that the church is conceived as embodying final and absolute authority, it would seem gratuitous to attempt to find any significant applicability to it of the democratic principle. I am told by Catholic friends that their church does not hold that democracy is applicable to its organization and government. On the other hand, Catholics affirm the validity of secular democratic government when constitutionally established—reserving, as do Protestants and Jews, the right of resistance to government on religious grounds.

Among the Protestant churches there is a widespread tendency to accommodate both doctrine and discipline to democratic assumptions; that is, to locate authority in the congregation or in the denominational body. This means, in theory at least, the laicizing of control. The Protestant principle of a universal priesthood has an obvious relation to the democratic principle, though with this important difference from the secular conception: it is not all men, but "all believers" who are priests in their own right. Not man in general, but redeemed man is a participant in this distributive sovereignty, so to speak, in spiritual affairs. There is more than a technical theological significance in the distinction. For it denotes capacity for participation in a spiritual community. This is, ethically speaking, the counterpart of that fitness for participation in the political community at which democratic education aims. I may remark in passing that the weakness of democracy in all its empirical forms centers in the unfitness of the average individual to participate in communal life at a level that insures order and progress. In an important sense the task of democratizing life is one of developing the kind of person who can be entrusted with responsibility in a free society. Perhaps the major contribution that religion can make to the growth of political and social democracy is in the development of the type of personality which it presupposes.

The limitations of organized religion in respect to the application of democracy to its own corporate life, I shall not pursue further. This subject will be discussed in a later lecture in this course.

This brings us to the question of the traditional vehicle of religious authority—revelation. I am not aware that anyone has attempted formally to reconcile the concept of revelation with a democratic philosophy. Broadly speaking, such accommodation as has taken place has been in the nature of a delimitation of spheres. Our religious traditions make much of the "givenness," so to speak, of basic religious truth. However, there are many Protestants who believe in the "progressive character of revelation" as against the concept of a "once-for-all given." It is probably safe to say that the progressive element here recognized has its locus in the development of the recipients, which continually alters the "record" of what is conceived as revealed, and of the understanding of it. Thus the student of scripture is continually applying the scholars' criteria of authenticity, and the use and interpretation of creeds are characterized by selective emphasis determined by the historical situation. It may be contended, of course, that since the record is the only concrete and objective datum of revelation, recognition of its changing character is equivalent to abandoning altogether the idea of an authentic revelation. Many oppose the progressive view on this ground. But its defenders are prepared to assert that revelation is no less definitely given merely because it is not once-for-all given. They insist that God reveals Himself in history. They differ as to whether this revealing is in the nature of an *invasion* or of a *pervasion*, but they all presumably find in it an intention.

The problem presented here may be stated thus: Is there a valid sense in which the idea of revealed truth is consistent with the democratic notion that ultimate authority resides in the people? And if so, does it require a restatement either of the concept of revelation or of the concept of democracy? Discussion of the question is bound to be inconclusive because neither concept in the present state of intellectual discourse furnishes a fixed point of reference. But the subject should not, I think, be avoided on that account.

Considering first the nature of revelation it seems clear that the more rigid traditional conception of it cannot be reconciled with any recognizable formulation of the democratic principle. The passive reception of a given truth, apart from a context of human activity and without co-operative participation in its discovery and interpretation, admits of no application of democracy in idea or in fact. The question, then, is narrowed to the modified concept of revelation to which I have referred. It seems clear that the "progressive" element that has entered into modern definitions of revelation definitely appeals to democratic sanctions. For the criteria of its determination are applied by corporate judgment that rests upon cumulative religious experience. Indeed, wherever the conciliar principle is applied in the prescription of beliefs, a democratic sanction is being appealed to. Thus even the most orthodox of churchmen have had to submit, willy-nilly, to decision by preponderant opinion as to just what God has said! It is strange that the settlement of great historic theological controversies by majority vote in church councils, should not have been more clearly seen as an inevitable recourse to democratic procedure.

Now, the fact that corporate bodies have to determine by the use of intelligence and conscience what the content of revelation is, results inevitably either in the negation of revelation or in the recognition of plural revelations. In his stimulating book, *The Meaning of Revelation*, H. Richard Niebuhr elaborates a "two-aspect" theory of history, in which a distinction is drawn between history as seen objectively and "our history," both of which are authentic in their own way. Revelation belongs to the latter category. Thus "we can speak of revelation only in connection with our own history without affirming or denying its reality in the history of other communities into whose inner life we cannot penetrate without abandoning ourselves and our community. The two-aspect theory allows us to understand how revelation can be in history and yet not be identifiable with miraculous events as visible to an external observer and how events that are revelatory in our history, sources of unconquerable certainty for us, can yet be analyzed in profane fashion by the observer."

An obvious criticism evoked by this, to my way of thinking, highly discerning statement is that Mr. Niebuhr has thrown out the baby with the bath. Many persons, among them both theologians and secular thinkers, will say that to admit the limited authority of a revelation is to surrender all that entitles it to that name. But is there not a fallacy in this? Continuity in human thought and communication would be destroyed by a reckless semanticism that calls for the abandonment of terms whenever their meaning is greatly altered. Mr. Niebuhr's discussion is pertinent here for two reasons. First, it deals with a *given* toward which the life of a group is oriented and by reference to which the experience of its members is interpreted. Thus to each member something is revealed that is beyond his individual, private competence to discover, something that is ultimate for him and for the fellowship to which he belongs. He believes that God has spoken to him and to his fellows a word that is authentic *for them*. Because of this reference to an ultimate spiritual source outside the group, the concept of revelation still applies, though the element of exclusiveness has disappeared. Secondly, this reference of revelation to a "confessional" group accents the empirical factor and makes the group the custodian of the revelation, which originated in the religious experience of the community. Group process is involved all the way. It would seem obvious that all this has meaning only for a democratic community; or at least that its significance increases with the democratic character of the community.

But if the relevance of democracy to revelation is deemed established in this way, is any modification of the conventional meaning of democracy involved? Only, I think, in the sense that a religious conception of democracy always differs from one that rests on no religious assumptions. Much confusion exists, I think, on this point. I have repeatedly said that a religious man has no right to claim that an avowed religious belief is essential to sincere devotion to the democratic way of life. But the ground of a wholly secular devotion to democracy is not identical with that which underlies the religious commitment. In the former case there is no appeal to cosmic support for faith in democracy. In the latter there is. In both cases faith is placed in a community of intelligence and good will, but the religious man grounds that faith in a divine destiny which the community of men is actualizing. The religious man who believes in the viability of democracy maintains that faith because he believes that humanity, by virtue of being human, is actualizing a purpose that informs all history. This enables him to believe in man. The thoroughgoing secularist, in the philosophical sense, feels no need of such cosmic support for a belief in the democratic principle. This, I think, is the ultimate distinction between a religious and a purely secular conception of democracy.

I am aware, of course, that, from a theological point of view, this discussion is an oversimplification and that, even so, it would be regarded by many theologians as less than accurate. What I have tried to do is to prick out the boundaries of a conception of revelation that recognizes its authentic meaning but to which the concept of democracy is in some important sense relevant, and at the same time to show that this relevance does require that the democratic concept be given some transcendental reference. But the latter assumption in no way limits co-operation for democratic ends between those who hold it and those earnest defenders of democratic institutions who have a different philosophic outlook.

I cannot forbear saying, however, that the ardent defenders of democracy on the basis of a thoroughgoing secular philosophy, have not taken seriously enough the task of making explicit the grounds of their belief. That the workings of the democratic theory are susceptible of experimental testing should go without argument. When the goods of life are agreed upon, many objective criteria appear by which to judge the procedures aimed at their attainment. This is true, by the way, of religion, and no religious person should object to the scientific testing of the techniques religion employs in the effort to develop the kind of individual and group behavior that it holds to be worthful. But the great moral imperatives under which a human being stands have to be responded to in an awful present, long before any conclusive experimental test of consequences can be applied. Men do not act courageously and sacrificially on the basis of a cool calculation of the probabilities. They act on a conviction that they *ought* so to act. There is no present validation of such momentous choices except the faith that is in them. The secular literature of democracy abounds in references to the democratic faith. I suggest that this is a blind sort of reference to an essentially religious conviction. There is something implicit here about the permanence of values that the religious man makes explicit as divine intention.

In his introduction to the late Carl Becker's book, *Freedom and Responsibility* (A. A. Knopf & Co.), Professor Sabine gives his interpretation of the philosophy of that great historian. For him, he says, "Faith in the ideals of democracy was of a piece with a larger faith, unfolding perhaps through the ages but certainly contained in the moral insight of the saints and sages, which was the clue to all that made life worth living." I have more than a suspicion that the average "secularist" harbors a faith whose outreach he shrinks from gauging. There is unfinished business here for the exponent of democracy who repudiates all religious sanctions.

Perhaps that is a digression; I do not know. At any rate, I will let it stand. The exposition offered in this address is not dependent on it, but to my mind it points up the experience which the religious man calls revelation.

I come now to the question whether prophecy as conceived in the Jewish and Christian religions is susceptible of a democratic interpretation. It should go without saying that I am not talking about prediction, which is a merely incidental aspect of prophecy in the scriptural sense, not an essential part of it. By prophecy, I mean the utterance of what the prophet believes to be the word of God directed at a particular human situation and at a level of historical significance.

Conceptions of Authority, Revelation, and Prophecy

Typically it involves a critical encounter with tradition and conventional moral judgments. The prophet stands "against the world." Thus the prophetic utterance seems at first blush a strikingly individual affair. The prophet seems to be laying claim to a special and private sanction. This is something quite different from the "revelation" we have been discussing at just that point, for the prophet seems to be standing *outside* the stream of communal experience in which revelation, as I have sought to interpret it, resides. Yet in reality I think this is a misconception of prophecy. I said in my last year's lecture in this series that prophecy is more than proclamation, and I should like to elaborate that statement here.

In the first place, let us note that Biblical history records the activity of false prophets as well as true prophets. Now what are the criteria of false prophecy? Certainly not the quality of intention, though evil intention obviously vitiates the utterance. A false word may be spoken in grand sincerity, as we all know. Nor is the contemporary judgment of those to whom the word is spoken a test of its validity, though this has a certain negative significance, for, if the prophet spoke what the majority of his hearers approved, we would not call him a prophet. Perhaps we might call him just an ordinary preacher! I submit that the only way the false prophet may be trapped is by the application of a social test—the verdict of history. When his utterance fails of confirmation in the developing conscience of the people, he is condemned. Theoretically, he may have been right, even though succeeding generations never validated his judgment. But this is to assume that history is wrong, that God has lost control of human destiny, and that would be a denial of religious faith.

Conversely, the criteria of true prophecy must be sought in the conscience of the community. It is only there that validation of the utterance can be realized. It may be a long time coming. It is the prophet's business to be scornful of time. But ultimately history brings him into his own. Is it not clear, then, that the true prophet stands firmly in the communal life, that his words are true because more deeply than others he has penetrated the meaning of human experience? If he stands alone, it is because the multitude itself is blind to the deepest realities of its own life.

But how does the prophet arrive at his insights? We who believe firmly in the techniques of religious devotion cannot fail to stress the inner resources of living—prayer, meditation, contemplation. We believe that moments of deliberate detachment from the temporal enable one the better to transcend the limitations of existence and attach himself to the timelessly worthful. The prophet must cultivate the sense of the eternal. Yet techniques of detachment may yield only mystical absorption and isolation. What the prophet speaks to men must spring from an intimate knowledge of human experience. He becomes the voice of the people's conscience. If he stirs them at all, it is because they sense an irresistibly authentic quality in his words. They are compelled to listen to him even though they may bitterly resent his denunciations and his admonitions. He is really appealing to something to which the voice of their own conscience says, Yea—though their stubborn wills may say, Nay. The appeal of the prophet is to what is deepest in the moral life of the community. He stands among the people and speaks not what they want to hear, but what in their sober reflection they know they ought to be willing to hear. Or if they are too deeply at war with their own best traditions, another generation, having rediscovered its heritage, will speak the confirmatory word. Such, at least, is the faith on which prophecy rests.

All this has important implications for a prophetic ministry in church and synagogue in our time. The man who would be a true prophet must be immersed in the spiritual tradition of his people. All too typically the minister is immersed in the temporal affairs, the immediate concerns, the ambitions and material involvements of his people. This makes him heir to a spiritual deficit rather than a spiritual heritage. The prophetic minister is truly representative of his people not in the sense of speaking their present mind for them but of making articulate those moral judgments and spiritual aspirations which arise out of their religious heritage and stand over against the temporal preoccupations of the moment.

It has been well said that the ordinary conception of representation in a democracy is erroneous. The representative of the people is no more than a robot if he represents only what is at the moment articulate and what is dominant. His business as a representative is to employ the detachment which his office allows for discovering the deeper meanings and continuing significance of day-to-day events in their relation to the enduring convictions and long-range commitments of the people he represents. This applies with especial force to the ministerial office. Again and again it will happen that in order to speak an authentic word, one that his hearers will increasingly cherish, he must say what at the moment is unwelcome for the very reason that he is the voice not of their ephemeral wants but of their continuing needs. It is not that he substitutes his judgment for theirs. Rather he makes it his business to articulate what he is able more quickly than they to discern as the true meaning of their spiritual strivings.

There is, then, no prophecy that does not rest upon what may truly be called a democratic principle. It springs from the communal life and gets its effective validation in the collective conscience of the community.

XV

DEMOCRACY AND ETHICAL REALISM

BY

JUSTIN WROE NIXON, D.D.

William Newton Clarke Professor of Christian Theology and Ethics, Colgate-Rochester Divinity School

In this discussion the term "democracy" represents the type of state in which government rests upon the support of a popular majority and exercises its powers under constitutional limitations that protect the rights of individuals and minority groups. The term "realism" has been used to describe views opposed to idealism in philosophy and romanticism in literature. In ordinary speech it is supposed to stand for a sobering estimate of the actualities of life as against fantasies of wishful thinking. The value of a term with such varied meanings is somewhat doubtful.

Nevertheless, the intention of those who framed this topic for our consideration is clear. Democracy, in America at least, is correlated with certain ethical views of human nature. As democrats we believe in the inherent dignity of man, which signifies that we regard men primarily as ends rather than means. We believe that men, by and large, have the capacity for self-development. Accordingly, we believe in liberty and equality. And because men develop their capacities best in a society characterized by consent rather than coercion, we believe in fraternal approaches to human problems. The democratic vision is the vision of a society where each individual has the largest possible opportunity to develop his talents in free co-operation with his fellows, who enjoy a similar opportunity.

But in practice the realization of the democratic vision is frustrated at many points. In practice men frequently do not co-operate as equals but use one another as superiors use inferiors. In practice some men have much liberty, others are hemmed in and thwarted by law and custom. In practice men are subject to many varieties of coercion, both within and without the law.

So there are gaps between the ethical ideals we profess and the actualities we face. The task of an ethical realism is to try to understand these gaps, and to enquire to what extent and by what means they can be bridged. Within the limits of this discussion we shall try only to call attention to some of the reasons for these gaps and to make a few suggestions as to the strategy to be employed in dealing with them.

I

First, let us look at this democratic state of which we are members and enquire what it is basically. Then let us ask what is the nature of the political ideals which are at variance with many of the practices of people within the state.

This democratic state, we would say quite arbitrarily, is basically a system of political power in more or less equilibrium. How does such a system of power emerge in human society? We would answer that the fundamental reason for its emergence is the existence of conflict between the desires of individuals and groups within the society.

There are certain persistent desires that appear in the conduct of men in western society, as it has developed over several millennia. There is the desire to exist, of which one may become conscious when one's life is at stake, a desire that may be so powerful that it will largely blank out the pain as a wounded man drags himself to safety across a battlefield. There is the desire for security in respect to whatever seems essential to life; food, habitat, occupation, the integrity of one's culture or nation. There is the desire for growth, for expansion in the use of one's capacities and in the pleasurable release of one's energies, a desire that is evident in all phases of the development of civilization. There is the desire for deference and social approval which easily becomes a desire for recognized superiority over others. The circumstances that secure deference for an individual differ from age to age and region to region, but the desire for deference itself is deeply rooted. And there is the desire to manipulate, manage, and master. Mastery is more complex than manipulation (especially the mastery of men), but the word stands for an urge we see in many powerful individuals.

These desires, as sources of social conflict, are described variously in the writing on this subject. Mark May says that the two things for which human beings will compete most keenly are possessions and prestige. Harold Lasswell suggests that income, deference, and safety are the rewards most sought after in our own society and that frustration at any of these points is serious. That is why the members of the lower-middle class, "the people who have some but not much income, deference, and safety and are struggling desperately to improve their status," are so prominent in aggressive social movements.

Moreover, these desires exist in individuals and groups in varying strength. Some are avid in their desires and press on relentlessly for ever-larger satisfaction. Others seem to acquiesce rather easily in conditions of great deprivation, as among the outcasts of India. Even the primary desire, the desire to exist, may be neutralized by the death-wish.

And the ways in which these desires express themselves, even when they are strong, differ to a marked degree. There may be direct, militant efforts to satisfy them, or indirect, long-circuited efforts. There is an immense amount of imagined compensation for the failure to achieve normal satisfactions, as in millennial movements. There may be deflections of desires and their discharge in unusual channels as in the contribution of sexual impulses to mystical states and humanitarian enthusiasms. There may be the multiplication of lodges and fraternities to atone for lack of recognition in economic and public affairs.

Now if human existence is to be tolerable, there must be established some kind of equilibrium among the desires of the individuals and groups that are in conflict. The achievement of this equilibrium is a primary objective of government. If these desires could be adjusted by agreement, or as the authors of the Federalist papers put it, "if men were angels, no government would be necessary."

The responsibility of achieving and maintaining this equilibrium draws the other essential characteristics of government after it. It must have the authority to draw up rules (laws) which limit and guide the actions of men where interests are in conflict, and to decide disputes which threaten disorder. It must have the power to give effect to its decisions, which means that it must have a monopoly of the use of force. (The collapse of the government of the Weimar Republic was due in part to the fact that its hold on the dominant force in that society, the army, had become uncertain.)

But no government can maintain itself permanently by force alone. It must begin to rely as soon as possible on habits of acquiescence on the part of the people in the rules of government. And acquiescence is willing in proportion as these rules are felt to serve the common interest or the common good. When the rules of government are no longer regarded as imposed by naked force to serve the special interests of a dominant group but as designed to serve the common good, then we have "justice" as distinguished from "power."

The common good appears repeatedly in history as the ultimate test of law and justice. It is the constant emphasis of St. Thomas Aquinas. It was the burden some time ago of an address by Professor Llewellyn of Columbia University at the Colorado Law School in which, referring to the work of the best lawyers of the past, he said: "Right and justice as they saw it had a rounded basis, it had a rooting in the felt interest of a whole." "Law work is not right work unless it makes sense for the whole as a wise man sees the whole." "The people have a deep and sure feeling about what law is for . . . it is for the whole and not for any single part or party."

Such is justice in theory. In practice it is never quite so perfect. In practice justice never entirely escapes the pressure of the special interests whose conflicts it is supposed to resolve in terms of the common interest or good. The rules of justice in any society that is a going concern have been made in part by dominant special interests; the interests of groups who have tended to think, as Nietzsche pointed out, that what is good for them is good for all. Justice in practice, accordingly, is relative to the *power* organization of a society. That is why Thrasymachus can argue in *The Republic* that "justice is the interest of the stronger," and why we have the proverb "might makes right."

We would not deny that other factors have entered into the making of the democratic state besides these desires whose conflicts compel men to seek an equilibrium through government. There are altruistic as well as egoistic elements in human nature, and the genius of man may enchannel a great variety of co-operative impulses through governmental administration. A government, accordingly, may become the educator of its people, the conserver of their culture, and increasingly the guarantor of the conditions of their economic well-being.

Here we are only concerned to point out that if we are seeking to understand the gap between the ethical ideals professed by the citizens of a democratic state and the actualities of practice, we must begin by realizing that the state itself—the political order—is not created by laying down certain ethical principles or ideals and then erecting a structure of power upon them. It is basically a structure of power consisting of forces operating in some sort of equilibrium.

This view of the state is supported by Emil Brunner in such words as the following: "The State is primarily not a moral institution, but an irrational product of history." ". . . It is 'there,' given, as a bit of the historical natural world in which we have been placed." "No state has ever sprung from the 'principles of justice.' But the existence of law always presupposes the existence of the State." This view is also in line with that of the late Archbishop of Canterbury, William Temple. "It has to be recognized," he said, "that society is made up of competing centers of power, and that the separate existence of contending vitalities, and not only human sinfulness, makes the elimination of power impossible. What has to be aimed at is such a distribution and balance of power that a measure of justice may be achieved even among those who are actuated in the main by egoistic and sinful impulses. It is a modest aim, but observance of political life leaves no doubt that this must be its primary concern."

II

So much for the nature of the state. Let us now ask what is the basic nature of the ideals that both inspire and rebuke our practices in the democratic state. What are these ideals of liberty, equality, and fraternity, or brotherhood? Again let us answer quite arbitrarily. These ideals are symbols drawn from the store of humanity's aspirations that have served the interests of particular groups of men in their struggle for a fuller life.

In form the ideals of liberty, equality, and fraternity are very old. They are rooted in the experiences of groups of kin around the world. They have been sanctioned by the teachings of philosophy and religion. Thus they belong to the common fund of things approved and honored by multitudes of people in western society.

But while these ideals appear now as universal abstractions, approved by almost everyone, they have come to the political influence they enjoy because they have been of value to specific groups of people struggling against specific oppressions and for specific advantages. Men fought against the arbitrary disposal of their persons and properties without due process of law. They fought against arbitrary taxation. They fought the intolerances that put their own faith at a disadvantage. They fought the trade restrictions of the mercantile system. They fought educational and political disabilities based on religion, sex, and race. They opposed the undue advantage enjoyed by the corporation in making agreements with single employees. We call this the struggle for "liberty." Actually it was a series of struggles for specific "liberties" that were of advantage to specific groups in improving their lot in life.

That "liberty" as an ideal rested upon the efforts of groups in behalf of their own "liberties," was clear to the framers of our Constitution. "In a free government," said James Madison, "the security for civil rights must be the same as that for religious rights. It consists in the one case in the multiplicity of interests, and in the other in the multiplicity of sects. The degree of security in both cases will depend on the number of interests and sects."

In the history of labor legislation the same connection between ideals and group pressures can be observed. William M. Leiserson, recently Chairman of the National Mediation Board, points this out in a discussion of how the employees of the railroads won the right to organize. The decisions of the Supreme Court, in such cases as

Adair *v.* the United States and Coppage *v.* Kansas, had seemed to deny the workers any legal claim to this right. So the workers said that the only way they could secure this right was to strike and tie up the commerce of the country. This they proceeded to do. What was the result? The train-service men—the engineers, firemen, and conductors—won the right to organize. Then Mr. Leiserson comments, "The other employees could not organize so easily. If the clerical employees or maintenance-of-way employees went on strike, that would not stop the trains from running, but if an engineer and conductor stopped, the trains would be stopped. So these train-service men won the right of organization by wars and threats of wars, and the others did not [at this stage] because they were in no position to wage wars."

The dependence of ideals for their effectiveness on the practical support that can be enlisted for them we do well to remember, when we are developing a charter of freedom for the whole world. Many are advocating, for instance, an international Bill of Rights. Sumner Welles says that this Bill of Rights "must guarantee for every individual of every race and creed in all countries the fundamental rights of life, liberty, and the pursuit of happiness." He maintains further that "no plea of sovereignty shall ever again be allowed to permit any nation to deprive those within its borders of those fundamental rights on the claim that these are matters of internal concern."

It is difficult to see how anyone with a democratic outlook could fail to want what Mr. Welles wants—the freedom of all men everywhere to worship in accordance with the dictates of their consciences and to have access to political, educational, and economic opportunities without regard to race or creed. We want that for Roman Catholics in Russia, for Jews in Germany, and for Protestants in Spain. But candor compels us to ask how valuable such a declaration of rights will be without the pressure of specific groups of people brought to bear at points where it can be transformed into some kind of political power.

The career of the Negro in America since the war of '61–'65 compels us to raise this question. The Negro has had the benefit of our own Bill of Rights embodied in the first ten Amendments to the

Constitution. In addition, he has had the special protection of the Fourteenth and Fifteenth Amendments, which were supposed to prevent any interference with his rights as a citizen and a voter. Everyone is aware of how these guarantees have been disregarded over wide areas. But now we are beginning to see something different. The Negro vote has been growing steadily in the northern industrial states and that vote is being used with balance-of-power tactics to secure the attention of politicians for the Negro's neglected rights. The effect of this growth in the political power of the Negro is being felt all over the Union and on many different issues.

Another illustration of the relationship between the effectiveness of an ideal and its utility to groups seeking practical ends, appears currently in the revived interest in the Kellogg-Briand Pact of 1928 for the outlawry of war. For years the Pact was a dead letter. It was regarded with contempt and observed only in the breach. Now it comes to life because in it is found a legal basis for the trial of war criminals at Nuremberg. The victorious powers now really need the Pact. If they continue to feel the need of it and the treaty becomes a valuable instrument of policy, the date of its signing may still become one of the great dates of history.

But is there nothing in an ideal but an "instrument of policy"? Is there nothing in the ideal of "liberty," for instance, but the pressure of specific groups for release from specific frustrations? On the assumption of a negative answer to these questions how can we explain the fact that such groups are always stating their aims in a generalized form? The Declaration of Independence is filled indeed with denunciations of specific acts of oppression, and the colonists were reaching out for the power to prevent them. But what are the authorities invoked by the colonists in justification of their revolt—merely their own desires? Not at all. It is to "the laws of Nature and of Nature's God" and to the "unalienable rights" of men that Jefferson makes his appeal. And the fiery eloquence of Tom Paine that so arouses the colonists is inspired by a similar appeal to a generalized good. "Freedom hath been hunted round the globe," Paine says. "Asia and Africa have long expelled her. Europe regards her like a stranger, and England hath given her warning to depart. O receive the fugitive, and prepare in time an asylum for mankind." From the Declaration of Independence to the Atlantic Charter, it is the vision of some universal embattled good that has sustained the morale of democratic Americans struggling to secure specific increments of that good for their own advantage, or that of others.

Why do men bring the general ideal to reinforce the pressure for power? Is not "pressure" enough? Apparently not. The general ideal is needed even to unify the group seeking its own advantage. It subordinates the conflicting selfish aims of the various members to the triumph of the cause as a whole. It heightens their self-respect by enabling them to identify their cause with great movements of an honored past. It enables the leaders to shift their specific goals in line with opportunities, providing the ideal remains the same. (Note Hitler's use of the ideal of *"Lebensraum"* to justify one conquest after another.) And it furnishes the leaders with dreams by which they may satisfy their followers when substantial rewards are not forthcoming.

Moreover, without a general ideal to cover their nakedness, sheer selfishness and the quest for advantage lack propaganda appeal to others. Thurman Arnold, one of our most realistic analysts of the political scene, gives an amusing illustration of that lack in the agitation of real-estate interests in New York against the erection of the buildings of Rockefeller Center. The competition of these new buildings was felt by these interests to be serious. They even brought suit against their erection. But to no purpose. Arnold explains the failure of the protestants as follows. "They could not find a magic inscription with which to fight Rockefeller Center and therefore could not give their selfish interests the color of a campaign for right, truth, and justice—even to themselves." "Had it been the Government which was erecting Rockefeller Center," Arnold continues in a semi-ironic vein, the protestants "would have had the backing of all right-thinking men and women who desired to preserve their ancient liberties."

There can be no doubt about the value to any group seeking its own advantage of a general ideal which has wide social approval. To ask why this is so would lead us into a study of man's inherent nature. Here we shall have to be content with saying in answer to the

"Why," that man seems to be a pattern-creating and pattern-cherishing creature. Patterns of muscular and mental activity save his energy. In dealing with new situations men use old patterns first; then, if necessary, they invent new ones. If the new ones are successful, they are reduced to habits as quickly as possible. Thoughtful men are ever seeking wider patterns to remove the inconsistencies in narrower ones. They reach out into the unknown and seek ultimate patterns of life that will give security to their highest values. Thus we have the birth of ethical philosophy and reflective religion.

It is inevitable that the struggle for advantage by individuals and groups should come up against the larger patterns of thought and purpose cherished by mankind. It has to make terms with these patterns. This is accomplished through the adoption of generalized ideals. Such ideals as liberty, equality, and fraternity provide continuity between present-day efforts and the honored efforts of other days. Unfortunately, they can also be used to camouflage the selfish and even sinister motives of those who organized the "Lincoln Legion," "Liberty League," and "100-per-cent Americans" of our recent past. But the abuse of an ideal is part of the price we pay for invoking it.

We are now ready to give an answer to the question with which we started—why the gaps between the ideals and the practices of the democratic state? Fundamental in the workings of such a state and in the achievement of ideals is the pressure of individuals and groups for their own advantage. These pressures constitute what we have called the power-structure of society. The state seeks to reduce these pressures to an endurable equilibrium through the instrumentalities of the common good (justice). Above and beyond power and actualized justice are our ideals in their generalized form. They have value now to this group and now to that, but they also have implications beyond all contemporary realizations of their value. The gaps between the practices of individuals and groups seeking their own interests and the implications of generalized ideals will never be entirely closed. What happens where democracy really works is that tension is successfully reduced at the points where it is most hostile to the equilibrium of the society and to its ideals and is transferred to points where it can be made tolerable, and even fruitful of progress.

III

What about the strategy to be employed in narrowing the gaps between ideals and practices? May we suggest what seem to be defensible angles of approach?

1. Since the democratic state is a structure of power, one of the ways to help a less-privileged group is to increase its power, and to encourage it to use its power, by organization and propaganda, to achieve a fuller life. This has been the logic behind the trade-union movement and the use of the ballot by Negroes to reduce their social disabilities. Idealists sometimes disapprove of the activities of groups in their own interest, but idealism alone does not usually win victories against privilege. The self-interest of the weak is almost always a factor in wresting their just dues from the strong.

2. One may work upon the gaps between ideals and practices from the point of view of the common good (justice). The state seeks to make these gaps tolerable through the instrumentalities of the common good (courts, legislatures, and administrative bodies). Here is the approach now being followed in respect to the problem of war. If the various peoples can be made to feel deeply that the common good represented in the peaceful settlement of difficulties is more important than any special interest to be served by violence, then we have a real chance to prevent war. And in labor disputes, if the party that threatens a strike or lockout can feel that it is able to get much of what it wants under the aegis of the common interest, it may forego the violent struggle in behalf of an exclusive interest. This approach involves the development of comradeship across the barriers that separate groups, the freeing of the channels of information that supply the general public, and constant political adjustments.

3. Where individuals and groups enjoy advantages at the expense of others, the ideals of our political and religious past may be so applied to specific situations as to develop an uneasy conscience on the part of the privileged. If by breaking down its moral defenses, the

position of the privileged can be reduced to one of naked power, it will be less tenable.

Here religious-minded folk may make a contribution without leaving the sphere of their particular responsibilities. All that is essential is that they see the pertinence of their general ideals to specific needs. (The Negroes, for instance, are justified in invoking the religious ideal of fraternity in their struggle against segregation.) And there is an inherent strength in religion that may be used for the realization of our democratic ideals as a whole. For, if an individual believes that the persistence of these ideals is due not merely to favorable social conditions but to a moral grain that runs deeply throughout the life of the world, he may hang on in the struggle to make these ideals real when others feel that the age of democracy is passed. He can give himself not to despair but to hope.

4. Finally, if the pressure for more power by various groups in society is not to become disruptive; if those who seek improvements in the instrumentalities of justice are not to become overconfident; if the idealist, abounding in good will but insensitive to the power structure of society, is not to become the unwitting ally of reaction, then a great need for clarification is upon us. One senses this need in the highest places in both church and state as, for instance, in the current condemnation of all balances of power, when balances of power constitute the *raison d'être* of government itself.

No one has described the consequences of the lack of clarity in respect to these issues with greater insight than Charles E. Merriam. "It is not merely," he says, "that good will is lacking among powerholders but rather that they grope for comprehension in an unintegrated world and, groping, are beset by an insecurity that accounts for their overreaction to the challenge of change, demagogic or scientific. An increase in social anomies may lead to an overreaction in the direction of overhierarchization, too great rigidity in the social and political structure, and eventually to a thunderous overexplosion in the society. To advocate merely a change of heart and of outlook is not enough. Alternative programs are indispensable."

If these words are true, there are few things more necessary right now than analyses of the functions of power, justice, and general ideals in promoting salutary social change. Unless these constituents of social equilibrium can be mixed in the right order and the right proportions, the danger of "overexplosion" in both domestic and international affairs will remain appalling.

XVI

ORGANIZED RELIGION AND THE PRACTICE OF DEMOCRACY

BY

H. PAUL DOUGLASS, D.D.

Director of the Committee for Co-operative Field Research of the Federal Council of the Churches of Christ in America and the Home Missions Council; Editor, Christendom

There are those who think that democracy was largely the product of religion. There was, however, a revolt in the church against what were believed to be tyrannical forms of authority. That revolt took a democratic form and largely inspired the democratic movement. Hence some would decide on equally good historical evidence that democracy was essentially a secular movement which was forced upon a reluctant church; that the churches which were democratic were so in a derivative rather than a religious sense. Thus the history is exceedingly tangled.

Certainly there was no one-way street. There was commerce back and forth between religion and secular democracy. Yet no one reading American history or the history of the great democracies—all of them—would argue that the experience of self-government in the church was not probably the most significant pattern that set the basic type of behavior enabling democracy in politics to succeed as well as it has done.

I think one could make a very strong case for the contribution to democracy of the church and of education, in spite of the fact that most of the church schools were started to propagandize or to perpetuate sectarian attitudes, to hold their own folk and to provide a succession of clergymen who were sound in their particular faith. The church schools very soon departed from that tradition and became schools of democracy, schools of free research, schools, particularly, that sought out poor boys and girls and gave them a part in the making of the American commonwealth from coast to coast, north and south. The influence of the church on education was democratic in the main. With regard to sensitiveness to social issues, with respect to pioneering in unpopular causes, you can make a strong case for the contribution of organized religion to democracy, and also to constructive community participation.

I have a sample here: a Cornell University research project carried on recently among the farmers of a certain county seeking to learn how participation in such constructive secular social movements as farm extension, health agencies, education, and the like, are related to church membership. There is a high correlation between membership, active as well as nominal, in the religious bodies and leadership in constructive social processes. In many ways the story might be and ought to be elaborated, and we should give praise where praise is due. But we should also have to note many things in which the church has been obstructionist with respect to democracy in the Western world.

Having dealt thus very superficially with these two areas, the influence of religion on democratic education and on social movements, I shall devote most of my time to two other aspects of the subject. The first is the democratic practices of the local church. Here is where my ignorance of communions other than the Protestant puts me at a disadvantage. But what I shall say is so largely a revelation of the stratification of American society, with which the church simply falls in, that the main inference will hit all of us. The illustrations used are largely from a study which I have been making in Jersey City.

Down under the hill in Jersey City where the railroad terminals are, about a third of the people live, and in every respect, without any qualification, they experience the rougher side of human existence. Under category after category, by criterion after criterion, they are the poorer people, whose situation is the more unstable in respect to occupational opportunities. There is a higher proportion of colored people. The educational level is lower. More of the housing is substandard. One need only remind himself how evils pyramid in the depressed areas to make such a judgment. Disasters come not singly, and the area is dark with sorrows. Our cities have sifted our people so that most of the people who have most of the troubles are in one place.

Up on the ridge is the other extreme in which in every respect we find coincidence of advantage, except the sole one of home ownership—which is a doubtful good, as those of us who own homes know. The stability that comes from home ownership does not reside in the apartment houses up on the ridge. However, in every other particular that I have measured there are all the advantages there, corresponding to all the disadvantages down below. Then in the two ends of the city are the lower middle-class working people whose status is just in between.

Now, I cite Jersey City because that is the last city I have looked at. Every American city is like that. There has been a sifting of people along the lines of economic and social advantage. I am studying a certain denomination in that city, a Protestant denomination, and I find that of its eleven churches all but two are highly local. They are class churches, every one of them, because they have no power to be anything else. They are not big enough or strong enough to draw people from farther than four or five blocks, or eight at the most. Most of their people live right around them. Human society in America has sifted the people so that only one kind of person lives anywhere near that church. That church is not strong enough to get outside that narrow orbit, and so it is a class church. And that is true of all but two of these churches.

The way that works out in my opinion—and this also is almost universally true—is to give the lie to the statement that Protestant churches are middle-class churches. I am now speaking of what I personally know. There are not nearly enough middle-class people to fill the existing churches. Repeated counts have shown that there is about a due proportion of churches on all levels of the social stratification. There are not as good churches in all places, but there are as many of them. And if democracy means that poor folk, doing for themselves religiously, have opportunity to create institutions of religion, then there is no part of the community which is not democratically provided for; and I think there is no part of the community which has numerically provided for itself so well as the colored people. Certainly they have plenty of churches.

We have, then, a stratification with which the church falls in, in the main, because it has no option. The local congregation has no choice other than to be the mirror of the immediate locality in which it finds itself. To be sure, two of the churches I have referred to had a certain option, and they have become more or less city-wide institutions. The undemocracy of the church is most largely exhibited not in the conformity to a pattern for which it is not responsible but in those situations where it has an option and where it is very apt to make a nondemocratic choice. One of the two churches of which I speak is located between the valley and the hill; on the hillside but right on the edge. It does not draw anybody from down hill in its ministry to the community, and it has the greatest membership and the greatest wealth and greatest capacity to minister; it serves exactly half of the circle in the center of which it is located. It does so unblushingly, accepting as a matter of course the idea that, if a church can draw almost entirely from the more advantageous localities and people, it does.

I studied all of the central churches in Seattle and I found, in the first place, that almost none of them had anything to do with anybody who lived within a mile of them. But if they did have to do with five, or fifteen, per cent there was this curious thing—which is often the pattern of the American city—that there was a certain corridor to respectability through the deteriorated areas between downtown and the polite suburbs. Sometimes it is automobile row, lined with automobile sales places, and the near in, rebuilt, high-class apartment houses are along that path.

Now, such a church has nothing to do with anybody within a mile, or, if it has, then it marches along that narrow corridor to respectability and draws on the high-class apartment houses, while with all of the poor people living in its neighborhood it has nothing to do. When these churches were confronted with the fact, they were very humble in their admission that it was all dead wrong. Nevertheless, that pattern is almost invariable. In studying parishes one finds these instances—most amusing if they were not so tragic, so morally wrong—of gerrymandered parishes where you just carve out a desirable spot within the undesirable.

Another church in Seattle that I recall has a long-string parish. It has nothing on either side. The other day the minister of a church in Minneapolis told me that there was a street one block from the church with a stone wall beyond which he had no members. That area was largely Jewish and Negro. As a matter of fact, he was drawing from just one quadrant. Virtually all of his people were in that one quarter of the circle surrounding the church; three quarters of it was not his kind of territory. And, while he admitted that it was not exactly a democratic expression of religion, yet he was satisfied as long as he could get success in that way.

What I have said, then, is that, in the first place, there is conformity to a social pattern which is undemocratic; and, secondly, when there is a choice, it is the choice of an undemocratic pattern in the church itself. Locally speaking, I am afraid I could not find very many exceptions.

I could show you not so far from here some Catholic churches which are just as definitely gerrymandered, so that all the poor are in one elongated area and the rich in another, and the parish is not at all a symmetrical parish. However, I think this is far less generally the Catholic than the Protestant pattern.

Now, on top of this, which so far has no necessary relation to race, there is the undemocratic pattern of race segregation in the church. Again, take the group with which I met yesterday, representing the eleven churches of which I spoke earlier. They said with the greatest sincerity that there was not one of the eleven churches which would not receive a Negro if he applied for church membership. As a matter of fact, the denominations have never segregated the Negroes by the act of setting up a separate church for Negroes. Nearly all the denominations have some Negroes. In Detroit a recent circularization revealed that five per cent of the Protestant churches of all denominations had Negro members. In the riot area in Detroit, where the Negro population movement had come up against the whole row of the great Woodward Avenue churches, a pastor said, "We have no difficulty in principle; for many years we had one Negro member. We said to him, 'Uncle Jim, why don't you belong to the big colored church, you and your wife?' And he said, 'They have a good deal of the truth, but up here we have all the truth.'"

There is, then, a tradition or a remnant of the paternal relationship of the white to the Negro race which permits a good many colored people to belong to the parishes of white churches. Many northern denominations have had in their parishes from time immemorial Negro members by two's and three's; nobody ever decided there was a limit, or quota, but that is how it was. However, it is very, very infrequently that an honest-to-goodness bi-racial church has appeared in American Protestantism.

I will cite one or two examples of bi-racial practice. In the Church of All Nations in Boston every Sunday and in weekday services in this finely equipped and well-supported church at least a third of the congregation is colored, and more than half of the choir. That is not exceptional; it is always like that. There has been recently organized in South Berkeley, California, a bi-racial congregational church, about two thirds colored and one third white.

But so far as I can gather from the colored leaders, their position in the main is that they do not desire to break down the great Negro denominations which are so powerful and significant an expression of their group life. They are "vitalities," as a Negro would call them; they have meat. And the racial grouping is as significant as the national: neither is eternal in the heavens, but they both have social meaning.

I think the Negro leaders want to have their cake and eat it, too, and I agree with them. That is, they want enough token bi-racial churches, so that the principle is well established, so that it ceases to be a strange or abnormal or difficult thing. They want enough churches around the country in which the two races are associated on terms of something like equality of membership, and in leadership and participation and Christian social fellowship, so that nobody can have any doubt as to what the rule of the religious-minded conscience is. But at the same time I think they wish to maintain, in the main, the power and the prestige and the opportunities of the great Negro denominations.

I may be wrong about that interpretation. I am right, however, in telling you that the situation is not as it should be, but that the conscience of the church is newly aroused on this point. I am, as a matter of fact, now digesting a group of reports from bi-racial churches of Protestant bodies in cities north and south, and I would say that easily four fifths of what they say is biased as to race, that half the rest is based on very recent experimentation, and about a seventh, or an eighth, perhaps, on established performance; that is the way it impresses me at the present reading. But even so, the situation is on the mind of the church as it has not been for a long time.

Personally, if I were asked for anything like a solution, I would say that you do not solve the problem of religious democracy apart from the problem of general democracy. The upgrading of these people who are socially stratified so that there will not be so much difference as there now is, the equalizing of opportunity and the removal of the causes of inequality, it seems to me, will have to be concomitant with an effort of religion on grounds of pure conscience to create equality.

I say that, because in having to give advisory opinions I have faced situations like this: A community on the edge of Dayton, where there was a fine type of old rural church, well-established, with an educated ministry and a good house of worship according to rural standards, found itself neighbor to a new high-class housing development which brought people whose standards were above the rural standards and whose type of education and of outlook on life was entirely different. The two cultures were not marked by racial or any essential difference; the rural people did not have any sense whatever of inferiority, but there was a distinct economic and cultural divergence. We had to ask the leaders of the group of churches to which that one belonged whether they thought the country church could take in the city people. Well, they said, they did not think it could, and I concurred. I concurred in the judgment that the cultural gulf, which had nothing at all to do with anyone looking down on anyone else, was nevertheless so great that different local churches were indicated in that situation.

Now, almost as near this rural church as the city incursion was, came a rural slum filled with hillbilly people who rushed into Dayton and started down the roads and, lacking streets and public facilities, brought a cultural level which was as much lower than the rural level as the urban level was above it. Again we had to ask whether the rural church could grade itself down culturally so as to deal with the hillbilly type of emotional religion that those people wanted. And again, the answer was No. There had to be three churches where, according to any pure and absolute interpretation of religious principles, there ought to have been one.

I have no answer, personally, to the question here raised, except that this is all part of the total struggle for equality and democracy in the world. At the moment, the church will do well if it makes good on token expressions of democracy, even though it cannot on a total expression.

I am going to have to shorten the treatment of my last point, which I wanted quite adequately expressed. It is the matter of religious democracy in relation to propaganda in nondemocratic nations. This has come to the fore in very crucial fashion in connection with proposals to coerce nondemocratic nations into permitting religious equality as democratically interpreted by the Western nations. Perhaps we can put the elements of the problem in a certain sequence.

First of all, the Wilsonian American democratic formula was that of self-determination for all nations. We do not hear so much about that now. Secondly, the actual program of dealing with conquered nations, the Nazis and the Japanese, indicates that we are not going to have a peace. We are going to have an armistice and then an indefinite control, the terms of which are not going to be fixed in advance; as soon as the Germans or Japanese get democracy enough to suit us, then we are going to turn them loose. It is a unilateral thing, the conditions of which are not going to be predetermined.

I suppose we shall justify this as Russia justified her failure to put the democratic aspects of the Soviet system into effect until the system was well established. China is doing exactly the same thing with respect to the democratic professions under her dominant one-party system. That is what we are doing. And that is the way Secretary Stettinius, rather lamely, I think, explained to the South American people the other day that, when we got order established, then the democratic aspects of our purposes would appear.

Here, then, is the working formula that we are going to use to coerce nondemocratic people into democratic ways. That is not a religious formula; that is a political formula. There is a strong disposition on the part of some churchmen, I think, to do the same thing with respect to freedom of religion in the nondemocratic nations. The Federal Council of Churches has adopted a significant report on religious liberty, from which I will quote: "We recognize the dignity of the human person as the image of God. We therefore urge that the civic rights which derive from that dignity be set forth in the agreements into which our country may enter looking toward the promotion of world order. . . ." Everybody agrees with that, I think. But are we going to put our form of democratic conviction into the world-order scheme and vindicate it in treaty agreements and in the functions and responsibilities assigned to international organization?

This idea was carried further in a great conference on world order in Cleveland about three weeks ago. The request was made to the conference at Dumbarton Oaks to include among the permanent commissions one on basic human freedoms, so that, along with the continuing work for economic and social progress, this commission, as part of the central world structure, would be dealing constantly with the problems of civic and religious liberty on a world scale. That is what the Protestants wanted to do. But this, I am glad to say—for I think there was great moral blindness in it—was never adopted by any churchmen so far as I am aware. A definite proposal was, in fact, put forward in the discussion, which said, in effect, to the nations of the world: If you will not do that, then you are outside the system of international security. Unless you incorporate our interpretation of religious liberty in your basic doctrine, then you are heathen and anybody can jump on you; you are not in the sphere of a mutual self-protected world order. That, as I have said, came up for discussion, but was not adopted. Yet it represents what I fear is a serious possibility as to the direction of our thinking.

Now, let us see just exactly what these religious leaders in the Federal Council, as the representative Protestant group, think religious liberty does include. Here is the statement which has gone to the President and the Department of State, which is actually a representative request on the part of this organ of the Protestant churches: "Religious liberty shall be interpreted to include freedom to worship according to the conscience and to bring up children in the faith of their parents; freedom for the individual to change his religion; freedom to preach, educate, publish, and carry on missionary activities; and freedom to organize with others, and to acquire and hold property, for these purposes."

Now how much coercion do we want to put behind that program in a nondemocratic nation? In a study pamphlet the Council goes on to illustrate the concrete situations with which it thinks it is being confronted: "Orthodox Islam is the contrary of religious liberty and finds no room for the concept as developed in Western lands. In the Sharia, or religious law, which is also the law of society and of the state, Islam controls the entire life of its members. In principle, it forbids apostasy under dire penalty and provides for change of faith only to Islam. This situation is especially aggravated in the Moslem countries of the Near East."

I think that this brings us to the most serious issue confronting religious bodies. All the mature religions believe that there is a certain absoluteness about the revelations in which they originate and from which they draw their sanctions. These they cannot compromise or deny. They willingly admit that their response to the revelation is very relative and fallible, and may be very faulty but, as to the absolute truth and authority of the revelation, I think they are all pretty much one.

Now we are dealing here with perhaps a less dogmatic but an equally stubborn form of conviction on the part, let us say, of the Moslems—I presume there are no Moslems here; perhaps there are—identical with this conviction on the part of all mature religions, which we represent. You must then hold for yourself and in some sense you must express to the world these convictions which derive, not in the sphere of your relative human historical experiences, but in the verities which are revealed from God. We have these differences of conviction, we know what those verities are, and we have to live together in the world. How are we going to do it?

The way of tolerance, just leaving each other alone, I think is not a feasible way. A year ago at the Conference on Science, Philosophy and Religion a Hindu put in the forefront of his criticisms of the Western world that it thought its religion superior. Well, every mature religion thinks that it is superior. This speaker said: Just as long as you feel that you are bigger than we are, that you are richer and stronger, your religion has an aura and complexion of superiority. "That," he said, "is cultural imperialism, and we don't like it." But, according to that reasoning, to cease to be an imperialist is to cease to believe in your religion as supremely good. This runs counter to the very nature of religion.

I would, therefore, like to close my discussion with a statement of what it seems to me we ought to do in order to live democratically as well as to keep faith with our fundamental convictions. One of the interesting recent suggestions is that instead of bushwhacking at each other we should set up religious embassies throughout the world. Put the matter on the high level of diplomacy and accredit an ambassador from one religion to another; he will have status and respectability, and interfaith communication will be carried on through recognized channels. That might have some interesting results.

Another suggestion, to which the Federal Council has become a party, is that we have a voluntarily adopted code of behavior between the faiths, so that in all matters of propaganda—and this is not confined to the Catholic-Protestant-Jewish triangle, but includes the great faiths of the Orient—there should be a gentlemen's agreement, a religious men's agreement, that there will be respect for one another's positions, and that behavior will be adjusted accordingly. I think this would not mean that pulpit propaganda would cease, but it would be understood and conducted in a more respectable fashion.

I must say, however, that my solution of the problem would be different. I think I could put up with the most ardent propagandist if I were impressed that he was really humble. And I think he would probably put up with me if he were very convinced that my motives had been purged of pride and self-interest and that what I was doing I was doing purely for the glory of God as I understood it. I think the real clash is not between fundamental convictions but that it results from the very human impediments and evils which attach thereto.

How are we going to convince one another that we are purged of pride and self-interest and that in our relations we are acting solely according to our faith and not according to our self-will and extraneous interests? I do not believe anybody can purify the human soul except the one God of all of us. But if we could together confront the greatness and goodness of God and lend ourselves to the leadership of the creative spirit, then in a thoroughly paradoxical world, as it seems to me to be, without reconciling all our basic convictions we might live together in a spirit of love that would cast out fear.

XVII

DEMOCRACY AND ZIONISM [1]

BY

MORDECAI M. KAPLAN, D.H.L.

Dean, Teachers Institute, and Professor of Homiletics, Jewish Theological Seminary of America

All that most people hear about the Jews these days has to do either with the diabolic plot of the Nazis to exterminate them or with the flare up of anti-Semitism in the democratic countries, largely as a result of the Nazi incendiarism of hate. That, however, is not the whole story. In this, the darkest period in the long annals of Jewish history, which abounds in tales of woe and tragedy, the Jewish people through its very struggle for existence is helping to keep alive the hope of a juster and kinder humanity. That contribution to civilization comes not alone from the vast number of Jews who are fighting in the ranks of all the armed forces of the Allies and are giving every spare ounce of their energy to the war effort, but principally from the collective enterprise of the Jewish people in the endeavor to reestablish its national home in Palestine. That enterprise holds a significance which far transcends the fortunes of the Jewish people. In so far as it is interwoven with interests of an international character, it constitutes resistance to those interests which are selfish and reactionary and offers aid and comfort to those which are enlightened and progressive.

The striving of the Jewish people to recover its national home can

---

[1] This address was included in the series in order that the Zionist project in Palestine might be described. Its original title was "Palestine, an Experiment in Democracy." The issues it raises are somewhat different in character from those of the rest of the volume, but it is included in its entirety as an earnest and authoritative defense of Zionism. Like the other addresses, it is to be taken as representing the personal views of the author.—The Editor.

meet with fulfilment only if the democratic nations will accord it their wholehearted consent. Such consent will come when the democratic nations learn to appreciate the need of having what is likely to become one of the world's most important crossroads inhabited by a people dedicated to democratic living. For the nations to regard with favor what the Jews are attempting in Palestine, presupposes on their part a deliberate commitment to democracy as the basis of international relations and a genuine interest in democracy as the basis of political and economic relations within each nation. If the Jews expect to elicit from the nations such a commitment and such interest, it is because the Palestinian project is animated by the ideal and method of democracy. By reason of its problematic future that project may, no doubt, be designated as still only an experiment in democracy. In that respect it is no worse off than many other promising movements which have appeared on the horizon. In a sense, all the occidental peoples are as yet only in the experimental stages of democracy. The fate of democracy is at present in the balance everywhere.

In order to ascertain wherein the movement to establish a Jewish national home in Palestine makes for democracy, it is necessary to have a definite idea of what we mean by democracy. We shall then be in a position to study the extent to which democracy has figured: (1) in the evolution of the aim to establish a Jewish national home; (2) in the steps taken to achieve that purpose; and (3) in the process of building the Jewish national home.

It is safer to define democracy from the standpoint of its end results than from that of its rationale. There is little likelihood that the end results which appear desirable should turn out to be undesirable, whereas the reasons we advance for their being desirable may upon close examination turn out to be untenable. Thus, in terms of rationale, the essence of democracy was assumed to be the principle that the primary unit in all political and economic problems should be the individual and not the nation or the state. The nation, from this point of view, is regarded as mechanically constituted of individual citizens, with each citizen entitled to the same rights and obligated to the same duties as every other. Any real understanding, however, of the workings of human society precludes this mechanical view, as it does the bare statement that all men are born equal. Nations are not mechanical organizations of individuals but social organisms, which are constituted of individuals with varying abilities and potentialities through which each one is rendered necessary to all and all to each.

These and other questions pertaining to the rationale of democracy, like the fiction of the social contract of the rights of property, of order *vs.* justice, or authority *vs.* freedom, do not touch the heart of the purpose which men seek to achieve when they are sincere in their appeal to democracy. That purpose is to have justice and kindness instead of tyranny and cruelty prevail in all human relationships. That purpose is to bring under control the inherent tendency of human beings to seek power and to exercise it for its own sake, regardless of the harm it does. One of the fatal mistakes of liberalism has been to commit democracy to some particular rationale rather than to concentrate on the objective of having human beings live in peace and mutual co-operation. Democracy should be viewed as aiming to help every human being to make the most out of life. Whether that can be achieved by treating the individual or the nation as primary, by means of a rational or a romantic approach to reality, through collectivism or individual enterprise, are questions of method and can be worked out peacefully, provided we do not lose sight of the aim.

Proceeding therefore to view democracy from the standpoint of its end results, we may identify it with the following three principles:

1. All exploitation and oppression of the weak by the strong must be dealt with as morally evil, economically ruinous, and politically intolerable. This applies to all human relations both individual and collective.

2. No exploitation or oppression should be regarded either as part of the divine government of mankind, in the sense of being a means of divine discipline or an expiation for sin, or of being an inherent part of the order of nature which it is futile to try to change.

3. Democracy cannot exist in a void; it is a quality of nationhood. Under its influence national solidarity functions as a means of fostering the maximum welfare and collaboration of all who compose the

nation, regardless of race, color, or creed. Such welfare and collaboration presuppose unity in diversity and freedom from oppression and exploitation.

I

With this conception of democracy in mind, the first question to which we shall address ourselves is: To what extent has this conception played a part in the evolution of the aim to establish a Jewish national home in Palestine? In answering that question we must call attention to the main facts which gave rise to Zionism. Zionism is not merely the revival of traditional Jewish Messianism. It is that Messianism recast into the pattern of modern democratic nationalism. Traditional Messianism coincided with democracy's aim of eliminating exploitation and oppression from human life. It held out the hope of the establishment of God's Kingdom of justice and love and the prospect of Israel as a nation restored to its ancient land. In that land Israel would demonstrate the potency of the Divine Kingdom through the social order which it would maintain there. But Messianism assumed that such a future would come about only through divine intervention of a miraculous nature. There was nothing that the Jews could do other than try to conform to the traditional teachings concerning the proper means to salvation. Included in the traditional teachings was the one which interpreted the exile of the Jews from their national home both as a means of expiation for the sins of their fathers and their own sins and as a means of discipline to render them worthy of redemption when the time for it would finally arrive. To take human measures for resuming national life in Palestine was traditionally condemned as sinful impatience.

It is this aspect of traditional Messianism which Jews have been unlearning during the past 150 years. They put in its place the assumption of democracy that no exploitation or oppression should be accepted as part of the divine purpose with man, and that it is more in accord with that purpose to throw off the yoke of oppression and to achieve the freedom to make the most of life in the here and now. What led Jews to adopt this assumption of democracy and to infer from it that to achieve redemption they must reclaim their ancient homeland? A knowledge of the circumstances under which they became acquainted with the spirit of modern democracy and of the way that spirit was either repudiated or lost in the shuffle in the various European countries, will supply the answer.

The revolutionary doctrines promulgated by Voltaire, Diderot, Rousseau, and Montesquieu and the political revolutions which took place in America and in France, mark the beginning of what is known as the era of enlightenment. When the limited number of Jews who happened to be in economic or cultural contact with the outer world learned of these new cultural and political developments, they readily made them part of their own outlook and hopes. These *illuminati,* as they chose to call themselves, became obsessed with the purpose of casting off everything that set them apart from the non-Jewish population, expecting in that way to remove the main obstacle to their being granted civic rights and being placed on an equal political footing with the rest of the population. Emancipation from the ghetto became their one dominant objective, which they sought to achieve for themselves and for their fellow Jews who still lived in a world of their own. Realizing what unlimited opportunities of achieving comfort, social status, and cultural enhancement civic freedom would open up to them, they were only too willing to surrender all traditional hopes of returning to Palestine. In addition, they lost all desire for the autonomy which had enabled the Jews throughout the centuries to retain their national solidarity, despite their dispersion.

In the early days of the era of enlightenment this surrender of Jewish nationhood was justified on the ground that it qualified the Jews to identify themselves with the general progressive trend toward cosmopolitanism, which held forth the hope that all national differences would be abolished. That was the case during the latter part of the eighteenth and the beginning of the nineteenth centuries. Cosmopolitanism was then far more fashionable than nationalism. Later, when nationalism displaced cosmopolitanism, the surrender of Jewish nationhood was urged as a manifestation of true patriotism. This process of self-dejudaization went on among the upper economic and cultural Jewish circles while the governments were either debating whether or not to give Jews civic rights, were granting them those rights grudgingly, or were continuing the old mediaeval policy of issuing against them oppressive and discriminatory laws. In France proper Jews were finally emancipated, with the proviso that they disavow their national aspirations. Germany, Austria, England, and Italy pursued almost to the end of the nineteenth century a policy of granting Jews civic rights in piecemeal fashion. The vast majority of European Jews, numbering from seven to eight million, resided in eastern Europe. There they remained without civic rights until the end of the First World War.

The Jewish *illuminati* of Russia were the first to be disillusioned in their hope that by dejudaizing themselves and acquiring the culture of their native country they would facilitate their emancipation. For a while they had been permitted to indulge themselves in their mistaken hope. That was during the reign of Czar Alexander II who evinced some signs of liberalism. In 1881 he was assassinated and was succeeded by his son Alexander III who reintroduced a spirit of reaction against all liberal tendencies. An integral part of the reactionary policy was to make the Jews the scapegoat for all the ills which had bred discontent against the Russian government. This diversion was effected not merely by propaganda but by organized incitement of the populace to pogromize the Jews. The first outbreak took place in the Ukraine soon after the assassination of Alexander II. That was the signal for a new series of oppressive measures against the Jews. They were driven out from many of the towns and villages where they lived and were pressed back upon themselves into the crowded pale of settlement. These events finally convinced the Jewish *illuminati* that they had been sadly mistaken in their policy of assimilationism. They then realized that, if they wanted to enjoy the blessings of democracy with its freedom from oppression and exploitation, they must follow the example of many of the newly risen nations and try to resume their own national life in a homeland of their own.

The first of the Russian-Jewish *illuminati* to give voice to this change of heart was Leon Pinsker, a surgeon in the Russian Army who had distinguished himself to the extent of earning special recognition from the government. He issued a call to the Jews to give up all hope of being emancipated by the other nations and to achieve self-emancipation by finding and purchasing land where they could resume their own national existence. The response to his call was quick in coming. The question was where to find such a land. Without much discussion, all thoughts turned at once to Palestine as the only logical place where the awakened yearning for normal living could be achieved in accord with the democratic vision which had transformed their ancient Messianic dream.

Immediately there arose, as if by magic, a movement to migrate to Palestine for the purpose of establishing there agricultural colonies. The determination to revive Jewish nationhood was accompanied by an enthusiastic faith in the physiocratic idea, enunciated during the callow years of the enlightenment era, that the cultivation of the soil was the only productive and normal method of living. The most notable response to this call to self-emancipation came from several hundred young Jewish students of universities who had become thoroughly Russified. They organized themselves into a colonizing body under the slogan of *Bilu*. That slogan represents the initials of the first words of the verse in Hebrew which reads: "O House of Jacob, come and let us go to the mountain of the Lord, to the House of the God of Jacob."

In central and western Europe, which harbored only about one quarter the number of Jews in eastern Europe, democracy had made considerable headway. It was formally recognized as the proper basis of government. But simultaneously with the progress of democracy there developed forces which threatened to undermine it, as in time they actually did. Those are the forces which have found their embodiment in nationalism. During the last decades of the nineteenth century nationalism acquired irresistible momentum. The original democratic conception of national solidarity as a means of furthering the maximum welfare and collaboration of all citizens, regardless of race, color, creed, or class, gave way to the utilization of national solidarity as a means of bolstering the monopoly of power in the hands of the possessing class, or of strengthening the nation in its struggle with other nations for markets and raw materials. Democratic nationalism was giving way to imperialistic nationalism.

In Germany and Austria, where political and religious conflicts had for a long time rendered national solidarity an unattainable desideratum, something more feasible and attainable than the ideal functions of democracy had to be found to achieve such solidarity. It was incomparably easier to appeal to fear, prejudice, and vanity. With the achievement of greater political and economic power as the nation's goal, and with the appeal to fear, prejudice, and vanity as means, modern nationalism of the German variety came into being. As a corollary of that movement came anti-Semitism. By focusing invidious attention upon Jews who had been recently admitted into citizenship and who had come to occupy important positions in the economic and cultural life of the country, it was easy to demonstrate to a discontented populace how national solidarity would help to rid them of troublesome competitors and interlopers.

This conception of nationalism and this method of fostering it spread from Germany to all countries where all who held the reins of political or economic power expected national sentiment to secure them against too close a scrutiny of their prerogatives. During the last decade of the nineteenth century, France, where the ideal of democracy originally arose as a movement to eliminate exploitation and oppression and to utilize national solidarity to that end, became infected with anti-Semitism. A military clique, together with a group of clericals, avowed royalists, and other reactionaries, plotted to seize control of the government by fanning nationalist sentiment into a flame that would consume the last vestiges of democracy. The Dreyfus affair, with its anti-Semitic assault on the Jews, was intended to be the spearhead of a movement to undermine the French Third Republic.

This entire course of events during the last two decades of the nineteenth century brought into sharp relief the contradiction between the hopes raised by the French Revolution for a free and just society, in which Jews would be treated as human beings on a basis of equality with all their fellow citizens, and the metamorphosis of those hopes into chauvinistic nationalism, with anti-Semitism as the principal means of inculcating it. Theodor Herzl, who happened to be on the staff of the *Wiener Neue Presse* and had acted as its reporter in Paris on the Dreyfus trial, was shocked into a realization of the hopeless position in which Jews found themselves. He arrived at the conclusion that the so-called emancipation of the Jews was bankrupt, and that anti-Semitism was bound to grow in extent and violence. Having tasted what new life and happiness true democracy might have conferred, Jews would no longer be able to endure the confines of the ghetto. Like Pinsker before him, and independently of him, Herzl saw but one way out—self-emancipation through the acquisition of some territory to which Jews could migrate *en masse,* and where they would establish their own state. As far as he was concerned, it might have been any available territory. But when he presented his plan to his fellow Jews, he became convinced that Palestine was the only place where Jews could experience national rebirth.

Herzl at first found very few sympathizers among the Jews in the western and central European countries. Despite the evident spread of anti-Semitism, the Jews in those countries continued to believe that it would soon subside. But when Herzl came with his project to east-European Jews, he immediately won a large and enthusiastic following. It was principally Herzl who created the movement known as "political Zionism" and who gave the democratic impulse to the forces that are driving Jews to rebuild their national home in Palestine. In his conception of the movement all of the three main principles of democracy constitute an integral part: (1) the reinterpretation of the Messianic ideal from that of passive waiting for a supernatural miracle to the exertion of initiative to throw off the yoke of oppression; (2) the refusal to continue the state of exile on the assumption that it is a divinely decreed expiation or a form of divine discipline; and (3) the decision to reinstate Jewish nationhood where it might function as a means of securing the maximum welfare and collaboration to all who come within its purview, in keeping with the highest ideals of democracy. Zionism has properly been defined as Jewish democracy in action.

II

Democracy as an orientation to life in which primacy is accorded to the purpose of combating all forms of exploitation and oppression and of furthering freedom and equality in all human relations, among individuals and groups, has operated not only in the evolution of the aim to acquire a Jewish national home in Palestine; it has also operated in the measures which have been taken to prepare the conditions necessary for the achievement of that aim. Those measures have been taken for the most part by Jews, but to a certain extent also by non-Jews.

1. The Zionist movement was bound to supplant a form of migration to Palestine that had existed since the thirteenth century and had drawn to Palestine men and women who had gone there in the spirit of a religious pilgrimage. They usually remained there and spent their days praying and engaging in religious exercises. They were supported by *Halukah,* moneys sent by, or collected from, Jews all over the world who considered their contributions as furthering a sacred cause. Probably the most harmless kind of parasitism, it was, nevertheless, bound to breed human relations unwholesome, from a democratic point of view. To have contributed to its virtual elimination is the least intended and least notable of Zionism's contributions, yet it deserves mention.

There was another form of philanthropy in Palestine, however, which clashed even more directly with the democratic spirit of Zionism, and which had to give way before it. That was the large-scale educational and philanthropic endeavor engaged in by the *Alliance Israelite Universelle* to westernize the Jews in the outlying countries. The organizers of the *Alliance* expected that such westernization would redeem considerable masses of Jews living in those countries from the squalor and ignorance of their surroundings. They included in their field of operations countries besides those in the French Empire. Palestine was one of them.

The principal activity of the *Alliance* was the establishment in 1870 of a farm school *Mikveh Israel* near Jaffa. The purpose of that school was to educate some of the younger generation of Jews whose parents lived on *Halukah,* to become farmers. Their training was conducted in French and in a spirit of loyalty to French institutions. No wonder that many of the trainees in the farm school later preferred the glamor of the Paris boulevards to toiling on some lonely farm in Palestine. Later a similar organization among well-to-do German Jews, known as *Das juedische Hilfsverein,* was also doing educational and philanthropic work in Palestine. Besides the unintentional aid they may have been giving to the imperial interests of their respective countries, these organizations were not helping the Jewish communities to feel the need of self-determination and self-reliance—the prime requisites of a spirit of democracy. Nothing less than the moral awakening that came with Zionism could achieve that.

2. On the other hand, a more deliberate manifestation of democracy is to be noted in the avowed aim of Zionism to have Jews achieve their own redemption as a matter of justice and not of pity, and by means of justifiable demands made in the name of the Jewish masses and not through political wirepulling of some individuals who happen to be favorites of, or influential with, the powers that be. In the past, these individuals, known as *shtadlanim* or intercessors, have had to come to the aid of the Jews every time there was trouble brewing. The fate of enslaved Jewish communities would often hang upon the whim of some nobleman or bishop and upon the willingness of the intercessor to humor him. This placed the community in the power of the *shtadlan*. Zionism has taught Jews not to entrust their fate to individuals, whether Jews or non-Jews, who might come to exercise arbitrary control, but to have faith in democratic procedure and in the justice of their cause. It put an end once and for all to the authority of self-appointed oligarchies, however beneficently disposed toward their fellow Jews.

This democratic attitude which Zionism has brought to all efforts involved in getting Jews to settle in Palestine and in creating there the conditions essential to their welfare, derives from Herzl's insistence that Zionism assume political form. That form has rendered Zionism an excellent training ground for the Jews in the art of self-government as a nation—something they have had no chance to exercise for over eighteen centuries. Political Zionism is based on the principle that the Jewish national home must be "publicly recognized and legally secured." So convinced was Herzl of the importance of public or international recognition as a prerequisite to the upbuilding of the Jewish national home that he deprecated the continuance of piecemeal colonization efforts, which had been in progress for almost fifteen years and which depended for their success upon the lethargy and corruptibility of the Turkish régime rather than upon its formal consent. What Herzl wanted was a charter which he hoped to obtain from the Sultan and which he expected to be duly guaranteed by the other European nations. He was determined to take the fate of the Jewish people out of the hands of any one government, however well-disposed, and to entrust it to the conscience of mankind. His idea, however, was finally realized only after his death, when the Balfour Declaration, to be referred to later, was embodied in the Palestine mandate.

The recognition and security which were to be the basis of political Zionism presupposed willingness on the part of the nations to do two things: (1) to carry on formal transactions with the Jews as a people through their duly authorized representatives, and (2) to concede to the Jews the right to a homeland of their own as a matter of moral and legal justice. Such willingness could not possibly be due to any political pressure, since Jews were in no position to exercise any kind of force. Herzl could have counted upon the public recognition and legal security of a national home for the Jews only on the basis of the inherent justice of his cause. The very fact that his purpose of placing the solution of the Jewish problem on the agenda of international affairs did not materialize before the end of the First World War, which was fought, to some extent at least, in order to make the world safe for democracy indicates how closely bound up the Zionist project is with the spirit of democracy. It may be asked: How, with the spread of anti-Semitism, could Herzl expect the governments to act in the spirit of democracy? The answer is that governments often act more justly than do their peoples. To be sure, in the instance of Zionism, they were unprepared at first to do so. But under favorable circumstances there could be, as there actually was, a break in the policy of calculating selfishness on the part of governments. Like their action in organizing the League of Nations itself, the incorporation of the Balfour Declaration in the Constitution of the League was no doubt due to a momentary inspiration of justice. Indeed, much of our best hoping and planning for a better world in the future has to depend upon such spurts of genuine justice and good will.

3. Political Zionism may, accordingly, be described as the application of democratic methods to the measures to be employed by Jews everywhere in their efforts to prepare the national home for those who want or have to go there. Its principal instrument is the World Zionist Organization, to which belong all Jews who subscribe to the above-mentioned aim of creating "for the Jewish people a home in Palestine secured by public law." That aim was formulated at the first Zionist Congress called together by Theodor Herzl in 1897. The World Zionist Organization has no way of enforcing any strict discipline, since its existence is necessarily based on voluntary membership. It represents a wide diversity of opinion in its congresses and in all of its working institutions. The only requirement besides subscribing to the main purpose of political Zionism is the payment of a shekel. That form of payment derives from the ancient Biblical tradition concerning the building of the Tabernacle in the wilderness. In the Bible the uniform payment of a half-shekel was intended to emphasize the equality of all Israelites. The reason for making it a half instead of a whole shekel is interpreted as symbolizing the incompleteness of the individual apart from the community.

The constituency of the World Zionist Congress is divided along party lines and into local federations. There are three main parties, the General Zionists, the Labor Zionists and the *Mizrachi*. The local federations are an accommodation to differences due to local conditions, but the division along party lines answers to the principle of democracy. The General Zionists take a position of neutrality toward the social and religious policies to be pursued in the actual process of upbuilding the national home. They are content to leave the determination of those policies entirely to those who are to engage in that process in Palestine. The Labor Zionists take the position that the Jewish national home must be planned and that the planning should begin with those who provide the initial moral and material support. They interpret planning to mean proceeding along the economic lines advocated by democratic socialism, the type of socialism promulgated by the Laborites in the British Parliament. The third party represented is *Mizrachi*. Their slogan is, "The Land of Israel for the people of Israel according to the Torah of Israel." They proceed from the assumption that, whatever be the economic or political policy which is to obtain in the Jewish national home, it must be committed to the practice of the traditional rites, principally the Sabbath and festivals, the dietary laws, and the continuance of ancient Jewish civil law.

In contrast with the General and Labor Zionists who envisage the Jewish national home as built on the lines usually favored in modern democratic countries, that of keeping the state and church separate, the *Mizrachi* maintain that such separation is incompatible with Judaism and the spirit of the Jewish people. This might point to the possibility that the Jewish national home might become a theocracy instead of a democracy. Such a possibility, however, is precluded by the actual proportions of the three main groups represented in the Zionist movement. The following numbers of the delegates at the Twentieth Zionist Congress which met in Zurich in 1937 represent a proportion which is not likely to vary to any considerable degree: General Zionists, 160, Labor Zionists, 230 and *Mizrachi* 83. This proportion gives the Labor Zionists predominance in all important issues and is a definite assurance that the Jewish national home will not harbor a theocracy.

What is particularly reassuring, from a democratic standpoint, is that the World Zionist Organization has demonstrated, for the first time in the history of the Jewish people, the possibility of getting groups religiously and socially divergent to collaborate. This democracy is all the more evident, in that there are some Zionist groups which hold religious and social views both so extremely rightist and so extremely leftist as to be precluded from collaborating with the main body of the Jewish people which is represented by the World Zionist Organization. But apart from their nuisance value or disvalue, they only help to emphasize the remarkable democratic achievement manifested in the large area of collaboration among the divergent groups within the World Zionist Organization.

4. To build a national home requires funds. The main part of these funds has to be used for those who do not possess the means to emigrate to Palestine and settle there, but who constitute the most valu-

Democracy and Zionism

able human material as colonizers and national-home builders. There would seem to be no special room for any manifestation of democracy in the gathering and distribution of such funds; the main problem is that of efficiency—incurring a minimum of waste and accomplishing a maximum of desirable results. But there is one fund in which the entire essence of democracy figures, with all the appeal of a great cause. This is the *Keren Kayemeth* or Jewish National Fund.

Long before political Zionism came on the scene, an east-European Jew, Herman Schapira, who started out in life as a Talmudic scholar and ended up as a mathematical genius who taught at Heidelberg, conceived the idea of establishing a fund to purchase land that would forever remain the property of the Jewish people. This, he maintained, would make it possible for the agricultural development in the Jewish homeland to take place in accordance with such ethical ideals as are expressed in the ancient agrarian laws of the Torah and have become the objective of most modern efforts in land reform. Thus both the Torah law of the jubilee year, which provided that all bought land should revert to the original owners, and the influence of Henry George's ideas about private land ownership as the main source of economic ills in civilized society, are reflected in the strenuous effort made by the Jews to forestall the evils of land speculation and mounting rents, to which any newly developed country is subject. In 1901, at the Fifth Zionist Congress under the leadership of Herzl, the Jewish National Fund (J.N.F.) was finally established. All National Fund land was then declared to be inalienable and capable of being leased only for forty-nine years, after which period the lease could be renewed. The lease to the land could be inherited. No more land was to be leased to any one settler than he was able to cultivate. Most significant of all was the principle that no hired labor would be permitted on National Fund land. In the cities, the J.N.F. acquires land for public buildings and workers' homes.

The manifold methods employed in collecting the Jewish National Fund are such as to enable all Jews, even the poorest, to feel that they share in it. With contributions ranging from endowments and bequests, which can come only from the well-to-do, to collections in charity boxes which are kept in the homes of the poorest, and with all manner of devices in between to give every one a chance to contribute to the Jewish National Fund, every Jew can be made to feel that he has a part in the rebuilding of the Land.

5. Unmistakable evidence of the democratic purpose and policy animating the Zionist movement was evinced in the set of principles which were formulated in 1923 at the Convention of the Zionist Organization of America and reaffirmed at subsequent conventions. They are the following: "1. Political and civil equality irrespective of race or sex or faith for all the inhabitants of the land. 2. To insure in the Jewish national home in Palestine equality of opportunity, we favor a policy which, with due regard to existing rights, shall tend to establish the ownership of the land and all natural resources and of all public utilities by the whole people. 3. All land owned or controlled by the whole people should be leased on such conditions as will insure the fullest opportunity of development and continuity of possession. 4. The co-operation principle should be applied as far as possible in the organization of all agricultural, industrial, commercial, and financial undertakings. 5. The fiscal policy should be framed so as to protect the people from the evils of speculation and from every other form of financial oppression. 6. The system of free public instruction which is to be established should embrace all grades and departments of education."

6. The most far-reaching effect of Zionism on democratic world tendencies made itself felt at the end of the First World War when, as a result of the idealism which Wilson had injected into the war purposes of the Allies, the atmosphere was electric with hopes that the peace would usher in a new and better world. Those hopes had been stimulated by the determination to remove the principal factor which had brought on the war. That factor was believed to be the domination exercised by the great powers over the small nations and the oppression of minority nationalities by the nations which harbored them. For the first time an attempt was made to give to democracy international scope by recognizing that nationalities, or historic groups which were conscious of a common destiny, were no less entitled to

Democracy and Zionism

freedom and equality than individual men and women. How to achieve that in practice, with so many nationalities unable to stand on their own feet, seemed to pose an insoluble problem. The problem of minority nationalities, though also far from being simple, at least had some earlier precedents and experience to fall back on. Already in the famous Council of Vienna of 1878 that problem had been dealt with. In the case of peoples constituting the majority populations on their own territories but incapable of self-government, there was as yet no internationally recognized means of assuring them help, without endangering their independence. In the democratic fervor which attended the organization of the League of Nations such a means was evolved. That was the system of mandates. The mandate system, which authorized a strong nation to act as guardian of a small and weak people, until such time as that people should attain to political maturity fitting it to become an independent nation, marked a radical break with imperialism. It was expected to put an end to the military domination and the exploitation of weaker peoples.

Zionism afforded the League an opportunity to demonstrate its adherence not only to the letter but also to the spirit of international democracy. The Jews constituted a nationality which had to get to the land of its origin before the mandatory power could exercise guardianship over it. But so strong and clear a case had been made out for the Jewish historic claim to Palestine that not one of the fifty-two nations in the League, or the United States, saw any reason for questioning the justice of including the Jewish people within the system of mandates. Accordingly, the Balfour Declaration, pledging the British Government to facilitate the establishment of a Jewish national home in Palestine, was duly incorporated in the mandate given under the League Covenant for the administration of Palestine. This act, judged by itself apart from any ulterior motives and mental reservations which may have been entertained by the mandatory power, very definitely constituted a most noteworthy development of democracy both in depth and scope. If eliciting the good in others is itself a contribution to the good life, then by eliciting from the nations such an avowal of democracy on an international scale, Zionism may be said to have made an important contribution to civilization.

III

With so much of the spirit of democracy manifest in the evolution of the aim to establish a Jewish national home in Palestine and in the measures being taken to get the Jews there, it is to be expected that the actual process of Jewish settlement in Palestine would translate that spirit into a way of life and embody it in institutional forms. How this expectation is being met in continually progressive degree in Palestine I shall now attempt to set forth.

1. The first element in the process of Jewish settlement in Palestine to be considered, from the standpoint of an experiment in democracy, is the creation of a new economic structure. In contrast to their experience in the United States, to which the frustration of their hopes for freedom and equality drove the Jews, and where they found a ready-made economy into which they had to fit themselves, the Jews who turned to Palestine to redeem their hopes realized that they were coming to a backward and neglected land. They regarded those very characteristics as an opportunity to demonstrate their ability to resume their national life, which had long been in a state of suspended animation. The fact that Palestine had been depleted of its natural fertility and that, except for patches of wretched cultivation, it was a land of denuded hills and swampy pestilential plains, was in itself a challenge to the Jews to provide the agricultural foundation of a new and progressive economy that would be able to harbor a vast population. The realization that this economy must be a Jewish creation, planned by the intelligence of Jews, and consummated by the treasure, toil, and sweat of Jews, is the soul and essence of Zionism. It is the one opportunity Jews have of nailing the lie that Jews can live off the economy created by others, but have no ability to create their own.

From the very beginning of the Jewish recolonization of Palestine, which began in 1882, the necessity of an agricultural foundation was apparent. But the early pioneers did not realize the full implication of an agricultural base for the creation of a new economy which would be capable of sustaining a national home. They thought all that was necessary was to acquire a farm, engage any cheap labor that could be obtained and exercise efficient management. There were plenty of Arab fellahin to be had, for, no matter how little the Jewish farmer was willing to pay, it was much more than the Arabs could ever hope to earn under native landlords. In the relatively short space of fifteen to twenty years, however, the ill effects of this shortsighted policy became visible and served as a warning to the leaders of the Zionist movement against any such private enterprise. The idealism of the first generation of pioneers and their great hopes of rebuilding the national life of their people survived in but a few of the second generation, and would have died out with the next. When political Zionism came along and gave larger vision and significance to the task of building a new economy which would be the Jews' own creation, it saved the first efforts of the early pioneers from being absorbed into the general background of native exploitation of the many by the few. The first thing political Zionism did was to establish the principle of nationally owned land on which no hired labor of any kind, Jewish or Arab, was to be permitted. In addition, the policy has been to encourage small farms. This policy has been described by Secretary of Agriculture of the United States, Claude E. Wickard, as making "for fairer distribution of farm income, for better care of soil, for better citizenship, and for happier living." Over two thirds of the settlement's six thousand Jewish citrus groves are of less than five acres each. The second thing was to foster a type of collective colonization which, in the opinion of so expert an authority as Walter Clay Lowdermilk, the noted American soil conservationist, may be regarded as "the most successful of modern times."

Co-operative colonization in Palestine has been a direct product of necessity and common sense. The extremely difficult conditions confronting the settlers and their inexperience in agriculture constitute the necessity. Their only assets are youth, social idealism, and devotion to Zionism. They are imbued to a profound degree with the teachings of socialism, but not to the point of being doctrinaire about it. The two main considerations have been: (1) ability to produce enough to be able to maintain a high standard of health and culture, and (2) the need of refraining from any form of exploitation, either individual or collective The degree of collectivism in these co-operative settlements varies from the complete absence of any private property and full submission to collective control and discipline to a mixed system of family ownership of the produce combined with co-operation in many other respects. Flexibility in type and degree of co-operation gives, on the one hand, free play to diverse human elements and distinctive characteristics and, on the other, makes possible unity of spirit amid a large variety of social and economic forms.

There are, in the main, three types of workers' collectives. (a) First is the *Kvutza,* or collective farm, which harbors memberships ranging from 150 to about 1200. It represents a synthesis of freedom and equality. All decisions touching fundamental policies are the result of free discussion on the part of all the adult members of each group. Each *Kvutza* consists of members who are considered likely to be mutually congenial. Increases in membership are made on the principle of congeniality. Generally, numbers of such collective farms organize themselves into larger units. With no formal sanctions to enforce any of the rules or policies democratically arrived at but with mutual good will, imperative as a means of holding together the members of each group, these collective farms demonstrate to what extent the problem of democracy is simplified by the elimination of the prospect of individual acquisition.

(b) The *Kvutza* mode of life, however, has one great drawback. It calls for the renunciation of virtually all privacy. Such renunciation is irksome to most people. They prize what is usually described as the possession of one's own soul. For such as these there is the type of small-holders' settlement, known as *Moshav,* which consists of a number of families each occupying its own home and cultivating its own little farm on National Fund land. They, too, are not permitted to hire others to work for them. That means that all adult members of a family must share the large variety of chores for which rural life calls. But there are children to be taken care of, farm products to be brought to market, purchases to be made, and various machines to be worked, which are beyond the ability of any one farmer to own. To all those items the co-operative principle is applied.

(c) There is a third kind of collective known as *Kibbutz.* The *Kibbutz* consists of manual workers who, in addition to having no agricultural experience, are in no position to start a farm collective of their own, yet are eager to have one. In that case, a number, say one hundred, organize as a unit. Most members of that unit continue to earn meager livelihoods in the towns, by working at various trades; but some, say from twenty-five to thirty, after having acquired the initial lessons in agriculture proceed to establish a *Kvutza* or farm collective. The earnings of all, both of the town workers and the rural workers, are pooled in a common fund from which all receive amounts in accordance with their minimal needs. This goes on until, one after another, the town workers are absorbed into the farm collective.

Collectivism as a method of settlement has been imperative for the Jews in Palestine. They would not have been able to cope with the hardships of the land had they attempted to do so on the basis of individual enterprise. They would not have been able to adjust themselves to the low standards of the Arab peasants, to which they would have been reduced had each one tried to eke out a livelihood for himself. They might, perhaps, have resigned themselves to the deprivation of all opportunities for cultural growth for themselves, but there is one thing they would not have been able to endure and that is to bring up their children without the education essential to the full development of their mental and moral powers. Such an education would be entirely unattainable without the collectivist economy which the Jewish pioneers in Palestine have adopted. That economy has made it possible to develop a type of education which is probably as fine an illustration of what is meant by translating democracy into educational terms, as there is anywhere in the world.

2. On an even larger scale than the collectives, which are laying the agricultural foundation of the country, the spirit of democracy is being promoted by the large network of co-operatives of all kinds, such as credit unions and co-operatives in insurance, in home-building, in buying, in marketing, in contracting, and in supplying services. At the end of June, 1944, there were 1050 active Jewish co-operatives with 140,000 members as compared with 210 Arab co-operatives with 10,000 members. Of the $25,000,000 capital and reserve reported by Palestine co-operatives only $250,000 belongs to the Arab

societies and the rest to the Jewish co-operatives.[2] Joint Arab-Jewish co-operatives—which are within the realm of the practicable—have not been tried because the English co-operative expert who visited Palestine in 1932 advised against it.

The fundamental purpose of these co-operatives is to build up the land without having to resort to the competitive system of capitalism, with all the attendant ills of speculation and crisis. The common earnings of all these co-operatives are shared equally. The significant fact about them is that they are not motivated merely by the desire to achieve greater economies or to make greater profits through the elimination of jobbery and middlemen. They constitute varied social experiments necessitated by the urge to build a new national economy. Otherwise, such a national economy could not come into being. Take as an example *Tnuva,* which is the largest marketing co-operative in the land and which has achieved phenomenal success. The *Tnuva* was organized as a result of the urgent need of marketing the products of the collective farms. The entire colonization effort would have collapsed, if the agricultural settlements had been unable to dispose of their products. The same is true of the contracting co-operative known as *Solel Boneh*. During the early twenties there was need to find employment for many immigrants who could not be settled on land. The *Solel Boneh* arose for the purpose of meeting that need. To be sure, it had to pay a high price for the undue zeal which led it to send workers who were not fully qualified for the jobs they were expected to do. That haste led to overexpansion and to poor quality of work. From failure the *Solel Boneh* learned its lesson, and has since achieved a stability which has somewhat narrowed its scope but has augmented its efficiency.

3. Of all manifestations of the democratic spirit in Palestine the most remarkable is, no doubt, that of the Workers' Federation (*Histadrut*). At the end of 1944 the *Histadrut* reported a membership of over one hundred thousand. Together with their families they constitute 38 per cent of the total Jewish population. It is an over-all organization of all workers in the collectives and co-

---

[2] These figures were given me by Harry Viteles, director of the Central Board of Cooperative Institutions in Palestine, Ltd., in Palestine.

operatives and of all white-collar workers who are unaffiliated with any other group—in a word, of all who earn their livelihood either through mental or manual labor. The essential requirement is that they shall live by their own labor and not exploit others. The general structure of the *Histadrut* is unique and reflects the unique character of the Palestinian experiment in democracy. The purpose of protecting the trade-union interests of its members is, though highly important, not the primary one. The primary purpose is to function as the principal land-building agency, and thus to pave the way for a workers' community in Palestine.

With that ambitious aim in view, the *Histadrut* engages in a wide range of activities such as no trade union could ever dream of attempting. The following is the list of some of its activities, as summed up by A. Revusky in his book *Jews in Palestine* (The Vanguard Press): "It establishes collective farms, supervises their progress and helps to provide them with funds—it organizes the sale of agricultural products and the co-operative purchase of consumers' goods; it conducts co-operatives in transportation and several lines of production; it operates contracting firms in various fields of rural and urban work; it organizes home-building groups and maintains a central office to co-ordinate their activities; it controls a labor bank and local credit unions; it possesses a country-wide health organization with its own clinics, hospitals, and sanitaria; it maintains workers' schools and encourages various cultural activities, including lectures, drama, music, etc.; it sponsors sports clubs, and in the case of Arab outbreaks, has actual control of Jewish self-defense; it regulates and organizes labor immigration by creating groups of pioneers (the *Halutzim*) in the Diaspora and preparing them for future tasks in Palestine."

This last function of regulating and organizing labor immigration differentiates it from all other trade unions in the world. Trade unions generally support a restrictive immigration policy. One can understand the reason for such a policy. Under the capitalistic system, immigration is attended by the lowering of wages and the standard of living. With no such fears, however, present in Palestine, because of the dominance of Labor Socialism, the advent of new manpower is counted on to raise the productivity of the country and the standard of living. With the purpose of strengthening the Jewish National Home uppermost in its mind, the Workers' Federation is bound to exert as much effort as possible to avert strikes and to bring about a better understanding between workers and employers. Of particular value is the success it has had in enforcing an equal distribution of work during periods of economic crisis. The recent action of the Palestine government in creating a Labor Department and engaging in the organizations of Arab workers in trade unions, is undoubtedly due to the activities of the *Histadrut*. The fact that the influence of the *Histadrut* reaches out to the neighboring counries, makes it perhaps a most important factor for democracy in the Near East.

4. The *Histadrut,* despite its predominant influence in the rebuilding of the Jewish homeland, does not monopolize what is, after all, the most important development in the life of the growing Jewish community in Palestine from the standpoint of democratic nationalism, that is, the capacity of a heterogeneous population to achieve self-government. We must remember that the majority of the Jewish population in Palestine lived until very recently under conditions and in a universe of thought virtually mediaeval. They have been catapulted, as it were, into the modern world where they can no longer expect uniformity of outlook or unanimity of opinion with regard to what is to be accepted as authoritative. Jews who are emancipated from the mediaeval ghettoes, or pales of settlement, need to become accustomed to having some of their number question the most sacrosanct traditions. Parents have to be able to bear the shock of having their most deeply rooted sentiments challenged by their children. When Jews from all parts of the world began coming to Palestine in large numbers, the problem arose whether they would be capable of achieving orderly self-government. Such self-government could no longer be of the theocratic type by which Jews had lived throughout the centuries. Those who were chiefly responsible for the reawakened Jewish life in Palestine would hear of no other than the democratic form of self-government.

The first practical moves to inaugurate Jewish autonomy were made in 1920. It took several years of passionate debate for the community to arrive at a common understanding. The most difficult issue that had to be fought out was woman suffrage. In traditional Jewish law, the woman did not have equal status with the man. To grant her political equality in the new Palestine was, in the opinion of the traditionalists, a violation of divine law. To be sure, not all of the difficulties in achieving autonomy were due to disagreement among the Jews. The British Administration afforded enough obstructive tactics of its own. The fact, however, that by 1928 the right of the Jewish community to exercise some degree of autonomy was formally recognized, is incontrovertible evidence of how speedily and effectively Jews as a people are capable of transforming themselves from an ancient theocracy to a modern democracy.

A small and vociferous group known as *Agudat Yisrael* representing extreme and militant orthodoxy has stayed out of the Jewish community, or *Kenesset Yisrael,* but it has been by-passed as a pocket of intransigent resistance to democracy, resistance that will no doubt in time disintegrate. Fortunately, the majority of the orthodox have refused to take such an intransigent attitude and are co-operating with the radical elements in the community. The composition of the *Asefat Hanivharim,* or Assembly of Deputies, in 1939 gives an idea of the diverse elements represented: Laborites, 34; Revisionists, 15; Sephardic, 6; General Zionists, 5; Women's Equal Rights, 3; Yemenites, 3. The *Astefat Hanivharim* is elected once every three years and meets once a year for a short session of a week or ten days. The executive committee of the Assembly known as the *Vaad Leumi,* or National Council, consists of 23 members and carries out the policies and plans of the Assembly.

5. The most knotty problem in the establishment of the Jewish national home is the bitter opposition to it on the part of the Palestinian Arabs. That opposition has been unrelenting, despite, and to a large degree because of, the fact that the Jews have been transforming Palestine from a barren and pestilential wilderness, which was slowly poisoning its half-starved population, into a highly cultivated and industrialized country capable of maintaining millions in comfort and happiness. It is of no avail to point to the historic

right of the Jews to the land, or to the fact that of all peoples driven from their lands the Jews have been the only people that has never renounced its claim to the land of its origin and has made a passionate religion of its hope to repossess that land. It is useless to argue that Feisal, the first leader of the pan-Arab movement, gave his approval to the transaction of the League of Nations, when it incorporated the Balfour Declaration into the mandate. It is a waste of breath to point to the fact that fifty-two nations have recognized the Jewish claim to a national home in Palestine. These and numerous other appeals to reason have been advanced by Jews and non-Jews to get the Arabs to sit down to discuss the problem. But one might as well try to reason with a stone wall. They will hear of nothing less than the complete repudiation of the Balfour Declaration, the stoppage of all Jewish immigration and all sale of land to Jews. The statement, "We do not accept the formula laid down by the Jews that there should be no domination by the Jews over Arabs, or by Arabs over Jews," sums up the official Arab position taken in 1936 before the Royal Commission.

In contrast with this uncompromising refusal even to negotiate, the Jews state clearly their position with regard to the place of the non-Jewish population in a Jewish Commonwealth. In a recent official answer by the Jewish Agency for Palestine to the specific question put to it concerning the guarantees for the personal religious and property rights of non-Jewish citizens, it was made clear that a Jewish Commonwealth was not regarded as being purely Jewish in composition. A considerable section of the population is expected to be non-Jewish. The status of non-Jewish citizens "would be exactly the same as that of Jews, all of them being subject to identical laws administered by a democratically elected government. Wide measures are envisaged for local self-government in urban and rural areas. Moslems and Christians would enjoy full communal autonomy as regards the management of their religious, educational, and social institutions. All citizens, without distinction of race or creed, would enjoy adult suffrage and be entitled to representation on the legislative and executive bodies. No citizen would be at a disadvantage as a candidate for public employment by reason of his race or religion. Fellahin and

Bedouin will enjoy the same status and rights as other citizens." The statement concludes that "the Jewish Commonwealth will not rest content with establishing merely formal equality, but will endeavor to bring about an increasing measure of real equality in education and standards of life by social legislation and economic development" (*Palestine,* Vol. I, No. 12, December, 1944).

No one can question the fact that more Arabs have been able to live in Palestine and to live a more civilized life as a result of the economy which the Jews have built up in that land. No one can question the fact that the national aspirations of the Arab people can be satisfied in the four adjacent domains covering an area one hundred times the size of Palestine. Moreover, by this time it has become evident that the national homelessness of the Jews is one of the most potent means which enemies of the democratic nations employ to sow hatred, dissension, and war. If ever there was an illustration on a world scale of the tragic consequences of the dog-in-the-manger policy, it is the case of the Arab leaders in and outside Palestine. It is inconceivable that the Allied nations, which are now preparing to establish a world order based on international justice and peace, should treat this dog-in-the-manger policy as sacrosanct and unalterable. Twenty-five years ago the British in solemn covenant declared Palestine as the one country which Jews may enter as of right and not merely on sufferance. Only shortly before the outbreak of this war the Mandate Commission of the League of Nations condemned Great Britain's White Paper as its interpretation of the Mandate did not conform to any prior, or possible, interpretation. For the nations now to condone the cruel obduracy of the Arab leaders in Palestine would be nothing less than a travesty on all law and justice and the signal to all the national egoisms and rivalries to come out of their hiding and resume their career of devastation. Let us hope that mankind will be spared such a tragic fate.

Thus, from whichever angle we view the movement to re-establish the Jewish national home in Palestine we can but see it as a unique experiment in democracy: the circumstances and forces which led to the adoption of that aim, the various measures which are being taken in order to prepare the conditions necessary to attain that aim, and the unparalleled achievements which the prospect of putting an end to the homelessness of the Jewish people has been able to elicit—all these attest to the creative power of democracy. The Jewish reclamation of Palestine may rate small in the affairs of mankind, but, as a social experiment, it is invaluable as a means of demonstrating that democracy is the only bridge from world chaos to world order.

INDEX

Abraham, 29, 30
Acton, Lord, 59, 170
Acts, Book of, 33
Adair v. the United States, 220
Adam, 27, 30
Adams, John, 60, 73, 75, 77n
Adelphi, The, 164
Administrative Theories of Hamilton and Jefferson (Caldwell), 113
agriculture: mechanized, 167; in Palestine, 248, 253-254, 256-259
Alexander II, 244
Alexander III, 244
All Quiet on the Western Front (Remarque), 88
Allen, J. W., quoted, 55
Alliance Israelite Universelle, 248
alternatives, choosing between, 187-188, 189-190
Ambrose, St., 37, 42
America. See Latin America; South America; United States
American Commonwealth, The (Bryce), 23
American Federation of Labor, 155, 156, 157, 158, 159, 160-161, 162
American Labor Party, 158
American literature, 100-107
American Renaissance (Matthiessen), 102
American Revolution, 110, 243
Americans, 105
Amos, 29
Anabaptists, 53
Anglicanism, 50
Anshen, R. N., 87, 93n
anti-Semitism, 239, 246-247, 250

Apology (Plato), 21
Apostles, the, 33, 44
Appeal from the New to the Old Whigs (Burke), 117
Aquinas, St. Thomas, 13, 36, 40, 41, 64, 76, 112
Arabs, and the Jews, 257, 259-260, 261, 262, 263-265
Arc, Jeanne d', 40
Areopagitica (Milton), 94
Aristotle, 11, 19, 20, 22-24, 25, 42, 72, 76, 77n, 80, 112, 118
Arminians, 48
Arnold, Thurman, 222
Arvin, Newton, 105
Asefat Hanivharim, 263
assimilationism, Jewish, 243-244
Associated Press, 167
Athens, Greek city-state, 20, 21, 23
Atlantic Charter, 222
Augustine, St., 36, 38, 39, 42
Australia, 166
Austria, 244, 245-246
authoritarianism, 202-203
authority, democratic conception of, 202-206, 207

Babbitt, Irving, 80
Balaam, 28-29
Balfour Declaration, 250, 255, 264
Bancroft, George, 48
Baptists, 53
Barnard, Chester I., 202
Baron, Hans, 57
Basic History of the United States (Beard), 7, 111, 116
Bavinck, H., 56

Index

Beard, Charles A., 7, 111, 113, 116; quoted, 16-17
Becker, Carl, 13, 210
Bernanos, Georges, 41
Bernard, St., 39-40
Beveridge, Sir William, 169
Beza, 58
Bible. *See* Scriptures
Bill of Rights, 128, 220-221
bi-racial churches, 231-233
Bismarck, 59
Blake, William, 96, 98
Bode, 173
Boissier, 35
Boissonade, 35
Book of Discipline (Westminster Assembly), 53
Borsodi, Ralph, 171
Bossuet, Bishop, 49
Boston, Mass., 232
Bridges, Harry, 160
brotherhood, 18-19, 26; as an ideal, 219, 223-225
Brunner, Emil, 218
Bryce, James, 23; quoted, 4-5
Bucer, Martin, 57
Buchanan, George, 58
Buchanan, Scott, lecture by, 177-191
Buckle, Henry, quoted, 48
Bunyan, Paul, 93
Burdach, 35
bureaucracy, 9-10
Burke, Edmund, 3-4, 117, 123
Burlamaqui, Jean Jacques, 112
Bush, Douglas, 93, 94-95
business, concentrated, 148-149, 167
By Blue Ontario's Shore (Whitman), quoted, 105-106
Byron, George Gordon, 98

Caesar, Julius, 77n
Caietanus, Cardinal, 51
Caldwell, Lincoln K., 113
California, and labor, 154
Calvin, John, 48, 49, 52, 55-60, 72, 76, 92, 94

"Calvin and Common Grace" (Bavinck), 56
Calvin and the Reformation, 56
Canada, United Church of, 154
Carpenters Union, 156
Carrington, Edward, 114
Caswell, Hollis L., 195-196
Catholic Church, 171, 204, 205, 231
chain stores, 167
Charles II, 60
Charles V, 57
Chesterton, Gilbert, 41
Chicago, Ill., 177
Chicago, University of, participants from, 44, 87
Chicago Tribune, 24
China, 234
Chinard, Gilbert, 43
Chisholm *v.* Georgia, 116-117
Christianity, 11, 72-76, 77-80, 83-84; and brotherhood, 18-19, 26; and literature, 91-105; medieval, 36-43; and the Reformation, 46-61. *See also* religion
church: and democracy, 192-195, 200-201, 227-234; and education, 181-182, 192-195, 200-201, 227-228; government in, 45, 50-61; and Jefferson, 73, 74; and the state, 37-40. *See also* religion
Church of All Nations, Boston, 232
church schools, 227-228
Cicero, 24-25, 56, 183
cities, growth of, 166-167
city government, corruption in, 10
city-state, Greek, 18, 19-24
civic rights, for Jews, 243-244
Clarke, M. V., 123
class war, 4, 160
classical origins, of democracy, 10-11, 18-26, 119
classics, 77-83, 94
Cleanthes, 26
Cleveland, Ohio, 235
closed shop, 153-155
Coe, George Albert, 175
Colet, John, 42

Index

Colgate-Rochester Divinity School, participant from, 214
collectivism, in Palestine, 254, 257-262
collectivist age, democracy in, 166-176
Colorado Law School, 217
Columbia University, 125, 217; participants from, 3, 26, 166
Columbian Orator, 90
communication: control of, 167-168, 173-174; difficulty in, 12-14
communism, 155, 157-158, 159
community: Christian attitude toward, 35-41; and the church, 228
community agencies, democracy in, 192-195, 197
competition, economic, 140-141
Conciliarism, 45-46, 51, 52
Conference on Science, Philosophy and Religion, 12-13, 88, 93, 237
Congregational churches, 53
Congress on Education for Democracy (1939), symposium on, 16-17
Congress of Industrial Organizations, 155, 156, 157, 158, 159, 160, 162-163, 174
Constitution, U.S., 6, 20, 22, 76, 109-110, 113, 114, 115-116, 118-119, 120, 122, 127-128, 166, 179, 219, 220-221
Constitutional Convention of 1787, 114, 115, 116, 119
consumer organizations, 174
Continental Congress, 76
Convocation of Canterbury, 50
Coolidge, Calvin, 10
co-operatives, 169, 174, 175; in Palestine, 259-260
Coppage v. Kansas, 220
Cornell University, 228
corruption, in government, 10, 21, 24
Council of Constance, 51
Council of Vienna, 255
county government, corruption in, 10
Croce, 98
Crusades, 40
curriculums, 193-194, 196
Curti, Professor, 101, 102

Daniel, Book of, 29
Dante, Alighieri, 43
Das juedische Hilfsverein, 248-249
Dayton, Ohio, 233-234
De Regimine Principuum (Aquinas), 41
decentralists, 171-172
Declaration of Independence, 6, 43, 63, 67-71, 73-74, 75, 76, 85, 92, 110, 112, 127, 181, 221, 222
Defence of the Constitution (Adams), 60
Defence against Tyrants, 58
democracy: and American history, 109-124; authority, revelation, and prophecy, 202-213; classical origins of, 10-11, 18-26, 119; in a collectivist age, 166-176; crisis in, 3-17; economic groups in, 151-165; and economic liberalism, 125-150; and education, 125, 150, 177-191; in educational practice, 16-17, 192-201; and ethical realism, 214-226; Hebrew sources of, 27-34; humanistic sources of, 62-86; literary sources of, 27, 87-108; meaning of, 62, 66-76, 86, 125-128, 193, 214, 240-242; medieval sources of, 35-43, 45-46, 51, 110-111, 112, 119, 120, 121; Reformation sources of, 44-61; and religion, 27-34, 36-43, 44-45, 46-61, 72-75, 201, 202-213, 225, 227-238; and Zionism, 239-266
Democracy and the Curriculum, 195
democratic collectivism, 172-176
democratic participation, 193-201
Democratic Party, 7
Democratic Spirit, The, 90
Denmark, 166
depressed areas, 228-229, 230
determinism, 92, 178-179
Detroit, Mich., 231-232
Diderot, Denis, 243
discrimination, 72, 159
divine right of kings, 204-205
Dixon, 175
Dominican order, 50
Dos Passos, John, 88-89
Douglas, Frederick, 90
Douglass, H. Paul, lecture by, 227-238

Index

Doumergue, E., 56
Dreyfus case, 246
Drucker, Peter, 9
Dubinsky, David, 41
Dumbarton Oaks, 235

Ecclesiastes, 30
Economic Development, Committee on, 168
economic groups, role in democracy of, 151-165
economic liberalism, and democracy, 125-150
economic liberty, 12
economic monopoly, 169-170, 171
economic status, equalizing of, 16
economics, meaning of, 128-129
Edman, Irwin, 48; lecture by, 18-26
education, 16-17, 125, 150, 177-191, 192-201; and the church, 181-182, 192-195, 200-201, 227-228; medieval, 40-41
Education for Freedom, Inc., 177
Education Between Two Worlds (Meiklejohn), 185-186
educational practice, democracy in, 16-17, 192-201
Egyptian belief, in resurrection, 28
elections: and political campaigns, 7-8, 9, 13-15; voting restrictions in, 8-9
Eliot, T. S., 80
Elliott, Harrison S., lecture by, 192-201
Emerson, Ralph Waldo, 96, 100, 102, 103-105
employment: freedom of, 131, 133-136, 141, 149-150, 151-156; full, 163, 168, 169
Encyclopedists, 43, 97-98
England, 45, 60, 111, 127, 244; collectivism in, 169. *See also* Great Britain
English literature, 91-100
Epictetus, 187, 189
Epicurean philosophy, 19, 24, 75
Epicurus, 75, 82
equality, 37, 71-76, 85-86, 114, 121, 214-215, 219-225, 233-234; in Declaration of Independence, 69-70, 73-76; in the Greek city-state, 20, 21-22; and the Jews, 240-241, 246-247, 251, 254, 256; Roman attitude toward, 25; Scriptural background of, 27-30, 33-34
Erasmus, Desiderius, 42, 79-80, 84
Essay on Milton (Macaulay), 11
ethical realism, and democracy, 214-226
ethnic status, equalizing of, 16
Europe, 45, 127; Jews in, 243-247; and labor, 157-158
Evangelische Ethik des Politischen (Wünsch), 59

Fairchild, H. N., 95
family: democracy in, 192-193, 195; society of, 23
farming. *See* agriculture
Fascism, 151, 155, 179
Federal Council of the Churches of Christ in America, 235-236, 237; participants from, 3, 227
Federalist papers, 115-116, 216
Feisal, 264
Fifteenth Amendment, 221
Filmer, 50
Finkelstein, Louis, 18, 19, 35; lecture by, 27-34
Fordham University, participant from, 109
foreign policy, and labor, 163
Fortune, 157
Founding Fathers, 6, 109-124, 151, 152, 179, 200
Fountainheads of Freedom (Edman), 48
Fourteenth Amendment, 221
France, 45, 181; American derivation from, 109-110; Jews in, 33, 244, 246; Protestant minority in, 58
franchise, limitation on, 8-9, 16
Francis, St., 40
Franciscan order, 50
Frank, Waldo, 41
fraternity. *See* brotherhood
free enterprise, 11-12, 135-140, 149, 150, 160-161, 169
free markets, 140-141

Index

freedom: basis of, 36; education for, 177-191; of employment, 131, 133-136, 141, 149-150, 151-156; literature of, 87-108; of opinion, 32-34; political, 12, 181, 184-186, 188; reconciling order and law with, 202-213; religious, 12, 181-184, 186, 187, 188, 235-238
Freedom, Its Meaning, 87, 93n
Freedom of a Christian Man, The (Luther), 47
Freedom and Responsibility (Becker), 210
French Declaration of the Rights of Man, 110
French Revolution, 99, 110, 111, 126, 243, 246
Freudian theory of frustration, 180
friendship, society of, 23
frustration, 216, 221; and the problem of freedom, 180-191
Fulbright, 4
Function of the Executive, The (Barnard), 202
Future of Industrial Man (Drucker), 9

Galileo, 40, 95
Gamaliel I, Rabban, 33
Gandhi, Mahatma, 171
General Motors Company, 152
Genesis, 27, 28, 29
George, Henry, 253
George III, 116
German Lutheranism, 48, 50-52, 57, 59, 60
Germany, 244, 245-246; and American derivation, 110; Jewish settlements in, 34; labor in, 157-158; totalitarianism of, 157-158, 171, 179, 239
Gershom, Rabbenu, 34
ghetto, emancipation from, 243, 247, 262
Gill, Eric, 41
God: concepts of, 64, 72-73, 74, 80, 81-82, 85-86; man in image of, 27-28, 29, 36, 235; as object of human love, 183-184
Gompers, Samuel, 162
Goodman, 55

government: under American Constitution, 109, 112-113, 115-124; centralization in, 161-163, 168-171, 172-173, 175; characteristics of, 216-218; church, 45, 50-61; corruption in, 10, 21, 24; in Declaration of Independence, 70-71; and economic activity, 132, 133-139, 144, 147, 150; as educational, 191; Jefferson on, 77n; in Palestine, 262-263; theory of, 10-12, 17
Great Britain, and Palestine, 255, 263, 265. *See also* England
Greek city-state, as political theme, 18, 19-24
Greek Commonwealth, The (Zimmern), 19
Greek literature, 77, 80
Greeks, as the elect, 72
groups: communication between, 12-14; conflicts of, 215-218, 222-225; economic, 151-165; utilization of, 15
Growth of American Thought, The, 101
guilds, 41

Haecker, Theodore, 38
Halukah contributions, 248
Hamilton, Alexander, 111, 113-116; quoted, 6
Hanna, Paul R., 201
Harding, Warren G., 9-10
Harpers' Magazine, 164
Hartley, 122-123
Hawthorne, Nathaniel, 100, 101-103
Heauton Timoroumenes (Menander), 182
Hebrew literature, and humanism, 77, 80, 83
Hebrew sources, of democracy, 27-34
Hebrew theocracy, 203-204
Hecker, Father, 92
Hegel, Georg W. F., 110, 117
Hellas (Shelley), 98
Herald Tribune Forum, 4
Herzl, Theodor, 246-247, 249-250, 251, 253
Hillel, School of, 28, 31-33
Himmler, Heinrich, 59

Histadrut, 260-262
History of Civilization in England, 48
History of Freedom (Acton), 59
History of Greater Britain, The (Major), 58
History of the United States, 48
Hitler, Adolf, 59, 61, 88, 157, 171, 222
Hobbes, Thomas, 94
Hopkins, L. Thomas, 198
Hotman, 58
Houston, George H., lecture by, 125-150
Hudson, W. S., 57
Hughes, Charles E., 203
human dignity, 16, 25, 27-30
humane spirit, 17
humanism, meaning of, 66, 76-86
humanistic sources, of democracy, 62-86
Hunter, A. Mitchell, quoted, 52
Hunter College, participant from, 35
Huss, John, 43
Hutcheson, William, 156
Hutchins, Robert, 177
Huxley, Aldous, 88
Hymn to Zeus (Cleanthes), 26

Iceland, 45
ideals, and practice, 214-215, 218-226
immortality, in relation to democracy, 27-29
imperialism, 162, 164, 255
Improvement of Understanding, The (Spinoza), 182
In Praise of Folly (Erasmus), 79
Independents, 53
India, 171
individual: conflicts of, 215-218, 222-225; in democracy, 125-128, 130, 131-132, 142, 148-150, 201, 240-241; in the Greek city-state, 19-20, 23; in organizations, 174-175; protection of, 19, 34
individual freedom, 181, 185, 186-191
Indulgences, the, 51
industrial revolution, 9
industry, concentration in, 166-168
Inquisition, 40

Institute for Religious and Social Studies, 91; participant from, 27
Institute for the Study of Group Dynamics, 175
Institutes (Calvin), 49, 56, 57, 58
intellect, individual freedom in, 188-191
Interaction: The Democratic Process (Hopkins), 198
International Federation of Trade Unions, 158
International Ladies' Garment Workers' Union, 159
International News Service, 167
Isaac, 30
Islam, 236
isolationism, in the Greek city-state, 24
Israel, 28, 29, 32, 72, 242, 251
Italy, 244

Jaeger, Werner, 80
James, Henry, 103
James, King, 49
James, William, 82, 85, 104
Jefferson, Thomas, 6, 18, 43, 60, 63-64, 66-67, 72, 73-76, 77n, 79, 98, 111, 113, 114-115, 116, 119, 127, 166, 169, 181-182, 221
Jefferson Bible, 74-75
Jerome, St., 37, 42
Jersey City, N.J., 228-229
Jerusalem, Temple in, 31
Jesus Christ, 74-75, 79-80
Jewish Agency for Palestine, 264-265
Jewish National Fund, 252-254, 258
Jewish Theological Seminary, participants from, 27, 239
Jewish tradition, democratic, 27-34
Jews, 72-73, 75; national home for, 239-266
Jews in Palestine (Revusky), quoted, 261
Joachim of Flores, 43
Job, 29, 30, 83-84
John, King, 204
John Ponet, Advocate of Limited Monarchy (Hudson), 57
Johnson, F. Ernest, lectures by, 3-17, 202-213

Index

Journal of Biblical Literature, 32
Judaism. See Jewish
Judeo-Christian tradition, 11, 15, 72-76, 77-80, 201; and literature, 91
justice, 241, 249; and the common good, 217-218, 223-226

Kallen, Horace M., lecture by, 62-86
Kant, Immanuel, 110, 178-179
Kaplan, Mordecai M., lecture by, 239-266
Kellogg-Briand Pact, 221
Keren Kayemeth, 252-254, 258
Kibbutz, 258-259
Kilwardby, 50
Knox, John, 55, 58, 60, 107
Koopman, S. Robert, 196
Kvutza, 258, 259

La Guardia, Fiorello, 166
labor legislation, 219-220
labor organization, in Palestine, 260-262
Labor Party (British), 169, 251
labor unions, 9, 141-143, 151-165, 169, 170, 174, 175
laissez-faire theory, 12, 115
Lambert, François, 51, 53
Languet, 58
Lasco, John à, 53
Laski, Harold, 4, 10, 170
Lasswell, Harold, 216
Latin America, 164
Latin literature, 77, 80
law: democratic interpretation of, 30-34; natural, 111-113, 118; Roman, 18, 24, 25-26
Lawrence, D. H., 103
laws, as object of human love, 183-184
Laws (Plato), 81
League of Nations, 250, 255, 264, 265
Lebensraum, 222
Lechler, G. V., 52
Leibnitz, 59
Leiserson, William M., 219-220
Lerner, Max, 9-10
Lewin, Kurt, 175
Lewis, John L., 157
liberal education, 177-191

Liberal Party, 158
liberalism, 11-12, 40, 241; economic, 125-150; meaning of, 129-130
liberties, "tripod" of, 12
liberty: economic, 12; as an ideal, 219-225; personal, 130-132. *See also* freedom
Likert, 174
Lilienthal, David, 172, 179, 188
Lincoln, Abraham, 152, 205
Lippmann, Walter, 25
literary sources, of democracy, 27, 87-108
literature, and the humanities, 77-85
Little Steel Wage Formula, 163
Lives (Plutarch), 90
Llewellyn, Professor, 217
Locke, John, 60, 97
Longshoremen's Union, 160
Los Angeles, Cal., 157
love, problem of, 182-184
Lowdermilk, Walter Clay, 257
Luther, Martin, 38, 46, 47-48, 50-52, 54-55, 57, 59, 76, 79-80, 92, 94, 107

McIntosh case, 203
McNeill, J. T., 48; lecture by, 44-61
Macaulay, Thomas, 11; quoted, 100-101
Machiavelli, 54
Madison, James, 73, 111, 114, 121, 166, 219
Magna Charta, 120, 204
Major, John, 58
majority rule, 14, 37, 75-76, 120-122, 125-128
man: concepts of, 112-113, 124; in God's image, 27-28, 29, 36, 235; and humanism, 82-83; and self-government, 11, 16
mandate system, 255
Manicheans, 38
Maritain, Jacques, 80, 81
Marsilius of Padua, 43
Massachusetts Institute of Technology, 175
Matthiessen, F. O., 102, 103
Maverick, Maury, 167
maximum production, 164-165

May, Mark, 216
Meaning of Revelation, The (Niebuhr), 207
Medieval Representation and Consent (Clarke), 123
medieval sources, of democracy, 35-43, 45-46, 51, 110-111, 112, 119, 120, 121
Meiklejohn, 185
Melanchthon, 51
Melville, Herman, 100, 101, 102, 103-104, 105
Menander, 82
Mennonites, 154
Merriam, Charles E., 225
Messianism, 242, 245, 247
Methodists, 53
Michelangelo, 42
Middle Ages. *See* medieval
Miel, Alice, 196
Mikveh Israel, 248
Mill, John Stuart, 20, 23
Millar, Moorhouse F. X., lecture by, 109-124
Milton, John, 93-95, 107
Minneapolis, Minn., 231
minority groups: labor discrimination against, 159; rights denied to, 75-76
minority nationalities, 254-255
Mishna, the, 28, 32
Misner, Paul J., 196
Modern Democracies (Bryce), 4-5
monarchic principle, 204-205
monogamy, and the Scriptures, 30
monopoly, economic, 169-170, 171
Monroe, James, 73, 114, 121
Montesquieu, Charles de, 97, 184-185, 188, 243
More, Paul Elmer, 80
More, Thomas, 42
Mornay, 58
Moscow, 143-144
Moses, Five Books of, 27
Moshav, 258
Moslems, 236
"mud-sill" theory, 152
Murry, John Middleton, 164
Musicians Union, 142

Muste, A. J., lecture by, 151-165
My Bondage and My Freedom (Douglas), 90

National Association of Manufacturers, 156, 169
National Industrial Recovery Act, 139
National Labor Relations Act, 126, 162
nationalism, 243, 245-246
natural law, 111-113, 118
"Natural Law in Luther's Thought," 55
Nazism, 157-158, 171, 179, 239
Negro: and ideals of rights, 75, 220-221, 224, 225; labor discrimination against, 159; and religion, 228-230, 231-233
Neo-Platonism, 38
Netherlands, 60
New Republic, 8
New School for Social Research, participant from, 62
New York, N.Y., 158, 166
New York Daily News, 24
New York Herald Tribune, 122
New York Times, 122
New Zealand, 166
newspapers, 167, 169
Nicomachean Ethics (Aristotle), 19, 23
Niebuhr, H. Richard, 44, 207-208
Niebuhr, Reinhold, 38
Nietzsche, Friedrich Wilhelm, 217
Nixon, Justin Wroe, lecture by, 214-226
Noah, Mordecai, 75
North Carolina, poll tax abolished in, 8
Norton, Charles Eliot, 103
Norway, 59
Notes on Virginia (Jefferson), 74
Nouvelle Héloïse (Rousseau), 97
Nuremberg trials, 221

Oldendorp, 59
oligarchy, 5
On Truth (Protagoras), 83
"ordinances of the communities," 33-34
organization: in business, 148-149; and the individual, 174-175; of labor, 151-165; and use of power, 224
Otis, James, 110

Index

P. E. N. Society, 88, 89
Paideia, the Ideals of Greek Culture, 81
Paine, Tom, 98, 221
Palestine, as experiment in democracy, 239-266
Palestine Mandate, 250, 255, 264, 265
Palestinian belief, in immortality, 28
Papacy, the, 45-46
Paradise Lost (Milton), 93-94, 95
Patristic era, 45
Paul, St., 26, 29, 101, 204
Paulicians, 38
Peasant War, 50, 51
Peckham, 50
Péguy, 41
Pennsylvania, Ratifying Convention of, 119
Pentateuch, 30
people, as used in American Constitution, 116-120
Pericles, 20
Petrarch, Francesco, 42, 78
Petrillo, James, 142
Pharisaism, 27-29, 30, 31, 32, 33
Philosophical Dictionary (Voltaire), 166
Pickman, 35, 36
Pico della Mirandola, 42
Pinsker, Leon, 244-245, 247
Plato, 5, 20-22, 23-24, 42, 72, 80-81, 82, 183
Plato or Protagoras (Schiller), 82
Plutarch, 90
PM, 9
police theory, of government, 10
Political Action Committee, 155, 174
political campaigns, 7-8, 9, 14-15
political freedom, 12, 181, 184-186, 188
political parties, 7-8, 14-15
political platforms, 8, 9, 15
political theory, classical, 18-26
politics: church, 45, 46, 50-61; in democracy, 4-5, 7-10, 13-16
poll tax, 8, 16
Ponet, John, 55, 57, 60
Poullain, Vallerand, 53
power, 9, 13-15, 170-171, 217-218, 222, 223-226, 241

predestination, doctrine of, 48-50
Prelude (Wordsworth), 99-100
Presbyterians, 53
pressure groups, 186
priesthood, hereditary authority of, 30-31
production, maximum, 164-165
Prometheus Unbound (Shelley), 98
propaganda, and religious democracy, 234-238
property: ownership of, 127, 129, 130, 132, 136-139, 143-147, 149, 150, 161-162; in Palestine, 254, 257-262
prophecy, democratic conception of, 202, 210-213
Protagoras, 82-83, 85
Protest of Speyer, 51
Protestants, 11, 204-206, 228-238; and literature, 92-105; Reformation, 48-61
Proverbs, 30
Provisional French Government, 145
Prussia, 158
public opinion, agencies of, 167-168, 173
public opinion polls, 174, 175
public school system, 173, 175, 193-194
Pufendorf, 59
Puritans, 11, 92, 100-105

Quakers, 53

Rabbinic concept, 27, 29
race segregation, in the church, 231-233
radio, 167-168, 173, 174
Railroad Brotherhoods, 155, 157, 159
railroads, nationalization of, 161
Raphael, 42
rationalism, 94, 96, 98
realism: ethical, 214-226; meanings of, 124
reason, as object of human love, 183
Reformation, and literature, 92-94, 100
Reformation doctrine, and government, 10
Reformation sources, of democracy, 44-61
Reformed Church, 48, 52-53, 57, 59, 60
religion: and democracy, 27-34, 36-43, 44-45, 46-61, 72-75, 201, 202-213, 225, 227-238; and education, 181-182,

Index

religion (*Continued*)
192-195, 200-201, 227-228; and humanism, 78-86; and labor, 165; in literature of freedom, 89, 91-106, 108; and politics, 14, 15
religious democracy, 206, 227-238
religious education, 192-195, 200-201, 227-228
religious freedom, 12, 181-184, 186, 187, 188, 235-238
Religious Trends in English Poetry (Fairchild), 95
Renaissance, 42, 94
representative government, 122-123
Representative Government (Mill), 23
Republic, The (Beard), 111
Republic, The (Plato), 21, 81, 217; quoted, 5
Republican Party, 7, 9
revelation, 236; democratic conception of, 202, 206-210
Revusky, A., 261
Rhineland, Jewish settlements in, 33
Rickenbacker, Eddie, 155
Rilke, 41
Rockefeller Center, 222
Roethlisberger, 175
Roman law, as political theme, 18, 24, 25-26
Romanticism, 94, 95, 96-100, 104
Rome, 41
Roosevelt Administration, 163
Rousseau, Jean Jacques, 43, 97-98, 179, 185, 186, 243
Rugg, Harold, 195
Rush, Benjamin, 74
Ruskin, John, 41
Russia, 244-245. *See also* Soviet Union

Sabine, Professor, 210
St. John's College, participant from, 177
Samson Agonistes (Milton), 93-94
Samuel, First Book of, 203-204
San Francisco, Cal., 157
Sarah, 29, 30
Savonarola, Girolamo, 40
Schapira, Herman, 253

Schiller, F. C. S., 82
Schmalkald Article of 1537, 51
Schnürer, 35
Scholasticism, 40-41, 117, 118
schools: church, 227-228; democracy in, 173, 175, 192-201. *See also* education
Science, Philosophy and Religion, conferences on, 12-13, 88, 93, 237
scientific method, 63
Scipionic circle, 82
Scotland, 45, 60
Scribes, 30
Scriptures, 49-50, 53, 54, 78-79, 83-84, 89-90, 92, 93, 106; and Jefferson, 74-75; as source of democracy, 27-34
Seattle, Wash., 157, 230-231
segregation, race, 231-233
Sehling, E., 51
Selective Service Administration, 156
self-determination, 234
seniority, 142-143, 149, 156
Seventeenth Century Backgrounds, The (Willey), 95
Shammai, School of, 28, 31-33
Sharia, 236
Shelley, Percy Bysshe, 95, 96, 98
Sherman, Stuart P., 105
shipbuilding unions, 162
Shorte Treatise on Politike Power (Ponet), 57
Shuster, George N., lecture by, 35-43
slavery, 19, 29-30, 76
Smith, Bernard, 90
Smith, Matthew, 143
Social Democrats, 157-158
social movements, and religion, 228
Social and Political Ideas of Some Great Thinkers of the Renaissance and Reformation, 55
social sciences, 63-66
social security, 168
socialism, 172
socialization, 137-138, 161
Socrates, 5, 21
Solel Boneh, 260
Solomon, Song of, 30
source, meanings of, 62-66

Index

South America, 234
South Berkeley, Cal., 232
Soviet Union, 16, 124, 135-136, 143-144, 145-146, 158, 169, 170, 233
Spinoza, Baruch, 178, 179, 182, 188
state: in American government, 115-120; and church, 37-40; democratic concept of, 240-241; function of, 10-11; Greek conception of, 21-24; Luther's ideas of, 54; nature of, 215-218; of totalitarianism, 170-171
Stettinius, Edward, 234
Stoics, 19, 24-25, 26, 76
strikes, 160, 220, 224
student self-government, 198-200
Suárez, 117
Summa Theologica (Aquinas), 13
Supreme Court, U.S., 116-117, 219-220
Sweden, 166
Switzerland, 45, 60, 166

Talmud, as source of democracy 27-34
Taylor, Father, 103
Teaching of Calvin, The (Hunter), 52
Teamsters Union, 156
television, 173
Temple, William, 218
Tennessee Valley Authority, 172, 175, 179, 188
tension, in a democracy, 13
Terence, 82, 85
theology, and the scientific method, 63
Thomasius, 59
Thoreau, Henry, 100, 102-103, 105, 171
Thrasymachus, 217
Thucydides, 20
Tiffany, I. H., 77n
Tnuva, 260
Tobin, Daniel, 156
Tocqueville, A. C. de, 23
Torah, the, 31, 32, 41, 251, 253
totalitarianism, 6-7, 21, 117, 126, 151, 153, 155, 157-158, 170-171, 176
Trinitarian theology, 38
Tucker, 122
Tudor period, 41
Turkey, 250

unemployment, 16
union-management cooperation, 160-162
Union Theological Seminary, participant from, 192
unions. *See* labor unions
Unitarians, 53
United Automobile Workers, 156
United Church of Canada, 154
United Mine Workers, 157, 158
United Nations, 168
United Press, 167
United States: Founding Fathers of, 6, 109-124, 151, 152, 179, 200; Jews in, 256; politics in, 4, 7-10; and slavery, 76
Unitive Protestantism (McNeill), 48

Vaad Leumi, 263
veterans, and labor, 155, 156
Vindiciae, 58
Virginia, and democracy, 73, 74
Virginia, University of, 77n, 181-182
Voltaire, François de, 166, 243
voting, limitations on, 8-9, 16, 263

Wagner Act, 162
Wallace, Henry A., 161
war: and labor, 163-165; and literature, 88; problem of, 224
war plants, 161-162
Washington, George, 111, 113, 115, 116
Waterhouse, Benjamin, 72
Watson, Goodwin B., lecture by, 166-176
Weber, 49
Weimar Republic, 217
welfare state, 11
Welles, Sumner, 220
Werke, Weimar Ausgabe (Luther), 48
White Paper, 265
Whitehead, Alfred North, 49, 87, 93n, 185
Whitman, Walt, 96, 100, 102-103, 104, 105-107
Whitman (Arvin), 105
Wickard, Claude E., 257
Wiener Neue Presse, 246
Wilder, Amos N., lecture by, 87-108
Will, Robert, 100
Will to Believe (James), 85

Index

Willey, Basil, 95
Wilson, James, 111, 115, 116-117, 118, 119
Wilson, Woodrow, 254
Winters, Yvor, 104
Wisconsin State Agricultural Society, 152
Witherspoon, 60
woman, emancipation of, 29
woman suffrage, in Palestine, 263
Wordsworth, William, 98-100
Workers' Federation, in Palestine, 260-262
World War I, 88, 250, 254
World War II, 163-164, 168, 239

World Zionist Organization, 251, 252
writers. *See* literary
Wünsch, G., 59

Youth Serves the Community (Hanna), 201

Zimmern, A. E., 19
Zionism, and democracy, 239-266
Zionist Congress, 251, 252, 253
Zionist Organization of America, Convention of, 254
Zionist party divisions, 251-252
Zwingli, Ulrich, 48, 59